Microsoft Dynamics Sure Step 2010

The smart guide to the successful delivery of Microsoft Dynamics Business Solutions

Chandru Shankar

Vincent Bellefroid

BIRMINGHAM - MUMBAI

Microsoft Dynamics Sure Step 2010

Copyright © 2011 Packt Publishing

First published: January 2011

Production Reference: 2010211

Published by Packt Publishing Ltd.
32 Lincoln Road
Olton
Birmingham, B27 6PA, UK.

ISBN 978-1-849681-10-0

www.packtpub.com

Cover Image by Mark Holland (MJH767@bham.ac.uk)

Credits

Foreword

Investing in a business application—be it managing one's customers, tracking inventory, coordinating global resources, or just being able to get real-time visibility to cash flow—has never been so important. Gone are the days when companies invested in business applications, such as CRM and ERP, to simply streamline their supply chain or manage their sales pipeline. And gone are the days when these business applications were selected, implemented, and deployed by the IT organizations alone. Companies, and individuals within them, are relying on these business solutions to provide them a competitive advantage—an advantage that includes not only using the facts and data to generate information, but also to transform it to the knowledge that can be applied to gain a deeper understanding of the environment and provide a reliable business operating system for enabled intuition. This intuition of where to invest, how to plan, and when to execute in a well-planned, analysis-rich, and coordinated manner is what provides a competitive advantage to today's organizations. The expectations of business transformation that business solutions can provide through product or service innovation, customer delight, and operational efficiency are making it even more critical to "get it right" and "provide the business backbone". Sales, marketing, operations, and services are joining the finance and IT organizations to enable this collaborative change. We need to ask ourselves what we can do to not only provide this competitive advantage to our customers, but also to provide a solution to our customers, for them to be able to manage their own customers and businesses with better decision making.

When Microsoft decided to invest in a methodology for Microsoft Dynamics solutions, there was one goal in mind—provide our customers with a Microsoft Dynamics purchase, implementation, and an ongoing experience that is unparalleled in the business solutions industry. We determined that we needed a Sure Step way to achieve this customer experience—an experience that is predicated on learning from successful implementations, and equally from the ones that went sideways due to a lack of integrated due diligence and execution approach.

Sure Step provides our partners, our value-added resellers (VARs), our independent software vendors (ISVs), and Microsoft Consulting Services and field teams, with valuable guidance on people, process, and technology aspects that need to come together in a timely, predictable, and disciplined manner to help our prospects and eventual customers "get it right". Microsoft Dynamics Sure Step is the culmination and ongoing journey to make this vision and experience real. Are we indeed investing in the success of our customers, and through that the success of the Microsoft eco-systems of partners and ISVs, keeping these principles in mind?

I have always believed (and known from first-hand experience!) that getting into college is only the first part of the arduous life-changing experience. Getting through college with the right skills, social temperament, informed career choices, and maybe, having fun through the experience, is often the most critical success factor for sustainable lifestyle. Investing in a business application such as Microsoft Dynamics CRM or one of the Microsoft Dynamics ERP products is not dissimilar. Making that right license purchase of software or signing up for the subscription of one of our online solutions is the key; making sure that the software indeed helps guide our customers to ensure their business success and meet their business goals is more critical. Understanding whether the solution is being analyzed, designed, developed, deployed, and eventually adopted and operated in context of the specific industry, with the right level of individual empowerment, in a relevant yet scalable manner to grow with the company, and eventually feel enamored and positively transformed by the experience, is what ensures success. Are we thinking about the customer investment and relationship we develop as transactional events, or as a strategic relationship we wish to develop and watch our customers graduate successfully from the implementation of the solution to reaping the rewards of their due diligence and implementation?

For our partners, Microsoft Services, and IT organizations of our customers, understanding the fundamental principles of any methodology, applying that framework to one's business, and driving adoption of a familiar albeit new way of managing customer expectations requires de-mystifying the method behind the perceived madness! It also becomes critical for each of you to understand how you can use the power and persuasion of Sure Step to not only adapt it to the needs of your organization, but also for the specifics of the customer engagement that you are managing, and as a result help provide you a competitive advantage against the other business applications that may provide the capabilities but may not provide the "customer-focused" approach to lifecycle management. Are you willing to invest time and effort in putting more discipline and accountability into the commitment that you are making for your customers' successes?

Chandru Shankar and Vincent Bellefroid have been loyal thought-leaders, advocates, and evangelists of Microsoft Dynamics Sure Step from the day we embarked on this journey of on-time, on-spec, on-budget Microsoft Dynamics engagements. Chandru Shankar has tapped into his extensive experience working in the partner channel implementing business solutions, and through the architecture of Microsoft Dynamics Sure Step, the deep insights, best-practice values, and the easy-to-comprehend guidance on why Microsoft Dynamics Sure Step recommends what to be done by whom, when, and how. He delves into the details and helps understand the value proposition of Sure Step not only from a sales or implementation perspective, but also ensuring that our customers are getting the most out of their investment now, and forever. The "brain behind the brawn" makes it an enjoyable journey (yes, for a methodology read!) through self discovery and relevant research that will hit close to home for many of you. Vincent Bellefroid has extensive experience dealing with the accolades and brickbats associated with going fearlessly where only the best and bravest readiness, adoption, and training experts can venture. He demystifies how you can embark on a journey of Sure Step adoption, and eventual excellence, within your organizations, by applying some time-tested techniques including Project and Change Management, real-life sales and deployment scenarios, and a roadmap of your success through structured roadmaps. It is hard for me think of a more qualified team to land the message, value, and approach of Microsoft Dynamics Sure Step for our business solutions-focused, business-savvy audiences.

Business-ready organizations are looking to unleash the power of their Microsoft Dynamics investments as they look to drive better decisions, based on operationally efficient business solutions. These organizations have managed their businesses to date. Can they now measure and improve? Do they have the solutions, people, and processes adopted, deployed, and executed in a manner that helps them drive the shift towards integrated end-to-end business management? This book will provide the understanding and approach you need to measure your success through the success of your customers and their business solutions.

Aditya Mohan – Director, Product Management, Microsoft Dynamics Sure Step

One of the most important avenues to a partner's business success—both short and long term—is their ability to manage customer expectations and deliver high quality solutions on time, on budget, and on spec. Sure Step encompasses a number of tools and guidance that enable partners to do just that—helping them drive profitable projects along with customer satisfaction and loyalty at the same time.

Partners with a proven methodology have a distinct competitive advantage, by offering customers peace-of-mind. We have been observing an increasing number of prospects asking for Sure Step-capable partners, so we absolutely recommend that existing as well as prospective Microsoft Dynamics partners adopt Sure Step. As an added benefit, partners will, instead of spending valuable resources developing and maintaining their own methodology, take full advantage of Microsoft's ongoing investments to make Sure Step even more comprehensive and robust. Partners who want to add their own flavor to Sure Step have the opportunity to do exactly that, by treating Sure Step as a methodology platform and developing "the last mile" themselves, much like ISVs build differentiating solutions on top of our ERP and CRM applications.

No matter how a partner plans to leverage Sure Step, this book should help not only explain what Sure Step is about, but also how to get it implemented and adopted within the partner's organization.

Anders Spatzek – Director, Microsoft Dynamics Services & Partner Readiness

Global organizations are typically geographically dispersed, and possess cross-functional teams with varying skill sets in different regions. Business solutions delivery for such organizations requires the ability to manage requirements and schedules, dictated by multiple forces. Also, influencers and power brokers can easily create scope creep and other issues to derail these important initiatives. A consistent methodology and taxonomy is an absolute must for dealing with the pulls and demands across these organizations, to ensure that the project stays on course.

Global delivery typically necessitates the involvement of multiple delivery teams, from the customer, to Microsoft, to partner organizations. Regardless of who owns the delivery of these engagements, it is of paramount importance that all the delivery resources are performing to the "same sheet of music". This is also where it is essential to have a common and consistent framework of delivery.

For our practice, Microsoft Dynamics Sure Step is the tool to ensure success not only for our global practice, but more importantly for our customers and partners. We require that our consulting organization is adept with the methodology, advocating certification on the methodology, and also selecting partners who can work well within these parameters. This book will be an additional asset to help our delivery resources understand the core principles behind the methodology.

Kundan Prakash – Director Business Solutions, Microsoft Services Global Delivery

Providing Microsoft's entrepreneurial partners and customers with industry best practices is vital for ensuring successful business growth. Microsoft Dynamics Sure Step is one of those tools that save time on implementations with the added benefit of bringing together the communication between a sales team and a consulting practice! Stocked with a multitude of templates aligned to a phased implementation process, you can find the right tools to use at each stage of a customer engagement.

In delivering the best knowledge to a global group of partners, Microsoft seeks out top business partners to provide insight and create new content that aligns to Microsoft product releases and industry direction. The result is a tool that brings over 800 pages of project management based guidance along with more than 700 templates, samples, and links to Microsoft resources.

As Sure Step can fit to any size of project, product line, a number of industry solutions, as well as both pre- and post-implementation activities, a new Dynamics team will benefit from guidance that will get them started down the right path to adopting Sure Step and applying it to their customer's lifecycles. This book is sure to find its way to the front of many consultants' bookshelves as the go-to reference for optimizing their use of Microsoft Dynamics Sure Step.

Lori Thalmann Pytlik – Sure Step R&D Manager

Successful ERP and CRM implementations are dependent as much on the product itself, as they are on the people and processes used to implement them. Accordingly, ERP and CRM sales processes are successful when, besides proving ease-of-use and showing relevant product feature sets, they help build confidence in the minds of the customers that a well-defined path exists to get their vision and objectives materialized. Simply put, Microsoft Dynamics Sure Step is the tool that provides the confidence in the pre-sales cycle and assurance during the delivery, which makes a difference.

For our Microsoft Dynamics practice in Microsoft Consulting Services (MCS), we require all our consultants and project managers to be fully proficient and certified in Microsoft Dynamics Sure Step methodology. This helps us in maintaining the high rate of customer satisfaction that we have in this business, as well as providing for an agile and responsive workforce that speaks the same language regardless of the project they are on, or at what point in the lifecycle of a project they were introduced.

This book does a great job in not only detailing out what Sure Step is, but how to best use it in various pre-sales and delivery situations to provide the confidence, consistency, and predictability in execution, so that it becomes one of the core differentiators.

Muhammad Alam – Dynamics US CTO, Microsoft Consulting Services

In order to provide world-class services in the business application space, it is paramount to use a standardized approach, particularly when multiple parties are involved in large and complex projects. This is why we consider Sure Step an important focus area for Microsoft Consulting Services (MCS)—not only do our consulting resources use the methodology extensively, but MCS also makes joint investments with the Microsoft Dynamics Business Group in the development of Sure Step and our offerings.

The MCS offerings for the Microsoft Dynamics AX and Microsoft Dynamics CRM products focus on four main areas, which are described in this book—the Decision Accelerator offerings to help customers with their due diligence, Optimization offerings to augment partner-led engagements, and Implementation and Upgrade offerings with end-to-end MCS involvement. We leverage Sure Step by building our offerings on the solid structure provided by the methodology, allowing us to be more predictable and consistent with our solution delivery process. We can clearly specify "Who" needs to do "What" in "Which Order", and also call out the "Responsible Party" for each step in the process.

Drawing on our field experience on hundreds of Microsoft Dynamics engagements, we continue to extend and improve Sure Step with artifacts and best practices gleaned from senior, knowledgeable resources. This book will help both our internal and external audiences better understand the structure of our offerings and our approach to solution delivery. It will also help highlight the MCS commitment represented in Sure Step, not just to our customers, but also to our partners.

Theo Gees – Sr. Director, Dynamics Program Office

About the Authors

Chandru Shankar is a Microsoft Services Director, responsible for driving solutions and offerings for the Microsoft Dynamics program office. He is also the architect of Microsoft Dynamics Sure Step, the implementation methodology for deploying the Microsoft family of ERP and CRM solutions, and is responsible for the functional design and content flow in the methodology.

Chandru has consulted for companies in a variety of industries, including aerospace, automotive, CPG/retail, high-tech, and manufacturing. He has undertaken multiple implementations of ERP and supply chain solutions, in numerous capacities, including Program/Project Manager, Solutions Architect, and Lead Consultant. His consulting skills are complemented by several years of manufacturing industry experience.

Chandru has also functioned as adjunct faculty for a major university, where he has covered topics including Supply Chain/e-Business Design, along with Strategy and Architecture for MBA students and Company Executives. He has spoken in multiple internal and external conferences over the years, as well as conducted training programs around the world.

Acknowledgement

My involvement with Sure Step began in 2007 with an interim (v1.5) internal release. Through all the subsequent releases, I have had the fortune of working with many individuals and partner organizations whose contributions were critical to the evolution of Sure Step. I often refer to Sure Step as a methodology by the field and for the field — the main reason for the continued adoption of Sure Step is the practical guidance provided by individuals with real-world experience in selling and delivering the Microsoft Dynamics business solutions.

There have been several partners who have contributed their thought leadership to Sure Step, and our sincere thanks to each of you for the content and continued evangelization of the solution. There have also been several Microsoft individuals who have played key roles in the evolution of Sure Step, including the Microsoft Consulting Services (MCS), Microsoft Global Solutions India (MGSI)/Microsoft Services Global Delivery, and Microsoft Dynamics Product and Field Teams. I thank each and every one of you, and would also like to call out a few individuals:

- **Version 1.0**: Laureen Leingaing for leading the development of the overall framework; Udo Burbank and Oliver Besler for the Editor tool.

- **V1.5 (Internal)**: Danny Nakagi for expanding the Cross Phase Processes into true swim lanes; Suneel Mathur for advice on the Enterprise Project Type; Bill Hylwa for expanding the Testing activities, especially for Enterprise projects; Eric Stathers and David Goad for leading the Decision Accelerator offerings; Jony Lawrence and MGSI for helping with the solution finalization.

- **V2**: Aditya Mohan and Mykola Konrad for their leadership and coordination of the overall program; Patrick Cooley and Rainer Nasch for the Client design; Philip Donald and Richard Grant for creating the Visio standards and the first subset of Process Maps for Microsoft Dynamics AX and CRM; Ronni Mattson, Mark Prazak, Maciej Pogoda, and Brian Bakke for helping with the Optimization offerings.

- **V2.6** and **V3.0**: Aditya Mohan and Lori Thalmann-Pytlik for their leadership and coordination of the overall program; Michael Hoffman for the AX and CRM Estimator Tools, Shaun Letley and Siva Surisetty for Agile Project Type; Cally Bauman for Public Sector industry coverage; Colin Silveira, Matt Koopmans and Rebecka Isaksson-Sehlstedt for OCM content.

I would like to thank the Microsoft Dynamics Leadership team, including Kirill Tatarinov, Michael Park, Hal Howard, and Doug Kennedy—your unwavering support for Microsoft Dynamics Sure Step clearly shows Microsoft's commitment to our customers and the Microsoft partner ecosystem. To my friend and Product Team counterpart, Aditya Mohan—your unabashed enthusiasm and evangelization for Microsoft Dynamics in general and Sure Step in particular continues to shine through. I also want to acknowledge the Microsoft Services leadership team, including Kathleen Hogan, Norm Judah, Kristen Johnson, and Paul Mirts—with your support, the services offerings not only leverage the great work done by the field, but they are also openly shared with the partner and customer ecosystems via Sure Step.

This book has been a culmination of many hours of labor. Given that it consumed almost all of my non-work time, I am grateful and thankful to my dear partner in crime, Vincent Bellefroid, for making this long journey enjoyable and worth the effort. Vincent, your knowledge of Sure Step and the partner and customer ecosystems for Microsoft Dynamics are evident in your practical explanations and scenarios that resonate with your audience. We couldn't be happier that you are a key part of our team!

Sincere thanks to our book reviewers, Jim Atkinson, Vjekoslav Babić, Ross Cook, and Aditya Mohan—your suggestions were important in creating a better product. Thanks also to the continued guidance from Kerry George and the rest of the Packt Publishing team—I cannot understate the importance of your help in addressing questions in a timely manner!

We would also like to acknowledge our Foreword writers, Aditya Mohan, Anders Spatzek, Kundan Prakash, Lori Thalmann Pytlik, Muhammad Alam, and Theo Gees. Thank you for your support of the book and the Sure Step program.

Last but not the least, I want to thank my past and present Microsoft mentors, Eric Stathers and Gayle Hoshino—your guidance has been a critical part of my development.

I would like to dedicate this book to my family—to my wife Veena, and my beautiful daughters Maya and Tara, you have given up so much of your personal lives during the development of this book, and I couldn't thank you enough for that. I would also like to thank my extended family—your support and encouragement drove me all the way. Special thanks to my father, L. Shankar, who even took some time to review a few sections and provide feedback.

And now, as one of my colleagues remarked, I look forward to getting my life back!

Vincent Bellefroid is a Microsoft Certified Trainer (MCT), founder, and co-owner of Plataan. Plataan is a Gold-Certified Partner of Microsoft, an independent training and consultancy bureau that specializes in Microsoft Dynamics and Project Management. Vincent is an experienced implementation consultant, who has worked with a number of customer and partner organizations, including global SIs. Building upon his distinguished ERP implementation career, Vincent is now responsible for the project management and quality control at Plataan.

Vincent was one of the early adopters of Sure Step in Europe and has been evangelizing the true value of Sure Step ever since. He has conducted multiple Sure Step training sessions, while helping the Microsoft Sure Step team develop the training materials and courseware. Vincent also guides Microsoft Dynamics partners through the certification and adoption process of Sure Step.

Acknowledgement

I co-authored this book because I wanted to help Microsoft Dynamics implementers and customers find their own way through due diligence, quality assurance, and satisfaction, guided by Microsoft Dynamics Sure Step principles. Each line of text in this book is based on what I learned in my career and still learn every day I teach and consult. Therefore, I want to thank all my trainees, customers, colleagues, and employers from whom I learn every day. I am a trainer and a student at the same time.

Stating that writing this book was an arduous task is squeezing the truth. The only way to get it done was to write for days on end. This book consumed my evenings, weekends, and holidays, which was time away from my precious family. Therefore I want to thank my wife Stien, and Stany and Lou, my lovely sons.

Planning to write a book is one thing, getting it done is a complete different ball game. But I could count on Chandru Shankar at all times. Chandru excels in his knowledge, knows Sure Step inside out, inspires, motivates, leads, and knows how to manage. He is a talented go-getter who guided me through every step of the way. Therefore, my deepest thank you to you, Chandru; I could not have managed this without you.

My thanks also go to Fotini Kaklamanou for introducing me to Sure Step many years ago and to Aditya Mohan for continuously inspiring so many people, including me, for this customer engagement methodology; your support for this book was crucial. Thanks to Bernadette Catherine Kelly for reviewing this book's proposal at the very beginning of the process.

Special thanks to all the reviewers who have contributed on this book. Thank you Swen Maes, Claude Verschueren, Jim Atkinson, and Vjekoslav Babić for fantastic contributions.

Thank you to all the Packt Publishing staff and Kerry George for your support and trust.

Finally, I want to dedicate this book to my father, Eric Bellefroid, currently retired. He excelled as a process optimization specialist and methodologist at Volvo Cars before those terms even existed.

About the Reviewers

Jim Atkinson is a Strategic Account Director with Sales Performance International (SPI). He helps his clients drive measurable and sustainable revenue and earnings growth by improving their overall sales performance. SPI's proven methodologies, training, and enablement programs, technology platforms, and professional services help clients transform their revenue engines to market and sell high-value solutions, enabling them to build a lasting foundation for sustained top-line growth. SPI is the exclusive owner of the Solution Selling® methodology and process.

Prior to SPI, Jim served as a senior-level Business Development Officer in the financial services industry, and as Managing Principal for a global human resources consulting firm. At SPI, he acts as the Subject Matter Expert on targeted territory planning.

Vjekoslav Babić is an independent Microsoft Dynamics NAV consultant, trainer, author, and blogger. He has close to 15 years of experience in IT, of which 8 years of experience is in the field of NAV.

As a Solutions Architect and a Project Manager with a leading Microsoft Dynamics President's Club service provider company, as a Microsoft Dynamics NAV Consultant with Microsoft Services, and as an independent consultant, he has been working on Microsoft Dynamics NAV implementations, ranging from tiny one-man-bands to international mega corporations, delivering services and trainings all over the world.

In 2008, Vjekoslav co-authored the acclaimed book *Implementing Microsoft Dynamics NAV 2009*, for Packt Publishing. Vjekoslav runs an active blog on NAV implementation, project management, and development best practices at http://navigateintosuccess.com/, acts as a columnist and editorial advisory board member at MSDynamicsWorld.com, and as a columnist in a number of other web or printed periodicals in Croatia and worldwide. Vjekoslav is also a frequent conference speaker at Microsoft and Microsoft Dynamics conferences.

Since spring 2010, Vjekoslav has held the prestigious Microsoft Most Valuable Professional (MVP) award for Microsoft Dynamics NAV.

Alain Krikilion has been working with Dynamics NAV (formerly "Navision Financials", "Navision Attain", "Microsoft Business Solutions Navision") since 1999, mostly solving technical problems in both small local projects and big international projects. He started working with NAV in a rainy Belgium and in June 2002 moved to a sunnier Italy.

Alain is also moderator of the mibuso.com forum where, aside from moderating, he also helps people solve (mostly technical) problems.

Alain Krikilion is a Microsoft Most Valued Professional (MVP) for the Microsoft Dynamics NAV product.

Swen Maes graduated in 1997 with a master in Applied Economics at the University of Antwerp. He started his career as a Project Manager at BT Belgium NV. He then went to work as a Distributor Systems Manager at Estée Lauder and then as a Business Consultant for two years at Stanley Europe. After seven years of experience in the IT sector, after having specialized in Project Management for ERP solutions, Swen decided to become a co-owner of iFacto Business Solutions. He is one of the promoters of Sure Step Methodology within his current organization.

One integrated solution that tunes and manages your business processes smoothly and efficiently—sound like music to your ears? Then iFacto Business Solutions is the partner your SME is looking for.

Over the years, iFacto has built an extensive expertise in software applications for various industries. With years of IT experience and thorough industry knowledge, iFacto Business Solutions offers the solution that meets the unique needs of your organization. iFacto is a young and dynamic company in full expansion. We continuously strive to optimize our services we offer to our customers, and every day we search for new opportunities in the market. Driven and motivated people are the key to be able to realize this ambition. A flat organizational structure, a strong corporate culture, and extensive opportunities in self development and career planning, are the major strengths of iFacto.

Aditya Mohan is the Director of Partner Solutions Management at Microsoft. He is responsible for providing Microsoft partners with business solutions to help monitor, manage, and scale their businesses, and drive productivity. These solutions include the Microsoft Dynamics Sure Step methodology and Microsoft Partner Business Systems. At Microsoft, Aditya has previously been the Business Program Manager driving the launch of Dynamics CRM Online, engaged in partner experience initiatives, and launched multiple other GTM initiatives.

Prior to Microsoft, Aditya worked in the IT industry and as a management consultant with Fortune 1000 companies and Mid-Market industry. He has managed a Software Strategy practice, SAP Small-to-Medium Business practices, and Customer experience initiatives at KPMG, BearingPoint, and Hitachi Consulting.

Outside work, Aditya is active in the high-tech and multi-cultural industry forums; loves to leverage his professional, social, and cultural skills; runs, skis, and attempts to be a role model to his three young girls. Aditya is proficient in the Japanese language, and graduated in Engineering from Arizona State University. He is passionate about providing Microsoft Dynamics customers with a purchase, implementation, and an ongoing experiences that are unparalleled in the business solutions industry; partner-ready solutions are key to achieving this goal!

I would like to thank my beautiful women at home—Sayoko, Ria, Keila, and Tara—for letting me be who I am, and keeping me honest that methodologies don't necessarily work in the house!

---

www.PacktPub.com

Support files, eBooks, discount offers and more

You might want to visit www.PacktPub.com for support files and downloads related to your book.

Did you know that Packt offers eBook versions of every book published, with PDF and ePub files available? You can upgrade to the eBook version at www.PacktPub.com and as a print book customer, you are entitled to a discount on t=he eBook copy. Get in touch with us at service@packtpub.com for more details.

At www.PacktPub.com, you can also read a collection of free technical articles, sign up for a range of free newsletters and receive exclusive discounts and offers on Packt books and eBooks.

http://PacktLib.PacktPub.com

Do you need instant solutions to your IT questions? PacktLib is Packt's online digital book library. Here, you can access, read and search across Packt's entire library of books.

Why Subscribe?

- Fully searchable across every book published by Packt
- Copy & paste, print and bookmark content
- On demand and accessible via web browser

Free Access for Packt account holders

If you have an account with Packt at www.PacktPub.com, you can use this to access PacktLib today and view nine entirely free books. Simply use your login credentials for immediate access.

Instant Updates on New Packt Books

Get notified! Find out when new books are published by following @PacktEnterprise on Twitter, or the Packt Enterprise Facebook page.

Table of Contents

Preface

Delivering business solutions is more than just product play. Software is often viewed as the enabler; however, the key to success is how the solution is implemented and how the implementations are managed. With this as the background, Microsoft has developed Sure Step as the full lifecycle methodology for the Microsoft Dynamics solutions portfolio.

This book details the use of Sure Step methodology beginning with the due diligence process for the customer that overlaps the solution selling cycle for the service provider, continuing through the solution implementation phases, and encompassing on-going maintenance and upgrades. Maximize your Microsoft Dynamics investments and increase your efficiency to select or sell, deliver, and operate and support your solution.

What this book covers

Chapter 1, Background and Concepts
In this chapter, we introduce the concept of Methodology and its importance in the selection and implementation of ERP/CRM solutions. A faulty selection process can derail any solution deployment, and it is important for the readers to understand what they can do to prevent this. Many implementations go awry because of poor scope, risk, and change management, and we will talk about this as well. Another topic of discussion for this chapter is Microsoft Dynamics—what solutions encompass this suite, the history behind the acquisitions, its position in the overall ecosystem, and so on.

Chapter 2, Solution Selling and Driving Due Diligence
The focus of this chapter is on selling business solutions. We talk about how solution selling is different from transaction sales, where you have to build a relationship with your customer and establish trust. We also represent two perspectives—from a partner perspective, they are helping drive the customer vision; from a customer perspective, they are doing their due diligence in selecting the right solution to meet their needs.

Chapter 3, Managing Projects
The focus of this chapter is introducing the value proposition for project management. We talk about managing projects from a result-driven and real-life perspective. This chapter sheds light on the resistance to project management and how to overcome that by unleashing the real value of project management. While introducing the reader to the four pillars of project success and explaining about project management essentials, we guide them to the benefits of smart projects. We also discuss project management adoption from an organizational perspective.

Chapter 4, Selling with Sure Step
This chapter builds on the introduction to selling in Chapter 2. In this chapter we talk about specifics on how Sure Step helps with selling Microsoft Dynamics solutions. We discuss the activities and cover in detail the Decision Accelerator offerings that help accelerate sales cycles and bring them to close, while also helping the customer with their due diligence process.

We also talk about how the Diagnostic phase sets the stage for a quality implementation by outlining the risks involved. We discuss the selection of the right approach for the deployment, as well as the roles that will be involved both from the partner and the customer teams.

Chapter 5, Implementing with Sure Step
The focus of this chapter is on the implementation lifecycle. This chapter discusses the different implementation phases and cross phases for implementing a Microsoft Dynamics solution using the waterfall approach, and covers the post-go-live stage as well. We concentrate on the real-life challenges that implementers and customers face when implementing ERP and CRM software solutions and propose solutions by demonstrating the true value of Sure Step in terms of methodology and supporting tools and templates. This chapter also introduces the reader to the agile approach and covers how this flexible and iterative approach is organized and supported by Sure Step.

Chapter 6, Quality Control and Optimization
In this chapter, we discuss some options for the partners and customers to ensure a quality implementation. In doing so, we introduce the Sure Step Optimization Roadmap, and discuss the Proactive and Post Go Live Review offerings.

Chapter 7, Upgrading with Sure Step
The focus of this chapter is on helping existing Microsoft Dynamics customers to upgrade their solution to the latest product release. We discuss how we begin with the Upgrade Assessment Decision Accelerator offering to ascertain the right approach, then explain the Sure Step Upgrade project type for technical upgrades. We also suggest approaches for adding new functionality during the upgrade process.

Chapter 8, Project and Change Management
The focus of this chapter is on the Project Management and Change Management disciplines in Sure Step. We discuss the key sub-disciplines of Project Management, such as Risk, Scope, Issue, and Communication management. We also explain why Organizational Change Management is a key area for customers and partners to consider when it comes to ERP/CRM engagements. In this chapter, we also cover the SharePoint feature built into Sure Step, to assist the solution delivery teams to effectively collaborate with each other.

Chapter 9, A Practical Guide to Sure Step Adoption
The focus of this chapter is on the adoption of Sure Step in Microsoft Dynamics partner organizations. We talk about how organizations can make their implementation methodology one of their core competencies. We also cover the Independent Software Vendor (ISV) perspective, and discuss how the ISV solution provider can leverage Sure Step.

Chapter 10, Summary and Takeaways
The intent of this chapter is the summarization of the book. We discuss the future of Sure Step and also provide a set of key action items that the readers can execute on in the near term.

What you need for this book

The only software component required for the methodology is the Microsoft Dynamics Sure Step 2010 application. The resources available to you are noted as follows:

- Download and install of the Sure Step 2010 application:
  - If you are Microsoft Dynamics Partner: Download from PartnerSource, at this direct link: `https://mbs.microsoft.com/partnersource/communities/consulting/resources/Consulting_SureStep_Methodology.htm`

- ○ If you are Microsoft Dynamics Customer: Download from CustomerSource, at this direct link: `https://mbs.microsoft.com/customersource/downloads/servicepacks/msdsurestep2010downloads.htm`

- ○ If you are a Microsoft resource: Download from ProductsWeb, via this link: `http://surestep`

- • Readiness materials and presentations:
  - ○ Leverage the Sure Step online training courses on the above sites
  - ○ Review the presentations and readiness materials
  - ○ Access the class schedules to find a classroom training course

- • Sure Step support:
  - ○ Connect with Sure Step peers on Partner and Customer Forums from the above sites

- • Adoption of Sure Step:
  - ○ Learn how Partners can identify a Sure Step Champion, and measure and drive adoption at `http://surestep.adoptionroadmap.com/`
  - ○ Learn how an organization with the right methodology can help the customer be more successful with Microsoft Dynamics at `http://www.microsoft.com/dynamics/en/us/implementation.aspx`

System Requirements:

- • Windows 7, Windows Vista, Windows Vista SP1, or Windows XP SP2 (or greater)
- • Microsoft Office 2007 or 2010
- • Internet Explorer 7 or 8
- • Microsoft .NET Framework 3.5 Service Pack 1
- • To use the SharePoint project creation feature, the following SharePoint versions are supported:
  - ○ Microsoft SharePoint Foundation 2010
  - ○ Microsoft SharePoint Server 2010
  - ○ Windows SharePoint Services 3.0
  - ○ Microsoft Office SharePoint Server 2007

Who this book is for

This book is aimed at newcomers to business solutions space, as well as experienced practitioners getting into the Microsoft Dynamics arena. If you are involved in one or more of the roles stated below, then this book is for you:

- If you are a Project Manager, Engagement Manager, Solution Architect or Consultant involved in delivering Microsoft Dynamics solutions, learn how you can improve the quality of your implementation with a consistent, repeatable process.

- If you are a Customer Project Manager, Subject Matter Expert, Key User, or End User involved in selecting the right business solution for your organization and delivering the Microsoft Dynamics solution, learn how the method facilitates the delivery of a solution that is aligned to your vision.

- If you are a Sales Executive, Services Sales Executive, Technical Sales Specialist, Pre-Sales Consultant, or Project Manager involved in sales of Microsoft Dynamics solutions, learn how you can leverage the guidance and artifacts to accelerate your sales cycle and bring them to a close.

- If you are the Customer Decision Maker, CxO, Buyer, or Project Manager who participates in the selection process for your business solution needs, learn how this process can help your due diligence exercise and set the stage for a quality implementation of the solution.

- If you are a Change Management expert, learn how you can help the customer manage their change during the business solution delivery process, and/or help service providers adopt a process for selling and delivering solutions.

- If you are an Independent Software Vendor (ISV) developing add-on solutions for Microsoft Dynamics, learn how the methodology can help you drive more successful engagements, and in turn, more customers.

Conventions

In this book, you will find a number of styles of text that distinguish between different kinds of information. Here are some examples of these styles, and an explanation of their meaning.

New terms and **important words** are shown in bold. Words that you see on the screen, in menus or dialog boxes for example, appear in the text like this: "The one technical post go-live offering, **Health Check**, is designed for the solutions that are already in operation for a certain period of time."

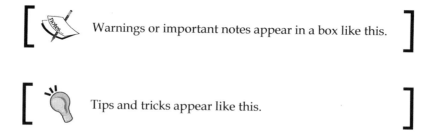

Warnings or important notes appear in a box like this.

Tips and tricks appear like this.

Reader feedback

Feedback from our readers is always welcome. Let us know what you think about this book—what you liked or may have disliked. Reader feedback is important for us to develop titles that you really get the most out of.

To send us general feedback, simply send an e-mail to feedback@packtpub.com, and mention the book title via the subject of your message.

If there is a book that you need and would like to see us publish, please send us a note in the **SUGGEST A TITLE** form on www.packtpub.com or e-mail suggest@packtpub.com.

If there is a topic that you have expertise in and you are interested in either writing or contributing to a book, see our author guide on www.packtpub.com/authors.

Customer support

Now that you are the proud owner of a Packt book, we have a number of things to help you to get the most from your purchase.

Errata

Although we have taken every care to ensure the accuracy of our content, mistakes do happen. If you find a mistake in one of our books—maybe a mistake in the text or the code—we would be grateful if you would report this to us. By doing so, you can save other readers from frustration and help us improve subsequent versions of this book. If you find any errata, please report them by visiting http://www.packtpub. com/support, selecting your book, clicking on the **errata submission form** link, and entering the details of your errata. Once your errata are verified, your submission will be accepted and the errata will be uploaded on our website, or added to any list of existing errata, under the Errata section of that title. Any existing errata can be viewed by selecting your title from http://www.packtpub.com/support.

Piracy

Piracy of copyright material on the Internet is an ongoing problem across all media. At Packt, we take the protection of our copyright and licenses very seriously. If you come across any illegal copies of our works, in any form, on the Internet, please provide us with the location address or website name immediately so that we can pursue a remedy.

Please contact us at copyright@packtpub.com with a link to the suspected pirated material.

We appreciate your help in protecting our authors, and our ability to bring you valuable content.

Questions

You can contact us at questions@packtpub.com if you are having a problem with any aspect of the book, and we will do our best to address it.

Background and Concepts

All companies must harness information to create competitive advantage. It is no longer possible to leverage information without technology, and both the information to be managed and the supporting technologies are continuously becoming more complex. Leading-edge IT implementations generally require special expertise from external service providers.

Gartner, Inc.

The success of a business solution, and specifically an **Enterprise Resource Planning (ERP)** and **Customer Relationship Management (CRM)** solution, isn't solely about technology. Experience tells that it is as much about the people and processes as it is about the software. Software is often viewed as the enabler, with the key to success lying in how the solution is implemented and how the implementations are managed. The transformation from the technological solution being the point of emphasis in the early days of the business software era to the solution becoming an enabler for business transformation has only been furthered by the ERP/CRM reports by independent organizations that decry deployment failures in great detail.

What stands out very clearly in these reports is the fact that ERP and CRM solution delivery is characterized by uncertainties and risks. Service providers have to balance time and budget constraints, while delivering the business value of the solution to their customers. Customer organizations need to understand that their involvement and collaboration is critical for the success of the delivery. They will need to invest time, provide relevant and accurate information, and manage the organizational changes to ensure that the solution is delivered as originally envisioned.

The need for seamless implementation and deployment of business software is even more accentuated in the current state of the economy with enterprise software sales going through a prolonged period of negative to stagnant growth over the last several quarters. Sales cycles are taking longer to execute, especially as the customers take advantage of the buyer's market and force software providers to prove their solution in the sales cycle before signing off on the purchase. In this market, a good solution delivery approach is critical. We have consistently heard words such as in-scope, within-budget, and on-time being tossed around in the industry. Service providers are still facing these demands; however, in the current context, budgets are tighter, timeframes are shorter, and the demand for a quick return on investment is becoming increasingly critical.

Microsoft has always understood that the value of the software is only as good as its implementation and adoption. Accordingly, Microsoft Dynamics Sure Step was developed as the methodology for positioning and deploying the Microsoft Dynamics ERP/CRM suite of products—AX, CRM, GP, NAV, and SL. In the vision of Sure Step, project management is not the prerogative of the project manager only. Sure Step is a partnership of consulting and customer resources, representing a very important triangulation of the collaboration between the software vendor, implementer, and customer, with the implementation methodology becoming a key element of the implemented application.

In this chapter, we will introduce the concepts and definitions used in this book, and lay the background for the ensuing chapters. We will also provide an overview of Microsoft Dynamics Sure Step, and the different aspects of the methodology that help both the implementer and the customer.

The business solutions market

The 2010 calendar year began with the global economy trying to crawl out of a recession. Still, businesses continued to invest in solutions, to leverage the power of information technology to drive down redundancy and waste in their internal processes. This was captured in a study by Gartner of the top industry CIOs, published in their annual report titled Gartner Perspective: IT Spending 2010. In spite of the recessionary pressures, organizations continued to list improving business processes, reducing costs, better use of information, and improving workforce effectiveness as their priorities for IT spending.

The Gartner study listed the following top 10 business priorities based on 2009 findings:

* Business process improvement
* Reducing enterprise costs

- Improving enterprise workforce effectiveness
- Attracting and retaining new customers
- Increasing the use of information/analytics
- Creating new products or services (innovation)
- Targeting customers and markets more effectively
- Managing change initiatives
- Expanding current customer relationships
- Expanding into new markets and geographies

The Gartner study listed the following top 10 technology priorities based on 2009 findings:

- Business intelligence
- Enterprise applications (ERP, CRM, and others)
- Servers and storage technologies (virtualization)
- Legacy application modernization
- Collaboration technologies
- Networking, voice, and data communications
- Technical infrastructure
- Security technologies
- Service-oriented applications and architecture
- Document management

[The source document for the previous two lists is: Gartner Executive Programs – CIO Agenda 2010.]

These are also some of the many reasons that companies, regardless of scale, implement ERP and CRM software, which again is evident from the top 10 technology priorities of the CIOs listed above. These demands, however, happen to be articulated even more strongly by small and medium businesses. For these businesses, an ERP/CRM solution can be a sizable percentage of their overall expense outlay, so they have to be especially vigilant about their spending—they just can't afford time and cost overruns as are sometimes visible in the Enterprise market. At the same time, the deployment of rich functionality software must realize a significant and clear advantage for their business. These trends are picked up and addressed by the IT vendors, who are constantly seeking and exploring new technological ingredients to address the **Small-to-Medium Enterprise** market demands.

The importance of a methodology

Having a predictable and reliable methodology is important for both the service provider (the implementer) and the users of the solution (the customer). This is especially true for ERP/CRM solution deployment, which can happen at intervals of anywhere from a couple of months to a couple of years, and the implementation team often comprises multiple individuals from the service provider and the customer. Therefore, it is very important that all the individuals are working off the same sheet of music, so to speak.

Methodology can be defined as:

The methods, rules, and hypothesis employed by, and the theory behind a given discipline

> or

The systematic study of the methods and processes applied within the discipline over time

Methodology can also be described as a collection of theories, concepts, and processes pertaining to a specific discipline or field. Rather than just a compilation of methods, methodology refers to the scientific method and the rationale behind it, as well as the assumptions underlying the definitions and components of the method.

The definitions we just saw are particularly relevant to the design/architecture of a methodology for ERP/CRM and business solutions. For these solutions, the methodology should not just provide the processes, but it should also provide a connection to the various disciplines and roles that are involved in the execution of the methodology. It should provide detailed guidance and assumptions for each of the components, so that the consumers of the methodology can discern to what extent they will need to employ all or certain aspects of it on a given engagement.

As such, a solid approach provides more than just a set of processes for solution deployment. For the service provider, a viable methodology can provide:

- End-to-end process flows for solution development and deployment, creating a repeatable process leading to excellence in execution
- Ability to link shell and sample templates, reference architecture, and other similar documentation to key activities
- A structure for creating an effective **Knowledge Management (KM)** system, facilitating easier harvesting, storing, retrieval, and reuse of content created by the field on customer engagements

- Ability to develop a rational structure for training of the consulting team members, including ramp-up of new employees
- Ability to align the quality assurance approach to the deployment process— important in organizations that use an independent QA process as oversight for consulting efforts
- Ability to develop a structured estimation process for solution development and deployment
- Creation of a structure for project scope control and management, and a process for early risk identification and mediation

For the customer, a viable methodology can provide:

- Clear end-to-end process flows for solution development that can be followed by the customer's key users and Subject Matter Experts (SMEs) assigned to the project
- Consistent terminology and taxonomy, especially where the SMEs may not have had prior experience with implementing systems of such magnitude, thus making it easier for everybody to be on the same page
- Ability to develop a good Knowledge Management system to capture lessons learned for future projects/upgrades
- Ability to develop a rational structure and documentation for end-user training and new employee ramp-up
- Creation of a structure for ensuring that the project stays within scope, including a process for early risk identification and mediation

In addition to the points listed here, having a "full lifecycle methodology" provides additional benefits in the sales-to-implementation continuum.

The benefits for the service providers include:

- Better alignment of the consulting teams with the sales teams
- A more scientific deal management and approval process that takes into account the potential risks
- Better processes to facilitate the transfer of customer knowledge, ascertained during the sales cycle, to the solution delivery team
- Ability to show the customer how the service provider has "done it before" and effectively establish trust that they can deliver the envisioned solution
- Clearly illustrating the business value of the solution to the customer
- Ability to integrate multiple software packages into an overall solution for the customer

- Ability to deliver the solution as originally envisioned within scope, on time, and within established budget

The benefits for the customers include:

- Ability to understand and articulate the business value of the solution to all stakeholders in the organization
- Ensuring that there is a clear solution blueprint established
- Ensuring that the solution is delivered as originally envisioned within scope, on time, and within established budget
- Ensuring an overall solution that can integrate multiple software packages

In summary, a good methodology creates a better overall ecosystem for the organizations. The points noted in the earlier lists are an indication of some of the ways that the benefits are manifested; as you leverage methodologies in your own organization, you may realize other benefits as well.

Why it is critical to have a solid approach for selecting and deploying ERP/CRM solutions

Business solutions delivery in general, and ERP/CRM consulting specifically, is very different from deploying other solutions such as an e-mail system. It goes without saying that e-mail communications are extremely important for companies in today's environment. Yet, a company could function for a foreseeable period without e-mail — people may actually have to resort to what now seems to be an archaic form of communication and pick up a phone to talk to other parties. As humorous as it may seem, it wouldn't be far from reality, and some employees would argue that their efficiencies may actually increase during that e-mail downtime as they are actually able to focus on their core job requirements.

In contrast to infrastructure solutions, ERP systems specifically, and CRM systems to an extent, form the backbone of the company. These systems support core functions such as quote-to-order entry, order fulfillment, receipts and payments, HR and payroll, inventory management, distribution/production planning, demand forecasting, and sales pipeline management, among other things. A company would be crippled if these systems were down for a long period of time. This is why, depending on the usage scenario, ERP/CRM systems are typically perceived as mission-critical systems, while infrastructure systems are most often seen as business-critical systems.

This is also the reason that customers take a long time to do the necessary due diligence before selecting the right solution to meet their needs. Given this criticality, it is easy to see how having a methodology that goes beyond solution delivery to help customers with their selection process can be perceived as beneficial by the customer. It is also why customers should go through the due diligence in selecting their solution provider or implementer as they do on the business application itself. It is critical that the solution provider follows a robust process as evidenced by the methodology that they employ, both in helping the customer select the right solution to meet their needs and in delivering the envisioned solution.

During the customer's selection/due diligence process, it is important that they are guided through their requirements gathering process, including understanding their current ("as-is") and future ("to-be") processes. Then the customer should be able to ascertain how each of the requirements fits within the proposed solution. Additionally, the customer should be able to determine all infrastructure components (hardware and any third-party software), as well as the release schedule (overall plan with resource needs from both the consulting and customer organization). The key output of the due diligence phase should be a solution blueprint that articulates the proposed solution for the customer, as well as a statement of work that explains how the solution blueprint will be executed.

From a solution delivery perspective, ERP/CRM engagements are also considerably different compared to an infrastructure project. The following illustration depicts some of the products in the Microsoft portfolio. As you go from left to right in this spectrum, the projected solution delivery effort as well as complexity increases exponentially.

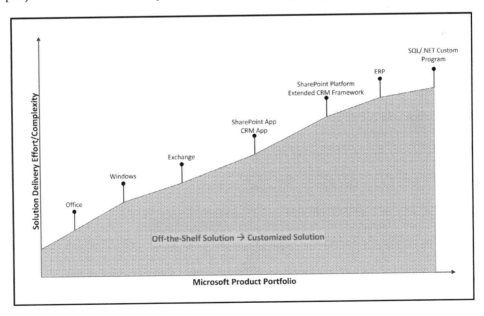

The key point in this graphical representation is that ERP/CRM solutions, on an average, require a level of customization that is far more than the typical infrastructure solutions. This is expected as these solutions are applied to multiple workflows within organizations in many different industries and verticals. As the customization need increases, so does the effort and complexity. This is not to say that all infrastructure projects will be straight off-the-shelf solutions, or that all ERP/CRM projects will be highly customized solutions. Any solution will have a range of complexity, from a quick, rapid deployment, to a longer, complex solution development and deployment. The point of emphasis is that this greater complexity implies a greater need for having an implementation methodology that ensures appropriate project and quality management during the solution delivery process. This is also what Sure Step delivers, which we will introduce in the next section.

What is Microsoft Dynamics Sure Step?

In the previous section, we discussed the criticality of having a solid approach for selecting and deploying ERP/CRM solutions. This is exactly where Sure Step fits in—as a method and process for customers and service providers alike. We will introduce Sure Step in this section, and in the rest of the book will talk about how it is designed to deliver on these promises to an organization.

Microsoft Dynamics Sure Step is a full customer lifecycle methodology for all Microsoft Dynamics® solutions. It provides service providers with comprehensive sales through delivery guidance, project management discipline alignment, and field-driven best practices, while facilitating the due diligence process and a high-quality solution delivery for the customer.

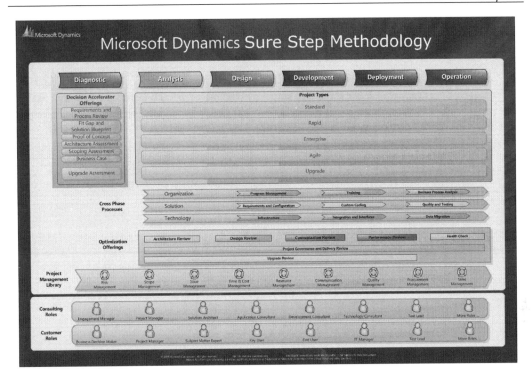

The first release of Sure Step was launched in 2007, and since then Sure Step has evolved to meet the demands of the Microsoft Dynamics ecosystem. Existing workflows have been modified and streamlined and new ones introduced. The methodology has also been expanded into a full lifecycle methodology that includes the customer's due diligence lifecycle as a precursor to the solution delivery process. Also, more content is being made available to the users, with the current release providing over a thousand content pieces, from guidance pages to templates to general project management libraries. The following are key characteristics of Sure Step, including some of the highlights of the Sure Step 2010 release.

- Using six phases, Sure Step covers not only delivery, but also solution positioning and selling. The first phase, **Diagnostic**, provides guidance and content for service providers to help customers with their due diligence process in selecting the right solution to meet their needs. The remaining phases, **Analysis**, **Design**, **Development**, **Deployment**, and **Operation**, provide workflows and content for solution delivery.

- Sure Step provides coverage for the entire Microsoft Dynamics solutions suite—Microsoft Dynamics AX, Microsoft Dynamics CRM, Microsoft Dynamics GP, Microsoft Dynamics NAV, and Microsoft Dynamics SL. With the latest release, Sure Step also extends the general coverage of this content into specific industry and cross-industry areas.

- Sure Step provides a very flexible approach for delivering the solution, with both waterfall and iterative approaches. The **Standard**, **Rapid**, and **Enterprise** project types scale up or down to match the customer engagement, and the **Upgrade** project type caters specifically to upgrading an existing solution. Also provided is the **Agile** project type for those engagements that lend themselves to an iterative solution delivery approach.

- The project types in Sure Step feature a structure that breaks down each engagement into cross phases or swim lanes. The Sure Step cross phases are **Program Management**, **Training**, **Business Process Analysis**, **Requirements and Configuration**, **Custom Coding**, **Quality and Testing**, **Infrastructure**, **Integration and Interfaces**, and **Data Migration**. These cross phases provide users with a very functional pivot to portray the activities or steps for delivering the solution.

- Sure Step includes additional guidance on optimizing an engagement with directed offerings, both during the implementation and post-go-live.

- Key process guidance, including project management and organizational change management disciplines, are provided in Sure Step.

- Sure Step covers the typical roles involved in an engagement, both from the consulting and the customer organizations.

- The Sure Step application also gives teams the ability to create projects with the starting templates in appropriate folders, either on their local machine or on a SharePoint server for bigger collaboration efforts.

Microsoft Dynamics overview

As discussed in the previous section, Sure Step covers the entire Microsoft Dynamics portfolio of solutions. In this section, we will provide an overview of those solutions, which is mainly intended to be a quick reference, or as a starting point for those readers who may not be familiar with all the solutions in the portfolio.

Microsoft Dynamics is Microsoft's line of business management solutions that provide Enterprise Resource Planning and Customer Relationship Management capabilities. The portfolio includes four ERP solutions, which were brought about by acquisition, and one CRM solution, the development of which was initiated in Microsoft.

Microsoft Dynamics GP (formerly known as Great Plains), and Microsoft Dynamics SL (formerly known as Solomon), were both acquired in 2001 from Great Plains Software, based in Fargo, North Dakota, USA. Great Plains was a mid-market business accounting software package popular in North America, while Solomon provided an ERP system with project management and project accounting functionality. Microsoft Dynamics AX (formerly known as Axapta), and Microsoft Dynamics NAV (formerly known as Navision), were both acquired in 2002 from Navision A/S, a company based in Denmark. Axapta and Navision were popular ERP solutions, especially for manufacturing and distribution midmarket companies in Europe. The ERP systems became the starting point for a new division in Microsoft called Microsoft Business Solutions, which also included Microsoft CRM. Microsoft CRM was primarily homegrown as noted earlier, and had its first launch (version 1.0) in 2003.

In 2005, Microsoft rebranded the products and created a suite of business solutions called Microsoft Dynamics. It includes the four ERP solutions—Microsoft Dynamics AX, Microsoft Dynamics GP, Microsoft Dynamics NAV, and Microsoft Dynamics SL—and one CRM solution—Microsoft Dynamics CRM. Microsoft SQL Server is the database technology used for the entire suite. The following diagram depicts the timeline:

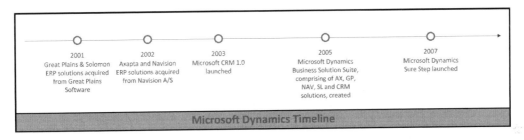

The Microsoft Dynamics solutions have been designed to be familiar to users, work easily with the existing systems that customers have already deployed, empower people and teams to be productive, and help organizations drive business success. The ERP suite provides functionality to help business in the areas of financial planning and accounting, supply chain, project accounting, field service, and human resources processes. On the other hand, the CRM solution allows companies to streamline the way their employees communicate and collaborate with their customers with features such as customer relationship, sales force automation, service management, marketing capabilities, and workflow automation and analytics.

In addition to the comprehensive financial and process management tools at the core of the Microsoft Dynamics solutions, **Independent Software Vendor (ISV)** partners offer a number of integrated, specialized solutions that provide versatile business software that address specialized industry needs.

The Microsoft Dynamics solution features (as of this writing) are as follows:

- Microsoft Dynamics AX is designed to help organizations operate across locations and countries by standardizing processes, providing visibility across the business, and helping to simplify compliance. It supports the needs of global organizations, featuring multi-language and localized functionality by country/region. Microsoft Dynamics AX supports the primary and secondary processes of organizations in multiple industries, including manufacturing, distribution, retail, and services.

- Microsoft Dynamics GP is a richly featured financial accounting and business management solution that provides organizations with fast and relevant access to information using familiar Microsoft tools. It features rapid, flexible deployment options, and a familiar user experience designed to maximize personal productivity.

- Microsoft Dynamics NAV is a solution for mid-sized organizations that is fast to implement, easy to configure, and simple to use. It features an innovative client that provides a user experience tailored to specific roles in the organization.

- Microsoft Dynamics SL is designed for project-driven organizations by connecting project management and accounting functions across company divisions and locations. It supports specialized customer, accounting, and regulatory requirements for professional services, government contractors, distribution, and construction management.

- Microsoft Dynamics CRM is a customer relationship management solution with core functionality, including sales, customer service, and marketing. It provides flexible deployment options, which feature a common code base for both online and on-premise solution deployments. In addition, Microsoft Dynamics CRM provides an xRM business application framework (also referred to as Extended CRM), featuring rapid application development, a high degree of flexibility, and consolidated systems management.

What is a project?

It looks like a simple question, but have we ever thought about what is essential to our business? Before we can start strategizing on how to manage and sell projects, we need to understand what a project is and, even more important, what it is not.

Most people respond to the question by talking about activities, planning, and meetings, due dates, documents, people, and objectives. This is how many of us think of a project, but can we call all engagements where people try to reach objectives by means of planned activities projects? Probably not. For example, in the production plants of automotive companies, people realize objectives and collaborate on planned activities, but we wouldn't classify those as projects.

Before we can speak about a project, we need to be certain about the unique and temporary character of our endeavor. Projects are temporary by definition, as they have well-defined start and end dates. Most of us are well informed about the starting date of our project; the end date can be more of a worry and is often confused with the go-live date of the brand-new software solution. Projects are also unique by nature—not only because they produce unique deliverables but also because the context for the execution is unique. Unique can mean that it has never been done before, or maybe it has been done in a very similar fashion before but never exactly in this way. Therefore, no two projects, by definition, can be the same.

In most of the definitions of a project that we can find in literature, these key elements are well absorbed.

The Project Management Body of Knowledge (PMBOK) defines a project as *a temporary endeavor undertaken to create a unique product, service or result. The temporary nature of projects indicates a definite beginning and end. The end is reached when the project's objectives have been achieved or when the project is terminated because its objectives will not or cannot be met, or when the need for the project no longer exists.*

By implementing Microsoft Dynamics solutions, we implement ERP or CRM software functionality, and from a product's point of view, many of these implementations are lookalikes. Then what makes these implementations unique?

Although we are implementing typical ERP or CRM functionalities, we need to implement unique business requirements for each customer. Every customer has unique demands for specific deliverables, such as internal reports and customized functionality, matching their unique organization of the business processes. But even more important to note is the fact that people make these implementations unique. Implementing the solution in a customer context is always unique because we are always working with different people. They always have a different background, knowledge level, expectations, goals, and their own unique way of working. We also work with changing consulting implementation teams, based on the availability of our consultants, resulting in a unique context. So yes, the Microsoft Dynamics implementations are projects because they are unique and they are meant to be temporary. We always need to deliver our projects in a limited timeframe and our engagements are never the same. However, this involves a lot of uncertainty and so our Microsoft Dynamics engagements are characterized by uncertainty going hand in hand with risk (in ISO 31000:2009 risk is defined as the effect of uncertainty on objectives).

Now that we have understood what a project is, we also need to understand what it is not. A project is not ongoing and repetitive; projects are not operations. Businesses driven by ongoing repetitive processes carry less risk because the context is much more controlled. In our projects, we do not have such controlled environments. We simply don't know who our key as well as end users will be and we also don't know how familiar they are with business processes and business solutions. We do not know how well they communicate and how they perform in teams. There is so much that we don't know when planning a new engagement.

What matters is to be aware of these risks and to be aware that the business we are in is completely different as compared to an operations-driven business. Only then we can really start strategizing on how to manage and sell projects. Therefore, we should review our future proposals and plans, bearing in mind that we are planning for a project, which ultimately means planning for risks. How well are these plans and strategies covering the uncertainties?

Most definitions of a project in literature include these elements of the unique and temporary character but do not outreach them. There are also few other questions that need to be answered:

Isn't it equally important to gain an understanding of the contractual and commercial matters:

- Are we delivering projects?
- How are we involved in projects?
- Do we have project responsibility?
- Do we carry the project risks and to which extent?

The answers to these questions prescribe and justify how we will sell and manage our projects. Just outsourcing resources to carry out project tasks does not call for the same management as carrying all project risks in a fixed-price project.

Implementing the solution

Ask any software vendor for their definition of a business solution and you will receive answers focusing on functionality designed to help automate business processes, empowering every aspect of the business, and ultimately accelerating an organization's success. Words such as insight, efficiency, flexibility, cost reduction, responsiveness, and many more are used to voice proven return on investment.

But what answers would you get when you pose the same questions to the customers? The first thing that you will notice is that the answers will not be so consistent. Most decision makers do have their own reasons why they want to have a software solution in their organization. What they want to achieve is related to the unique history of that company, their incomparable way of doing things, and the industry sector to which they belong. Their objectives also have a direct link with the company's business plan and strategic objectives. This means a customer's definition of a business solution is never universal but always specific.

Although business solutions are designed to achieve the same results within organizations, customers usually seek for very specific solutions for resolving their unique problems and supporting the business challenges as envisioned by them. No matter how rich the functionality of the solution is, unique customer's expectations cannot just be delivered off the shelf. This gap needs to be bridged by the implementation process.

One might think that implementing business solutions in small and mid-sized companies is less complex compared to the large-scaled implementations in corporations. Be careful not to jump to conclusions here. In general, business processes are less standardized in these types of businesses. Instead, you will find a rich and interesting variety of procedures representing the unique way of doing things. This makes the need for a unique business solution even greater and demands a streamlined implementation process.

By now, you will have understood that the implementation process is a key part of the overall solution. But before you march into your customer's premises to start implementing, it could be wise to give some thought to the meaning of all this for your customer. Imagine yourself in your customer's situation and don't take things for granted. How will your implementation strategy affect this organization? Can they conceive what an implementation process is, and even more important, what added value it means for them? Are they aware of the risks, and do they know that it needs both parties to work together to implement a project successfully? Are they aware what their role would be?

Business solution implementations are rife with challenges. Even consultants, who have been delivering these solutions for a number of years, run into issues on projects that they may not have previously encountered. No matter the years of training and shadowing experienced colleagues, unique challenges are bound to come up. Having this in mind, it is not surprising that our customers sometimes cannot estimate the level of effort that they need to put into this implementation and that they are not aware of the importance of their involvement. It is then important for the consulting teams to make sure the customer understands their expectations in the overall solution delivery process.

Technology Evaluation Centers (TEC) is a research organization that has several publications on ERP/CRM solutions. In their research whitepaper titled *5 Tips to Assure a Successful ERP Implementation*, they bring up some key points for the customer's implementation team.

Management buy-in is also considered one of the keys to successful implementations. TEC believes that it is essential that corporate management is actively involved in the system selection decision by naming an executive sponsor who participates and provides the necessary support for the project. A senior management sponsor to champion the expected organizational change is highlighted as "a critical, must-have step" for successful implementations.

Ensuring the participation of a cross-functional team is another key to success noted by TEC. A team comprised of all functional divisions and management levels within the organization facilitates active ownership of the project by the entire user community. This also ensures that the implementation team will be able to reflect the requirements of the users, thereby maximizing the value delivered by the solution.

These are good points for the customer team to keep in mind, so that they understand their responsibilities for implementing the solution. As the next section will illustrate, teams that ignore these lessons do so at their own peril.

ERP and CRM implementations—facts and figures

Over the years, most of the reports on CRM and ERP implementations endorsed the existence of gaps between customer expectations and actual results. The studies also pointed out that time and cost performance still remain an undeniable point for improvement.

You need to be careful while interpreting these statistics. Most studies do not measure exactly the same things, they have different types of respondents, and the methodological approach may vary as well.

In the early nineties, *Standish's Chaos Report* shocked the industry, when it reported a 16 percent success factor on software development projects. The same report called 53 percent of the projects to be challenged on implementation, and 31 percent to have failed. Although considered to be controversial, this report managed to attract worldwide attention for solution delivery issues.

About sixteen years later, we still have Chaos Reports, now accompanied by many others. The 2009 statistics of the Chaos Report showed 32 percent success, 24 percent failure, and 44 percent projects to be challenged. Investigations of other research companies show slightly better statistics; however, they all conclude that there is still opportunity for improvement as most of our ERP and CRM projects take longer and cost more than expected.

While these facts and figures may shed a poor light, these statistics are not intended to discourage a relatively young industry sector or to put off executives from undertaking ERP and CRM projects. Instead, these should be viewed as lessons learned from failed and challenged projects, which the stakeholders involved in the solution implementations can use as input for continuous improvement efforts.

It also seems easy to transfer the responsibility for all failed implementations to the service provider. But as we have noted in the previous sections, a solution is made up of many components, including the product (software vendor), the service provider, and the user of the solution (the customer). While it might be easy to blame the implementer for all failures, it is not entirely justifiable. For instance, recent reports also offer insight into how customers impede their own projects.

Microsoft's own research into customer escalations of Microsoft Dynamics engagements has shown that almost half of the escalations were due to implementation issues. Further research indicated factors such as lack of formal processes within the teams, communication issues, and scope management, corroborating the need for a good methodology for solution delivery.

Many factors decide whether or not a customer perceives a project as successful. Time and cost are two of the most important criteria, but there is another parameter that is important but ignored sometimes—business value. Recent studies allege that ERP/CRM implementations under-deliver business value, and the organizational changes of the solution are reported as ineffectively managed. This again underscores the need for a good delivery process, one that begins with the organization clearly determining success factors for a project before undertaking it. For instance, Microsoft Services requires an understanding of the **Conditions of Satisfaction (COS)** to be noted within the Project Charter or similar project documentation, and signed off by the customer at the outset of the engagement. COS can be excellent measures of project success, but the key to measuring this is to clearly establish:

- Baseline metrics—the values that exist before the project is initiated
- Projected metrics—the goals for the engagement

When these metrics are measured after the engagement, the teams can clearly determine success or failure of the project.

Nucleus Research released a guidebook, titled *Maximizing success delivering Microsoft Dynamics*, in October 2009. According to the guidebook:

> When deployed properly, Microsoft Dynamics ERP and CRM solutions can deliver significant returns to customers – however, that is often dependent on selecting a partner that can deliver the project on time and on budget with minimal changes from the initial project scope and planning.

Nucleus also noted that:

> While a structured implementation methodology delivers the greatest success for Microsoft partners, partners also needed to be flexible enough to meet the specific needs of customers and to evolve over time as business dynamics changed... Structured methodologies like Sure Step can help partners balance their approach to diagnosing, implementing, and optimizing solutions for customers. The skills and guidance of implementation partners are a key factor in Microsoft Dynamics's customer success, and those that are most successful have moved beyond ad-hoc diagnostic, communication, and project management to follow a more structured implementation approach such as Sure Step. They reap the benefits through improved communication, greater customer satisfaction, and ultimately through greater profitability and growth.

Summary

This chapter serves as an introduction to the rest of the book. We began with a discussion of the needs and priorities of the business solutions market. We then explained how, depending on the usage scenario, ERP solutions, and to an extent CRM solutions, can be mission critical to the customer organizations. This criticality underscores the need for a dependable approach for selecting the right solution to meet the customer's needs, a method that builds on the knowledge gained in the envisioning stage to deliver a solution that meets the requirements. We also introduced Sure Step as a methodology designed to fulfill these needs.

The chapter also includes a brief overview of the Microsoft Dynamics solution portfolio. We also introduced the notion of a project within the business solution arena, and discussed implementing these solutions and lessons learned from past implementations.

The next chapter covers the body of knowledge behind solution selling and how it aligns well with the customer's due diligence process. We will illustrate the benefits of this approach for both the service provider and the customer.

References

- Gartner Perspective: IT Spending 2010. Gartner, Inc.
- Microsoft ERP and CRM Solutions: `www.microsoft.com/dynamics`

2
Solution Selling and Driving Due Diligence

In the previous chapter, we discussed the importance of having a methodology for the selection and delivery of business solutions. In the context of business solutions, a methodology benefits both the service provider and the customer. Not only does a methodology provide a consistent and repeatable approach via workflows and processes, but it also provides a connection to the various disciplines and roles that are involved in executing the methodology to ensure successful solution delivery.

For business solutions, and specifically for ERP/CRM solutions, we also introduced the notion of full lifecycle methodologies. A customer lifecycle methodology encompasses the solution discovery phase, the solution delivery phases, and continues through the operation and any future upgrades of the solution. By beginning with the discovery phase, a full lifecycle methodology provides a structured process for solution evaluation, as well as proper dissemination of the knowledge captured during the diagnostic phase through to the solution delivery phases, thereby ensuring that the final solution aligns with the original solution vision.

The diagnostic/discovery phase sets the stage for success, and it is important that customers and partners do not take shortcuts in this stage. There have been many publications that decry the need for companies to thoroughly carry out their vetting process to select the right solution in order to meet their organizational needs.

This chapter will focus on the solution selection and due diligence aspect in the discovery/diagnostic phase. In this chapter, we will discuss the following:

- How this diagnostic process drives value for both the customer and the solution provider
- What an organization needs to do in order to be solution centric

- What solution selling means to the service provider's sales cycles and to the customer's due diligence process
- Microsoft's method to support the solution selling process

Driving value for the customer and the solution provider

A business solution should be about driving value in the customer's organization. Period! As we discussed in the first chapter, ERP solutions specifically, and CRM solutions to an extent, are mission critical because of the number of core functions they support, such as Quote-to-Order Entry, Order Fulfillment, Receipts and Payments, HR and Payroll, Inventory Management, Demand forecasting and sales pipeline management, among others. When you see the applicability of the system to multiple workflows within the organization, it should then not be a stretch to understand and determine the impact of the system on that organization. A good sales team will try their best to articulate this value during the sales cycle, regardless of whether or not the customer is looking for those kinds of metrics.

A question can be asked as to why this is important. It is easier to drive executive support for a project when there is a value associated with the solution. Executive support is absolutely critical for a project of such magnitude. Additionally, during the implementation of the solution, the solution delivery team is bound to go through peaks and valleys. When there are clearly defined value projections, these will be excellent motivation factors for the team to keep forging ahead through its struggles.

The most important aspect of driving value for the customer is ensuring that the right solution is being positioned to meet the organizational requirements. A good sales team always keeps its customer's needs at the forefront. Always strive to do what's best for the customer and their organization, even if it means walking away from an opportunity if you determine that it is not the right fit to your solution. This is where ethics come in, but when sales teams follow this thought process, they will have appreciative customers. And over the long run, they will end up on the winning side and be able to feel good about their accomplishments.

Stephen R. Covey published a gem titled *The 7 Habits of Highly Effective People* in the 1990s. This book received world acclaim for its easy-to-do approach to ethical and moral issues in our day-to-day lives. One of the habits that Covey espouses is *Think Win/Win*, which is applicable to our discussion as well. Highly effective sales personnel will strive for win-win deals because both parties will be better off and will profit in the end.

A business solution sale should not be about filling the sales period quota, but should be about helping the customer organization. There is of course no denying the influence of quotas and bonuses on sales behavior. However, by aligning the right solution for the customer, the sales personnel can get their individual goals accomplished while also helping organizations achieve their potential. This should give them a sense of gratification that extends well beyond the period-end bonuses. Long-term value can be achieved through a due-diligence process that engages and informs the customer through the sales process. Solution providers that establish such a culture and inculcate these values in their organizations are in turn successful in the long run.

Value realization and measurement

During the customer's due diligence process, the service provider strives to gain an understanding of where the customer organization is currently at and their vision for the future. The proposed solution will bridge the customer's gap from their as-is state to their to-be state—an effective value realization process begins early in this cycle and is executed in sync with the solution visioning and delivery process.

As the service provider develops the blueprint for the proposed solution, they should begin to define the value that the solution will provide. While this will include, in part, the determination of the conditions of satisfaction for the customer, the critical component to determining value will be to understand the business drivers for the organization's change to the proposed solution.

Microsoft, in its training curriculum, defines a business driver as:

> *a brief statement that defines clearly and specifically the desired business outcomes of the organization along with the necessary activities to reach them.*

Business drivers help communicate the vision and strategy of an organization. Business drivers clearly articulate the goals and objectives for moving the organization from its current (as-is) state to its desired future (to-be) state.

Business drivers can also help in the alignment of the business priorities to the organization strategy. In turn, they can explicitly align each initiative to the organization's strategic objectives, while also helping with the measurement of the desired outcomes.

Simply put, a business driver is something that should result in quantifiable savings for the organization. As such, the business drivers should have SMART attributes:

- **S**pecific
- **M**easurable
- **A**ggressive but attainable
- **R**esults-oriented
- **T**ime-bound

Microsoft provides a straightforward technique to define or write a business driver. Start with a "verb", and add to that the "element to measure" and the "focus or area of emphasis".

 Business Driver = Verb + Element to Measure + Focus or Area of Emphasis

Using this definition, the following are some of the examples of business drivers:

- Increase the sales for product ABC
- Reduce the average inventory in Plant XYZ
- Improve the **Days of Sales Outstanding (DSO)** in the Area Office
- Accelerate the time to market for new product introductions

Once the business drivers have been defined, it is important to capture the metrics that will enable the measurement of the value. This is where the above definition also helps, as the "element to measure" translates into the metric or **Key Performance Indicator (KPI)** to measure.

Microsoft defines a KPI as:

an instrument to monitor, predict and manage performance needed to achieve a specific target.

The value measurement statement then includes the KPI and a "threshold value".

 Value Measurement = Key Performance Indicator (KPI) + Threshold Value

The following are examples of value measurement statements that include the metrics or KPIs for the business drivers:

- Sales of product ABC to increase by $5M
- Average inventory in plant XYZ to be reduced by 15%
- DSO in the Area Office to be improved by 5 days
- Time to market for new product introductions accelerated by 30 days

With the business drivers and KPIs defined, the next step is to measure and capture the baseline metrics—the values of the KPIs in the current (as-is) state. Without establishing the baseline metrics, you cannot quantify the effect of the new solution on the drivers, so this step is very important.

Related to the determination of the KPIs, it is also important to define the timing and frequency of when the measurements will be taken. The actual execution of measuring the results will typically happen only when the solution is actually in operation for a given period, but the teams should decide up front when the measurements will occur. They should also decide the frequency of the measurements for the corresponding KPIs.

The solution delivery process is then set up to ensure that value realization is accelerated and maximized. After the solution has been deployed and has gone through a period of stabilization, the actual outcome or metrics can be measured.

The following diagram summarizes the value realization and measurement process in the context of business solutions:

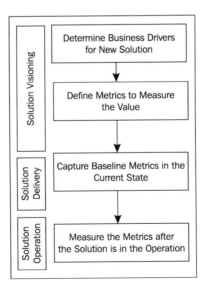

In the following sections, we will discuss how this concept of value realization is enabled by a solution-centric approach. We will also discuss how solution selling helps the customer identify the right solution, and sets the stage for the solution implementation so as to realize the projected value from that solution.

What it means to be solution centric

Let's begin this discussion by expounding on the definition of a "solution". Quite simply, the word solution means an answer to a problem. But the English Thesaurus offers us other terms such as key, clarification, elucidation, explanation, resolution, and result. All of these definitions fit quite nicely into the constructs of business solution selling, and therein is the crux of the issue — "solution" can mean different things to different people. Because a solution has applicability to multiple contexts, it is a commonly used word in organizations, necessitating that the organizations must clearly define the usage of the term.

In his book, *The New Solution Selling*, Keith Eades, who founded the **Sales Performance International (SPI)** organization, discusses the definition of "solution". He describes a solution as: "a mutually agreed-upon answer to a recognized problem, with a specific emphasis on the need for the problem to be acknowledged by both parties, the buyers (customers) and the sellers (solution provider)". The second aspect of a solution highlighted in the book is that it should "provide some measurable improvement". With that, Eades provides a complete definition of a solution as:

> *a mutually shared answer to a recognized problem, and the answer provides measurable improvement.*

For some organizations, it has become very fashionable to say that they have "solutions" and that they are "solutions-focused", as this apparently takes away the negative connotation associated with the term "products". A product is viewed as an offering that the selling company is forcing on the marketplace, while a solution is viewed as something the marketplace is actively seeking, with the solution being that answer the sellers can offer to the buyers. So, is the product the antithesis of a solution? Far from it! In many cases, and especially in the context of business solutions, the product can be the primary driver of the solution. But it is in the usage or delivery of that product that can truly define the success or failure of the solution for the customer. And the up-front positioning of the solution is the key to a successful delivery, which is where the solution-centric approach comes in.

For an organization to be truly solution focused, Eades explains that they need "more than superficial packaging manipulations or bundling services with products". Solution-centric should not be treated as buzz words to be thrown around by the organization. In the book titled *The Solution-Centric Organization*, Eades states that "solution–centric organizations define themselves by the problems they solve for customers, versus by the products or services they make, sell or deliver". Solution-centric should be a philosophy that permeates throughout the organization so that teams such as sales, marketing, services, and so on are all aligned around a common approach and model.

The need to be truly solution-centric is even more important in mature marketplaces such as ERP/CRM solutions. In this market, many of the top solution providers offer products that have been around and used by many organizations. Each of these products includes a range of features and functionality that are hard to differentiate from the competition. SPI terms this **differentiation blur**, which is a result of the product being perceived as commoditized, or the product becoming too complex and feature rich for the industry to be able to differentiate it. To combat this issue, companies start to bundle their products with services and deem these as solutions. But what they have really achieved is creating what SPI labels as "pseudo solutions".

Such approaches neither help the customers looking for a solution, nor do they help the solution provider develop a consistent approach to selling. This is further corroborated by a market research by industry analysts, who found only a ten percent effectiveness rate of value positioning by these solution providers. The research also points to other findings that are endemic in a pseudo-solution company. In these companies, a high percentage (70 to 80 percent) of the marketing materials remain unused, highlighting the disconnect between the sales and the marketing teams. Another finding in these companies is that they revert to sales training to solve the problem, and they often find the shelf life of unreinforced sales training to be about six to eight weeks.

So how then does a company become truly solution centric? As SPI puts it, for a true solution-centric approach, organizations need to embrace a sustained business model to market, sell, and deliver customer transformation. They need to identify the problems they solve rather than the products they offer, align all of the aspects of their marketing with the solution framework, and systemically adopt and reinforce the solution selling and solution-centric disciplines across the entire organization. Companies doing this will find themselves able to consistently position the value of their solutions to their customers, to clearly differentiate the value vis-à-vis their competition, and create a business model for sustainable growth.

Solution selling concepts

In the previous section, we discussed what a company needs to do within its overall organization to become solution centric. We now shift our focus toward solution selling. We will see how solution selling not only helps the sales teams of these companies, but also how this approach ensures that the solution providers are helping their customers realize and maximize the value from their solutions.

Solution selling and driving due diligence are mutually dependent courses of action. While the former is a better process for the service providers' sales personnel, the latter is a better mechanism for the customers in their product selection process. So, when a service provider starts implementing solution selling, innately they are also assisting the customer and ensuring a thorough due diligence process, granted that there will always be the likelihood that the process will be skewed toward the product that the service provider is representing; however, if the process is conducted properly, the customer should be able to clearly determine the extent to which there is fit between their requirements and the solution, as well as what their future solution will look like.

Let's begin by looking at solution selling from the perspective of the solution provider or the seller of the solution. In his book, *The New Solution Selling*, Eades talks about the areas where solution selling helps the seller—as a philosophy, as a map, as a methodology, and as a management system.

Solution selling is a philosophy that can permeate the culture of the organization because it places the customer as the focal point. Solving the customer's business problems and achieving positive results are the key elements of this philosophy.

Solution selling provides a map with the steps for achieving the end goal of the selling organization. This includes the ability to identify and qualify opportunities, diagnose the customer's problems and pain, analyze the needs, develop the solution vision, and manage the process to a successful closure.

Solution selling can be seen as a methodology that provides a collection of tools, job aids, techniques, and procedures. When utilized correctly, the approach will result in higher customer satisfaction and increased sales productivity.

Solution selling also creates a Sales Management System that provides coaching skills for sales and executive management by instituting a high-performance sales culture in the selling organization. As such, it also provides an effective measurement tool for the overall sales performance.

Solution selling—buyer's perspective

So far we have looked at solution selling from the seller's viewpoint. Let's now look at solution selling from the perspective of the buyer. Three of the four areas noted above directly impact the customer as well.

The solution selling philosophy places the customer at the forefront. Any seller who is using this technique then automatically has the customer's interests in mind. This approach creates a trusted relationship between the buyer and the seller, and a more cohesive approach toward delivering the results expected of the solution.

The steps in the solution selling map include diagnosing problems, analyzing the needs, and developing the solution vision. These steps intrinsically help the customer with their due diligence in selecting the right solution to meet their needs.

Solution selling provides a methodology to deliver higher customer satisfaction. Using a consistent, time-tested process helps the sales teams use their prior experience in similar situations, which the customer can leverage for their own benefit.

In the next sections, we will discuss two key aspects of solution selling—building the trust between the buyer and the seller, and building the vision of the solution.

Building the trust

In general, a buying process is optimal when the buyer believes that the product or service that they are acquiring is the best solution to their problem, and they are getting it at the best possible price. As the magnitude of the purchase increases, so does the buyer's inclination to research the marketplace to seek out the right solution at the right price for their needs. Essentially, the length of the due diligence process for the buyer increases exponentially with the importance of their requirement. However, there is one more factor that can affect the buyer's due diligence process, and it is **trust**. Trust that the solution will meet their needs, trust in the seller that they are providing the best price, trust that the seller will deliver the promised solution, and trust that the seller has the wherewithal to support the solution should any problems arise after the delivery.

Trust is especially essential for business solutions. As we noted earlier, business solutions are mission critical, so intrinsically there is high risk associated with any kind of wrong steps or failure in the realization of the solution. It is then easy to understand the importance of having a trusting buyer-seller relationship.

More often than not, trust is something that needs to be earned. In the business solutions arena, an organization that has a methodical process in place will succeed more consistently. By showing the buyer that you have a well thought-out, repeatable process, you give them the comfort factor that you have experienced success with other customers, thereby building that trust. The solution selling process is one such process that allows you to inculcate the trust factor in your customer, by moving the dial away from "transactional selling" to "relationship selling".

Trust can have economic implications as well. In his book *The Speed of Trust*, Stephen M. R. Covey talks about developing trust and also illustrates how trust can be an economic driver. His formula is based on the observation that trust always affects two outcomes — speed and cost.

When trust goes down, the decision making speed goes down, which makes the costs go up:

$$[\quad \downarrow\text{Trust} = \downarrow\text{Speed} \uparrow\text{Cost} \quad]$$

When trust goes up, the speed of decision-making increases and correspondingly the costs go down:

$$[\quad \uparrow\text{Trust} = \uparrow\text{Speed} \downarrow\text{Cost} \quad]$$

Covey goes on to talk about the impact of trust in the form of a tax or dividend. He incorporates trust into the traditional business formula, expanding it as follows:

$$[\quad (\text{Strategy} \times \text{Execution}) \, \text{Trust} = \text{Results} \quad]$$

This discussion and these formulas imply that trust implications should be an important consideration for sales personnel. Beyond the ethical reasons, trust obviously also has an economic impact on the cost of sales for an organization. Covey sums up the impact of trust in the following words:

> *the ability to establish, grow, extend, and restore trust with all stakeholders – customers, business partners, investors, and coworkers – is the key leadership competency of the global economy.*

We can see the impact of trust in our customer transactions as well. When a new seller approaches a customer with a solution, the buyer seeks proof that their solution has been successful, without which the buyer would turn toward a more established provider. Why is that? This is because the customers do not have the same level of trust in the new provider as they would with an established one. This is all the more important reason for the selling organizations to adopt solution selling as a philosophy. Solution selling is one of the best techniques available for the sellers to establish credibility and trust with their buyers, which, as we have seen, can positively impact their success ratio.

Building the vision

A key aspect of solution selling, and one of the most pervasive and permeating themes of solution selling, is the notion of the seller building a shared vision of the solution with the buyer. When the solution is truly articulated from the buyer's perspective, the perceived risk in the solution is much lower for the customer, thereby making it a lot easier for them to buy off on the solution.

Michael Bosworth is one of the original pioneers of solution selling. He authored the book titled *Solution Selling*, and he was also the original founder of the organization that is currently run by Keith Eades. Bosworth discusses the notion of creating a vision at length in his book, and he ascribes high importance to the vision creation process. In Bosworth's view, *people buy from people who can create visions for them* and *a solution is equivalent to the buyer's vision.*

The notion that people buy from people is commonplace for big ticket items such as business solutions. These are not transactions that you would expect somebody to make over the Internet or by some other "sight unseen" method. Customers will want to establish that the solution is credible, the team delivering the solution is trustworthy, and the organization supporting the solution will be around for the long haul. But let's assume that all things are equal or close enough that the differentiation is not obvious—for example, the competition also has a mature solution, as well as trustworthy and personable sales personnel. The key point in Bosworth's notion is that when the sellers can make the buyers feel that the solution is theirs and matches their vision, the buyers feel that they are in control of the process and they are empowered.

Bosworth's teaching ties the buyer's needs to the solution visioning process. As the customers move through their buying cycle, their concerns change over time. It is then important that the seller stays aligned with the customers, and advances the vision in lock-step with the buyer. When the buyer is able to clearly visualize and articulate the future outcomes of the seller's solution, the sale becomes less complicated, resulting in shorter sales cycles and higher close ratios.

In 1943, Albert Maslow wrote a classic paper on our hierarchy of needs, titled *A Theory of Human Motivation*. Maslow's hierarchy progressed from the lowest need level to the highest, as noted here.

- **Physiological needs**: This is the first level and includes the basic human needs such as air, water, and food.

- **Safety needs**: Personal and financial security, health, and well-being are characteristics of the second level.

- **Love and belonging needs**: The third level involves social and emotional needs such as friendship, family, and intimacy.

- **Esteem needs**: The fourth level is about the need to be respected, including self-esteem (respect of others) and self-respect (inner strength).

- **Self-actualization needs**: This level pertains to an individual realizing their potential to the fullest.

One of the key points of this hierarchy is the progression of needs — from the first level, to the second, and so on. According to Maslow, if a human is unable to meet his/her basic needs such as food and shelter, they will be less inclined to pursue higher needs such as prestige and status. Some have criticized the hierarchy, but it has also become the basis of many subjects, and the hierarchy has been applied to many areas. For example, marketing has many teachings on understanding consumer buying behavior on the basis of the Maslow's needs hierarchy. Correlation is visible in business and sales management as well, including through fields such as transpersonal business studies.

Bosworth also used the Maslow's hierarchy as the basis to develop the buyer needs cycle in the perspective of solution selling. The next diagram depicts the progression of this needs cycle from latent need to solution vision:

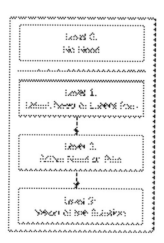

- At **Level 0**, the buyer has **no need** for the product or solution, and the seller recognizes that—for example, you would not look to sell a heat lamp in the Saharan region. This level is obviously outside the solution selling realm.

- At **Level 1**, the seller sees a need in the marketplace but the buyer does not as yet recognize the need. So the **latent need** for the solution is in the mind of the seller, not the buyer. Or in other words, it is a **latent pain** for the buyer. Sellers functioning at this level do so by projecting their vision of the need for the solution on the buyer.

- At **Level 2**, the buyer is cognizant of their need or pain, but they do not know of a solution for the problem. At this stage, as the need or pain is recognized but unsatisfied, there is potential for a solution sale between the buyer and the right seller. If the buyer believes that there is a potential solution, they will actively seek a solution and the need becomes an active need. However, if the buyer does not think that there is a solution to their problem, the need can become suppressed and go back to Level 1 as a latent need.

- At **Level 3**, the buyer sees the **vision of the solution**. The buyer's needs have progressed from latent to active, to a point where they can foresee the solution that solves their issues. At this stage, the buyer is looking to buy the solution and has a well-developed vision that includes four components —who will be taking what action, when in time, via a capability of a seller's product or service.

A key point in this progression of the buyer's needs is that at Level 2, the buyer understands the potential for a solution, but those needs have not yet been acted upon by a seller and so they are "undeveloped needs". If, at this stage, the seller thrusts their vision on the buyer, a suboptimal situation arises with the buyer having to trust the seller to solve their problem. It is therefore very important for the seller to get the buyer to admit their pain at this stage, which is proof to the seller that the buyer views them as trustworthy and has the ability to provide the right solution.

Another key point is that for the opportunity to be considered as qualified, the buyer must agree to participate actively together to develop the solution vision. The buyer must either be able to articulate the requirements of the solution or agree to participate in the needs assessment process.

If sellers find themselves in a situation where the vision has already been created, and they are merely comparing their offering to that of the competition, they are in danger of becoming another check mark in the buyer's decision-making process. It is very likely that the buyer is already aligned with a competitor who helped them develop their requirements, and is just looking for additional proof points or pricing leverage, before completing the purchase with them.

When the buyer is able to see the specific solution capabilities to address their needs, they will be able to articulate the solution vision and act on their problem.

When to discuss feature/functionality or demo the solution

Another habit that Stephen R. Covey discusses in his book, The *7 Habits of Highly Effective People*, is "seek first to understand, then to be understood". This habit is one of the core notions of solution selling: to patiently cultivate interest in the solution by first understanding the customer's problems that they are trying to solve. To develop a win-win relationship with your customer, you must understand what it means for them to win, or in other words, what a successful solution means to them. Follow the "principles of empathetic communication" by outlining the objectives in terms of the customer's needs and wants. This allows you to craft the solution vision in terms of the customer's objectives, facilitating an easier buy-in of your solution.

For solution selling, Michael Bosworth has a simple message: *diagnose before you prescribe*. Prescribing is when the seller leads with presentations on their company, product, or services. Instead of the focus being on the customer's organizational needs and benefits, the seller's message is "you need....". The problem here is in the understanding of the seller, who assumes that the buyer already is aware about what value their offerings are going to bring to him/her.

Being disciplined to listen first before talking is easier said than done, as in real life we are often impatient. When we know the answer, we find it hard to hold back or have empathy for the customer who does not know the information we know. Bosworth calls this seller impatience "premature elaboration", and he thinks that it is one of the primary reasons for killing a sale. Also, impatience is counterproductive to the solution seller's goal of building relationships between the buyer and the seller.

When sellers lead with feature-functionality, they play right into the hands of the competition. Remember that unless you operate in a very unique industry where you have a monopoly over the market, your competition is very likely to have a set of compelling features and functionality. Bosworth believes that *the role of the product in a sale should be proof – not in interest arousal, education, or need development*. The product should be used to prove that the solution indeed matches the customer's vision.

This approach benefits the seller in many ways. Early product demos could result in the buyer feeling that he or she was being "sold to". If the customer has yet to detail out their requirements, discussing product features with the customer can come across as the seller trying to impose their solution on the buyer, not to mention that it feeds into the hands of the competition that comes afterwards and can put its own spin.

Showing the product early can also lead to the seller having to get into discussions on features that the customer didn't have any interest in. However, during the demo, questions can arise that require the sales team to defend their product—something that could have been avoided if the seller had already determined exactly which features the buyer was interested in, and focused the demo only on those solution components.

Another reason to wait to do full-fledged solution demo is that the customer could request a proof-of-concept after the solution vision has been developed. Also, the seller can avoid having to discuss any pricing questions that may come up during the demo. Until the customer buys into the solution vision, the seller should avoid any discussions of price. When the customer sees the solution vision and the value of the solution, pricing negotiations can be much smoother and you can avoid any unnecessary acrimony.

So, how do you prevent the urge to start with show-and-tell? The answer lies in solution selling, where you methodically diagnose the customer's requirements and, in concert with the buyer, you build the solution blueprint, which will of course be biased toward your solution. Also, in using this approach, you will develop a solution selling benefit statement, which is a composite statement of the features, advantages, and benefits of the solution.

A solution selling benefit statement tells the buyer that the seller's solution addresses the vision that was developed through active participation by both the buyer and the seller. As Bosworth puts it, the statement will indicate to the prospect: *who will be doing what, when in time via a product or service.* So, in effect, the seller has corroborated with the buyer that there is a level-3 need, meaning that the buyer has participated in the development of the solution vision. If the buyer is still at level 2 or before, and the need or pain is still undeveloped or latent, the best the seller can do is to develop an advantage statement. The **advantage statement** can list only the benefits from the eyes of the seller, as they still don't know the detailed pain points of the buyer. And that is the fundamental difference between an advantage statement and the benefit statement that results from the solution selling approach.

Staying aligned with the buyer

One of the essential techniques offered by solution selling is keeping the seller in strategic alignment with the buyer. To stay aligned, the seller must be able to understand the thought process of the buyer so as to be able to predict their behavior.

Based on his years of sales experience, Michael Bosworth was able to break down what a buyer goes through into a series of steps. As the buyer's needs go from latent need, to active need, to solution vision, Bosworth found that buyers have four primary concerns:

- Is there a **need**?
- Is it the right **solution** to meet the need?
- What is the **cost** of the solution?
- What is the **risk** associated with acquiring the solution?

The presence of a need initiates the buying cycle. The need must be in the foreground of the buyer's mind for him or her to initiate the cycle. However, a seller can adversely affect the sale by putting undue pressure on the buyer in this stage. To prevent that, the seller should get the buyer to acknowledge their need. Once the buyer acknowledges their pain, they progress to their next concern—cost.

Cost is a key concern for most buyers. However, it is important for the seller to recognize at what stage the buyer is. If it is early in the buying cycle, the seller is better off avoiding all cost discussions as they have yet to determine if there is a need associated with their solution. When the buyer achieves solution vision and is able to understand the value of the solution to their organization, cost implications change to price association, and the seller is in more favorable position to have this discussion.

In the typical marketplace, a buyer has many options; selecting the right solution from that mix is a pressing concern for the buyer. This is where value justification comes in. The sellers who have done their homework are prepared with business drivers for the solution, and can perform a **Return on Investment (ROI)** analysis for the customer to prove the value of the solution. Customer case studies can be used by the seller as additional proof points at this stage. Also, for the patient sellers, this is the stage at which they show their customers a full-fledged product demonstration to highlight how the features meet the customer's requirements.

The more important the initiative, the more risk rises to the top of the buyer's concerns at the later stages of the buying cycle. This includes the perceived risk of not having selected the best solution as well as obtaining the best price for the solution. Risk can also extend into solution support—the perceived risk of the service provider going out of business and not being able to support a solution in operation. Sellers should use sales methods and techniques that include risk management disciplines to identify, analyze, and respond to the perceived risks in a timely manner.

While analyzing these four concerns even further, Bosworth also found that they clearly fall into three phases in the buying cycle.

- Phase 1: Determination of need
- Phase 2: Evaluation of alternatives
- Phase 3: Evaluation of risk

In the following screenshot, Bosworth depicts the four buyer concerns as they shift within the three buying cycle phases. This tool is used extensively in solution selling as a means of anticipating buyers' behavior, so that the seller can stay aligned to the expectations.

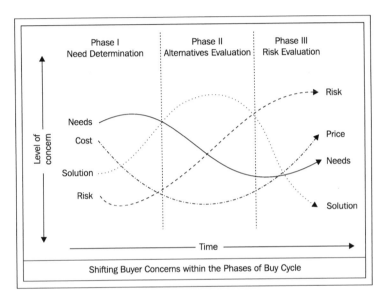

Shifting Buyer Concerns within the Phases of Buy Cycle

As seen in the screenshot, the buyer's primary concerns in the early stages of the buying cycle are need and cost. As the buyer moves towards the end of the cycle, risk and price take over as higher concerns, as the needs have been determined and a solution has been identified by that time.

For the seller, phase I is about helping the customer determine their needs, but with a bias towards the seller's solution. In phase II, the seller shows proof that their solution meets the customer's needs, in the form of product presentations, customer evidence, ROI analysis, and so on. Finally, in phase III, the seller seeks to mitigate any and all risk factors perceived by the buyer, and moves to close the sale. By acting as a "buying facilitator", the seller allows the buyer to perceive that they own the process, while also ensuring that their sales process is executed efficiently.

Vision processing—creation and reengineering

There are many sales tools and techniques available to help the seller guide the buyer through the development of the solution vision. For example, Bosworth espouses a technique called the *9-Block Vision Processing Model*, where the seller moves the buyer from pain to vision through a series of questions that gradually build upon each other. As seen in the next diagram, sellers begin with **Open** questions—open-ended questions fashioned in a way to give the buyer a sense of control throughout the process. Open questions then lead to the **Control** questions that allow the seller to probe into specific subject matter areas. The final set of questions, the **Confirm** questions, lead to the summarization of the buyer's needs and pain, ensuring that the seller has a good understanding of the situation.

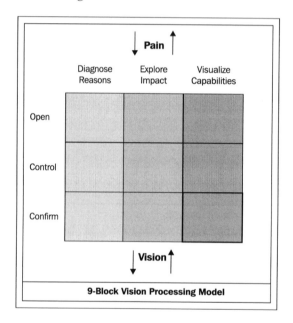

9-Block Vision Processing Model

The Open, Control, and Confirm questions in the 9-Block Vision Processing Model are noted vertically. From left to right, the model leads the seller to **Diagnose Reasons**, **Explore Impact**, and **Visualize Capabilities**. In the left vertical block, the seller uses his/her Open, Control, and Confirm questions to diagnose the customer's latent pain and get them to admit the pain. In the middle vertical block, the seller determines the organizational interdependencies, and the impact they have on the issues. The seller is able to determine which issues are more critical, and who are the power players or influencers for the requirements. The last vertical block helps the seller crystallize the solution selling benefits and vision, by getting the buyer to take responsibility for solving their needs, preferably with a bias towards the seller's solution.

While much of our discussion to this point has been about creating the vision as the seller is starting anew with the buyer, it is important to understand that these techniques also apply to situations where the buyer already has an initial vision in mind. This is a key point, especially in the business solutions arena where it is becoming commonplace for a solution provider to get engaged at the **Request for Proposal (RFP)** or **Request for Information (RFI)** stage. At this stage, the customer may have already engaged with an independent third-party consulting group to come up with their initial requirements. It is also possible that they could have engaged with a competitor for this. Obviously the latter situation is not ideal, as the requirements are already fashioned with a bias towards the competitor's solution, and the seller needs to do some investigation to ascertain that it is indeed still fair competition at that point. Keep in mind that if the buyer is merely going through the exercise to show their management that they completed the requisite steps for their due diligence by analyzing "n" solutions, it may be better for the seller to not waste too much of their time. But if it is still open competition, then the seller can still use the same techniques offered here to "reengineer the vision".

The Microsoft Solution Selling Process

In the previous sections, we have seen how effective the solution selling concepts can be to align the seller with the customer's needs. Solution selling helps the solution provider build a trusting relationship with their buyer, and facilitates a working relationship between the seller and buyer to craft a common solution vision for the mutual benefit of each other. As a company, Microsoft prides itself in ensuring that the customer's needs are at its forefront, and in turn helping its vast partner ecosystem to also operate by this credo. To facilitate that mission, Microsoft adopted the solution selling method and fashioned it within the constructs of its internal and partner sales mechanisms. This method, known as the **Microsoft Solution Selling Process (MSSP)**, is the subject of this section.

Specifically within the business solutions arena, MSSP has been systematized to help Microsoft Dynamics Partners and Microsoft's internal teams through their sales cycles. The method gives selling teams a structure for creating and delivering value at each step of the sales cycle. Sales teams are provided with an effective process to understand the customer's needs and critical business issues. The process also facilitates the sales resources to work closely with the customer's subject matter experts for determining and developing the right Microsoft solution to fit their requirements.

MSSP aligns the account teams with the customer's decision-making process in their buying cycle and creates an emphasis on driving real business value through Microsoft solutions. It helps the sales teams evaluate their progress on their sales cycles, and it affords the sales and leadership teams a means to develop business plans, drive resource allocation and utilization, and develop viable forecasts for effective decision making.

The stages of MSSP are shown in the following diagram. Also shown in the diagram is a mapping of MSSP to the buying cycle described in the solution selling concepts section, which we will also discuss below.

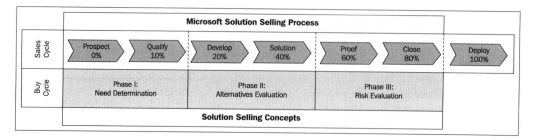

The first stage (**0%**) of MSSP is the **Prospect** stage. The goal of this stage is to identify prospects for the business solutions via sales calls, mailers, internet marketing, conferences, or other means to arouse interest in the solutions. Sales teams create account plans and research typical customer pain points in the industry. They also gather customer success stories as evidence of past success in the space.

The next stage (**10%**) is the **Qualify** stage where the sales teams ensure that the prospect has a real need for a solution. In this stage, the customer will have identified their pain areas, while the sales teams may also detect potential latent needs. The sales team helps the customer by ascertaining the business drivers and starts working towards developing a shared vision. This is also the stage where the sales teams will ensure that there is a business sponsor for the initiative, as well as look to negotiate access to the power sponsor.

The **Prospect** and **Qualify** stages correspond to **Phase I** of the buying cycle. The actions by the sales teams assist the customer to unearth the needs for the solution.

Develop is the next stage (**20%**) of MSSP. The sales team understands the high-level solution requirements and conducts detailed requirements gathering sessions to craft the solution vision. The customer has admitted to their business pain, and is aware of the consequences of not going through with the solution deployment. The sales team will also want to meet personally with the power sponsor in this stage. They will also want to gauge the competitors involved, as well as gain an understanding of the customer's decision-making process.

The next selling stage (**40%**) is **Solution**. The goal of this stage is to develop a solution blueprint that matches the customer's requirements. The sales team has linked the solution to business need, and has identified the business metrics or KPIs for the solution value measurement. Hardware and any third-party software needs for the solution are also determined. A high-level cost estimate has been developed, shared with the customer, and acknowledged. The sales team also begins to plan for any solution demonstrations that it may anticipate in the next stage.

The **Develop** and **Solution** stages correspond to **Phase II** of the buying cycle. The sales teams assist the customer to understand how the solution fits their needs during these stages. It also bears mention that the customer teams may run parallel exercises with the competitors to evaluate alternatives.

The next MSSP stage (60%) is **Proof**. In this stage, the sales teams mitigate any perceived risks for the customer, with detailed product demonstrations, showing proof that the solution meets the requirements. Detailed value proposition analysis for the solution is also conducted to help the customer articulate the projected savings associated with the solution, as well as the timeline as to when they can recoup their investment. In this stage, the sales team also provides the initial proposal to the customer.

Close is the last stage (**80%**) in the sales cycle before the deployment of the solution begins. The goal of this stage is to finalize and get sign-off on all the contracts— this includes contracts for the software and the **Statement of Work** (**SOW**) for the solution delivery. The solution implementation plan is presented and acknowledged by the customer. The solution team also begins to finalize the appropriate resources for the solution delivery.

The **Proof** and **Close** stages correspond to **Phase III** of the buying cycle. The steps taken by the sales teams help alleviate any risks identified by the customer, leading to the final approval of the solution.

The final stage (**100%**) of MSSP is the **Deploy** stage. This stage begins with the transition of knowledge from the sales to the delivery team. The delivery team then takes over responsibility for the solution. The sales teams conduct internal reviews of the sales cycle and document key learning for future opportunities.

Summary

In this chapter we introduced and discussed the concepts of solution selling. Solution selling helps the seller stay aligned with their buyers by building a trusting relationship and a common vision of the solution that meets the customer's needs. We also presented the different techniques afforded to enable solution selling, including value measurement, vision processing, and the phases of the buying cycle. Finally, we covered MSSP, the solution selling process that Microsoft designed to help its partners and internal sales teams.

In the next chapter, we will focus on project management and talk about managing projects from a result-driven and real-life perspective. We will then come back to solution selling in *Chapter 4, Selling with Sure Step,* to explain how solution selling is enabled by the Microsoft Dynamics Sure Step methodology.

References

- Bosworth, Michael (1994). *Solution Selling*. New York, NY: McGraw-Hill.

- Covey, Stephen R. (1989). *The 7 Habits of Highly Effective People*. New York, NY: Free Press.

- Covey, Stephen M. R. (2006). *The Speed of Trust*. New York, NY: Free Press.

- Eades, Keith M. (2003). *The New Solution Selling*. New York, NY: McGraw Hill.

- Eades, Keith M. and Kear, Robert E. (2006). The Solution-Centric Organization. New York, NY: McGraw Hill.

- Maslow, Abraham (1943). A Theory of Human Motivation. *Psychological Review*, Volume 50(4), 370–396.

3
Managing Projects

In the previous chapter, you examined solution selling and driving due diligence concepts. This chapter will walk you through the fascinating discipline of managing projects. The profession of project management is emerging because quality has become a competitive instrument over the years. The **Project Management Institute (PMI)** defines project management as the application of knowledge, skills, tools, and techniques to project activities to meet project requirements. Being a project manager in charge of software implementation projects is a challenging and demanding responsibility. Good project managers combine various skills in a balanced way. They need to bring into practice leadership, communication, negotiation, problem solving, and influencing capabilities in a unique and temporary environment. And when things go wrong, project managers usually find themselves in the eye of the storm. Nevertheless, managing projects brings great rewards. Successfully implementing business solutions implies that your customer organization will benefit from more efficiency in its daily routines because of your team's effort and quality. At the same time, you create and manage a context in which consultants can realize their professional ambitions.

In this chapter you will discover:

- About projects and Project Management
- The four pillars of project success
- Project management essentials
- Project management adoption
- The indispensable organizational benefits

About projects and project management

In this section, we will discuss and argue against some widespread resistance for project management and provide you with food for thought on topics such as the need and alternatives for project management.

Myths and resistance

We need to grant the skeptics some credit for their stiff resistance. Resistance for project management is omnipresent and sometimes embedded in hard-to-shatter myths. The onus of proof rests with the plaintiff and so we need to plead the project management's cause for every assignment—a glaring contrast to the tolerance for the unstructured approach. Now what kind of resistance do we face? The opinion that project management is a lot of overhead is widespread. At the same time, it is often seen as an obstacle to flexibility. Many people consider project management as the theorizer's way of doing things diametrically opposed to the management's prime directive of getting things done.

Project management is also labeled as unsalable like a dead stock. These kinds of arguments make you think twice before shouting your project management ambitions from the rooftops. But how strong is the skeptics' case?

Is project management overhead?

What is overhead? From a cost accounting perspective, overhead costs are the costs incurred for operating a business but that do not generate revenues or profits directly. Typical overhead costs include accounting fees, advertising, depreciation, insurance, interest, legal fees, rent, repairs, supplies, taxes, telephone bills, travel, and utilities costs. In this logic, the question of whether or not project management is overhead leads to another question: do we send invoices to our customers for the project management services that we provide? However, is this the crucial question? According to this line of reasoning, we should categorize our sales teams as overhead and should not be invoicing their services. And if we would partly invoice our project managers, does this make the overhead question redundant?

When the skeptics refer to project management as overhead, they often think about a mountain of papers and quite a few procedures and administrative tasks associated with the project management discipline. This criticism can be legitimate when their project management practice is not scaled to the size and complexity of the projects or to their organizational structure. Ignorance is usually at the basis of these failing project management procedures.

To answer the overhead question, we need to assess the benefits of our project management practice. Does it contribute to our project's profit and quality? Does it add value to our customers and team? If the answer to these two questions is positive, then it is clearly not an overhead. If you cannot extract these benefits, then your project management practice may be labeled as overhead. Project management is what you and your organization make of it, and it can either turn into an overhead or a value-added service.

So when the skeptics cry out that project management is overhead, they are probably right. But it tells you more about their project management practice than about project management in general.

Is project management an obstacle to flexibility?

You often meet people who claim to support the project management practice, but they instantly add that they fear the impact on the organizational flexibility. They think that project management procedures will decrease their ability to respond to unpredicted changes, and it doesn't take long before their reasoning sets project management against a pragmatic approach. So, isn't project management concerned with practical matters? Do we lose the capability of change, and does project management stand in the way of progress in our projects? These are the questions to be answered when testing the accuracy of this proposition.

The project management discipline would be in great difficulty if this all were to be true. Who on earth would even consider implementing a project management practice knowing that it will paralyze the organization's effectiveness? Are the millions of project management practitioners laboring under a misapprehension? This looks like an untenable proposition.

Mostly, this aversion towards project management finds its breeding ground in the inability to separate essentials from side issues. People struggling with this dilemma overemphasize the importance of all the described project management tools, documents, and steps of a methodology. They spend too much time in administering and describing the project, losing valuable time for the real management of the project and its practical matters. A bureaucratic vision on project management is causing the contrast with the "let's just get on with the job" approach.

Good project management practice is all about managing change, practical matters, and flexibility. By keeping it result driven, lean, and mean, it will empower you to make the project happen. A good project manager is not a bureaucrat, but is a tight-rope walker, balancing the need for administration, steps, and tools in each project. Now that's easier said than done, and it takes a seasoned project manager with thorough knowledge of the project management discipline to realize structured flexibility. Although unskilled and inexperienced project managers tend to grasp hold of rigid procedures, company executives cannot go scot-free either when speaking about obstacles to flexibility. They are responsible for the company's culture and this culture represents the limit of what is achievable for the company.

Is project management unsalable?

The previous chapter on solution selling will probably enable you to answer this question by yourself. A project management practice that unleashes value and benefits for the customer must be salable. If you can't get it sold, you struggle to sell the value of your methodology and/or you cannot convince the customer for the need of it, this can be related to the intrinsic values of your methodology or to a failing sales process. We are used to selling our software, business consultancy services, as well as development expertise, but how familiar are we with selling a project management service? Do we have a good selling strategy in place for valuing this type of service? If you want to get project management sold, it must be a real element of your adaptable value proposition, necessary for good bridge selling. Your customer or prospect might not be familiar with the landscape of implementation projects and the need for project management, and they might be nervous or even frightened in crossing. Your value proposition for project management services needs to be flexible and adaptable to variations in each opportunity. A notable fact is that those who claim not to be able to sell project management have no adaptable value proposition for it, but yet price their project managers as the most expensive individuals on the team. This way, they create their own obstacles.

Why project management?

This is the key question that needs to be asked before we even consider implementing a project. A good project management practice needs to address the issues we want to see resolved or improved. In general, there is only one common goal that needs to be realized—to make projects profitable and successful. You want and need to make profit from your projects and, at the same time, deliver value to your customers as expected. This is a matter of economic survival.

You must have heard this before but did you give it some thought? Delivering software projects that lose money is fairly easy. All you need is customer buy-in, some resources, and there you go. Some people don't even realize that their projects weren't lucrative until the end of the fiscal year when accountants call executives to account. A project is a synonym for risk and, if you want to realize the essential goals of profitability and customer satisfaction, you need to manage the risks. This is why you need project management, not as a side-issue but as an essential vehicle for your project business.

Now we know that you need project management because your projects need to be on time, and within budget and scope. But are these goals smart enough?
If you want a project management practice that is pragmatic, you need to define pragmatic goals as well. What does it need to succeed in your organization and your specific projects? How can it be valuable to your people and your customers? Be specific about it. Most companies have a set of specific metrics for their sales, marketing, finance, and operational systems and services based on well-considered and specific objectives. If projects are the essential component of your services business, you need to have these objectives as well for your project management practice. Without them, it's a hard road to improve on your project's profit and customer satisfaction. Yes, on time and within budget is measurable, but can you measure within scope and quality expectations? How much is your current project management practice contributing to these goals? What would be the effect if your current project management procedures are put on hold? How can you improve your project management practice in the future, or will you still be working with exactly the same procedures in a few years? There's room for smarter objectives if you are really seeking for a value-adding project management practice. So, before you start beating your brains out on how to implement a project management methodology, start defining why you need it and what it needs to achieve. Now, where do you start?

Of course it is not so easy to define how your project management practice must contribute to your company's success. It demands a strong vision on your service delivery strategy, your company's strengths and weaknesses, your customer portfolio and sector, and your employee mix and your project history. Your project management goals need to be embedded in this context and, at the same time, need to be very specific in different disciplines. You can start by developing a breakdown of areas where you will define objectives to be realized and measured. A good starting point could be the nine knowledge areas as described in the **Project Management Body of Knowledge (PMBOK)**:

- Project Integration Management
- Project Scope Management
- Project Time Management

- Project Cost Management
- Project Quality Management
- Project Human Resource Management
- Project Communications Management
- Project Risk Management
- Project Procurement Management

Take those as categories for your objectives and prioritize them. Which areas match with your SWOT analysis outcome and align with your service strategy key points? Then envision within each of these categories what will help your organization to improve your service. What are the known issues and what needs to be resolved? What tools and procedures do you need to achieve that and what will be the resulting business improvements? Who will benefit from it and to what extent? This is just an example of a breakdown for your objectives; you can make it in any kind of way as long as it is valuable for you and your company. The key message is: you need to know exactly why you need project management if you want to adapt to a helpful project methodology.

The alternative

Let's assume that you want to deliver your projects without a standard project management methodology; where would you end up? One of the first symptoms is that most of your colleagues will fill in their project roles in their own way. Each consultant, developer, and project manager will have their own tools, templates, steps, quality standards, and even their own jargon. You will find it difficult to work in harmony with your colleagues as it is hard to envision what and how they will deliver. Then how can you manage the team's activities and deliverables in a proactive way? How will the team members know what is expected from them? Different project managers in your company might set completely different objectives, quality standards, and deliverables in their projects. Imagine that you are engaged as a consultant or developer, working on two projects with various project managers expressing completely different expectations in terms of what and how to deliver. How difficult and inefficient is that? How can you communicate to your customer what they might expect?

With such a modus operandi, the success of your projects will be a gamble. Some projects will turn out to be successes while others get stuck in general discontent. As a company, you leave the probability of your company's project success entirely to individuals and there will be no way to improve your overall quality and profit in a structured way. Companies working in this way usually see only one way to improve their quality — by replacing resources. They find comfort in the idea that a few people were responsible for the project's failure and reassure themselves that with other resources this could not have happened. It usually doesn't take long before they are facing the same problems all over again in a new project. Chaos is ruling in these companies and it is discouraging to all involved.

Some companies associate formal project management usage to compensation. If the customer is willing to pay for these services on their engagements, the implementation will be guided by a project manager. In these cases, they make the deployment of project management principles on their projects dependent on the ability to sell the project and on the customer's ability to understand the need for project management. Failing to get a customer budget for project management implies an unmanaged implementation. You certainly know these cases where a sales manager communicates that there is little (if any) budget for project management. Then what happens? It's a remarkable fact that in these circumstances, a project manager will be assigned. No budget means lacking project management, but nevertheless a project manager is assigned. Who wants to be in this person's shoes? Usually, the consultant seasoned with a track record of product experience gets the honors in managing this assignment. This person needs to be the doer as well as the manager at the same time, requiring a complex straddle that is hard to perform even when a significant number of days for the task are available. Now this poor project manager needs to go through this exercise, knowing that there is no official project management time available. Don't forget that risks are not dependent on reward. Our seasoned product specialist will face the same level of risks as when a significant project management budget is available. In most of these cases, no clear and formal agreements are made in terms of the project risks. The customer will transfer the risk as much as possible to the vendor, and you will be forced to deliver in line with expectations.

What kind of outcome can we expect? Along with the regular application consultant's task, our poor seasoned application consultant fulfilling the project manager's role will probably be queuing numerous internal and customer meetings, negotiations, additional analysis activities, scope changes, planning and scheduling, among others.

By now our consultant is up to his neck in work and cannot focus enough on the regular consultant's tasks. This will bring about quality issues, causing even more meetings, negotiations, and rework. To get out of this vicious circle, you probably need a mix of sales along with project management skills and guidance. So in the end, you did work for which you didn't have any budget and excluded as a service to your customer. Unfortunately, it was not really efficient or proactive, and it ended up costing much more than what a well thought-out project management would have costed if it had been in place. In the best case, the organization is aware of this extra time spent on the specific project, but in many cases, people try to cover up by creative reporting in their timesheets. In that case, you will probably notice, by the end of the fiscal year, that your projects were not as lucrative as expected—a not-so-nice surprise.

The customers don't benefit from this scenario either. They started an ERP or CRM implementation to improve their business processes, to empower their people with efficient tools enabling them to be more effective in their jobs. Ending up with numerous meetings, dead-end discussions, and a grumbling workforce is far away from the envisioned objectives. They should be made aware about the risk factor as an essential element of implementation projects. Customers have a distinct interest in the positive outcome of the project and must accept the necessity of project management.

So, what's really the alternative? Don't forget that risks are not dependent on reward.

Using our own methodology

Full marks to those companies that invested time to develop their own implementation methodology. It is not obvious to envision a quality strategy for your projects, not to mention the work involved in transferring this vision into a workable set of procedures, guidance, and tools while encouraging the organization to adapt to it. However, it is a joy to see this rough journey guiding an entire company to project success, profitability, and satisfied customers and employees. For these partners, the implemented structured project management methodology will be the starting point and key instrument for continuous improvements and the center of their competitive advantage.

In all fairness, we have to add that not all companies who claim to have a project methodology of their own really do have one. Some are aware, others just can't see that what they have in place is not adding any value and can't be considered as a project management methodology. Let's focus on this last category—those who think they have a solid methodology. Why are they on the wrong track? The first thing to check is who is really using it in the organization. If nobody is using the methodology, it is of no value no matter how good the intrinsic value is. If your methodology exists only on paper and in presentations, it doesn't really exist. How can you know? This is a simple question with a simple answer: by checking or (even better) by controlling. Questions such as "are you using the methodology" will not give great solace. You need to dig a bit deeper, by inspecting on a regular basis, who is using what in terms of the methodology. This quality control will reveal the real usage of your methodology.

A second question that you need to ask is what value your methodology delivers. Does it really makes a difference or what is the intrinsic value of it? Sometimes it looks as if some people are content with the phase-based approach. As long as we have defined phases, we are on the safe side, is their reasoning. The phases symbolize the company's know-how in project matters and guarantee that not all work is done at the same time. They indicate that planning and milestones are crucial elements of the company's implementation approach. This methodology can be summarized in three words: phases, planning, and milestones. We all know that these are valuable elements of a project management methodology, but they don't make up the complete value offering of a methodology. You cannot conclude that you have a house when only the shell of your building was realized. At this stage, the construction does not yet provide you with the functions that we expect from a house. It does not protect and it cannot give any comfort yet. An approach, including only these three elements, cannot be called a project management approach. This is because it cannot supply basic proactive functions along with effective procedures and tools to realize our project objectives.

Why quality-driven companies prefer project management

Quality-driven companies seek to improve their quality levels in services and products continuously. In doing so, they have come a long way making use of modern methods for quality control and improvement. You have probably encountered customer organizations where methods such as ISO, Total Quality Management, Six Sigma, Kaizen, or Deming Cycle are used. These days, quality awareness is the rule rather than the exception as quality became a competitive instrument over the years. One of the best examples illustrating this is Toyota. They became the largest car manufacturer in the world, owing a great part of this success to their quality management strategy and the branding of it. Many others followed, either inspired by the example of successful quality companies such as Toyota, or even because they were forced to do so. Today, many suppliers don't even have a choice but have to conform to standards such as ISO. And as IT professionals, we do not have to look far to see quality management arising in our daily jobs as well. **Information Technology Infrastructure Library (ITIL)**, a widely adopted and consistent documentation of best practice for IT Service Management, and **Capability Maturity Model Integration (CMMI)**, a process improvement approach that helps organizations improve their performance, are the models that describe how IT departments function today.

Over the years, the focus of quality control and assurance processes has also shifted. Quality managers want to prevent defects rather than just detect them. They want to manage proactively by continuously learning from previous experiences. So when you plan to implement a software solution in this type of a company, it should not come as a surprise if they are looking for a quality approach demonstrating proactive ability. To do so, you not only need to have a good implementation methodology in place but also need to be able to capture, demonstrate, and realize the real value of this methodology. A few slides on phases, meetings, and a planning sheet will no longer be sufficient. Let's not mince matters—quality management is on the rise and this will have a significant impact on how customers will expect you to manage your projects. You can no longer sell quality by means of individual efforts and heroics, but need to demonstrate a repeatable, integrated, and standardized approach.

The four pillars of project success

In the previous section, we discussed the reasons why we need project management and how can we overcome the resistance to it. In this section, the most important elements constituting the intrinsic value of a project methodology will be discussed.

People can quite easily get lost in details when evaluating different methodologies to support their project delivery strategy. Overwhelmed by many procedures, steps, activities, and documents, they grope around in the dark for the true intrinsic value. This section will provide you with four valuable indicators in your search for a supporting implementation methodology.

Communication matters

We all know how important communication is in terms of our project success. When we think about some of our less successful, or even failed projects (a minority of course), we frequently blame it on bad communication. We usually do not walk around blaming the project's failure on an incorrect formula in our spreadsheet or on a system error in our planning software product, but bad communication is always a valid reason. Now, what do we mean by this? Does this mean we did not speak enough? Didn't we have enough meetings or should we have called our customers much more? What actually is good communication?

Communication is everything; it is omnipresent in everything we do. It is estimated that three-quarters of our day is spent communicating in some way. By communication we steer and manage the things we do. The lion's share is taken by speaking and listening, while only a minority of that time goes to reading and writing.

Agreed, reading and writing project documents is important, but that doesn't mean we really are communicating as this involves speaking and listening as well. Being a good listener is an essential element for good communication. Epictetus, a Greek Stoic philosopher once said: "nature has given us one tongue but two ears, so that we may hear twice as much as we speak".

Most of us have experienced this already in our daily project work. We manage our projects by communicating. Phone calls, e-mails, meetings, live meetings, and chat are all vital elements of our project management toolset. Nobody usually speaks about it, but there is a good deal of complaint about those project documents that nobody ever appears to read. Sometimes it feels like filling a library, where nobody ever comes with books.

What do we need to consider when planning for effective project communication? Of course we need communication skills, but even the most gifted speaker or active listener will not be able to fulfill communication needs in a project that does not allow effective communications.

The following four rules of thumb are indispensable for effective communications.

Rule number 1: Communication requires interaction

Communication is a two-way activity between two or more people. It is usually triggered by an interaction or an event. To make good communication possible, you need to plan your project interactions accordingly. Without customer interaction, good communication will be hard to achieve. The following diagram illustrates typical planned customer interaction levels in real-life implementations.

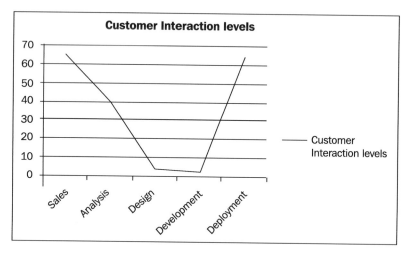

We usually have many interactions with our customers or prospects during the sales process. Meetings, follow-up calls, demonstrations, customer interviews, account management visits are all part of planned interaction management to close the deal. Because of these interactions, we also have the possibility to have good communication with our customer's stakeholders. Interacting with them means that we can speak with and listen to them, basic conditions for effective communication.

When the real implementation project kicks off with the *analysis* phase, we typically still have sufficient planned interactions by means of kick-off meetings, workshops, and interview sessions. However, after these activities, interaction levels may drop significantly. We tend to isolate ourselves during design and development phases when working on technical and functional designs and executing development activities. Some people blame this on the involvement of technical consultants in these stages of the project lifecycle; it is due to the stereotype view people have about technical consultants. These consultants start to become quite active during design and development activities and are known for not being the best communicators. If this is what you were thinking, you'll have to think again. The problem is not that some people carry out their tasks in a concentrated way for which they need an isolated environment; the problem is that no other activities triggering customer interactions are planned. This kind of planning, lacking a sufficient planned level of customer interactions, is endangering your project communication. This creates a "communication black hole" that can be quite big if the durations of your design and develop phases are significantly long. Think about the impact: no customer interaction means no communication and no customer involvement.

When we start preparing for the go-live of the new system, the customer interaction level suddenly starts to rise again. That is because we often have an over-planned deployment phase. Everything we didn't plan for in the design and development phases needs to be done in the deployment phase, resulting in many customer interactions. So maybe after months of low levels of customer interaction and communication, we suddenly need to communicate and interact ceaselessly. This won't be easy for the consulting and customer teams as they are missing communication routines and culture by now. In this kind of scenario, you also need to communicate too much in too little time. The receiver of your communication will experience problems in continuing to comprehend everything and might build up some (additional) resistance because of this.

Interactive communication must be equally spread over the complete project lifecycle and not concentrated in a few moments. The existence of such communications depends on your planning. The cause of failed project communications is not necessarily found in the lack of communication skills of your people, but it might be the organization of the project lifecycle itself.

Rule number 2: E-mail does not equal project communication

Sometimes you would think that people use e-mail communication because this allows them to stay within their comfort zone. Delivering bad news, informing about decisions, and asking for accountability is far more easily done from a comfortable chair and desk than in face–to-face conversations. No need to change places. You just write down what you want to say, your machine will not criticize your message, and you can send your message exactly as you intend—easy, quick, and efficient.

Yes, e-mail communication is without any doubt convenient in all possible ways. This makes it indispensable and there is nothing wrong in using e-mail for communication. However, because of its convenient character, it has known pitfalls as well. E-mail is addictive and we tend to use it all the time—in all circumstances and for all communications. This addiction will not make our project communications any better. Good project communication also requires regular interactions, including active listening and speaking along with non-verbal communications.

Facial expressions, body language, and intonation can provide you with a treasury of information on people's emotions, motivation, stress level, and much more. Studies show that when we communicate, 80% of the information we receive comes in the form of non-verbal communication. This is also expressed in a Chinese saying: *Beware of the man whose belly does not shake when he laughs.* If you use only e-mails as the means of communication, you will not identify such things and miss the opportunity to respond appropriately. Sir Karl Popper stated that it is impossible to speak in such a way that you cannot be misunderstood. When using e-mail, the chances of getting misunderstood are clearly higher. As a project manager, you need to motivate stakeholders and team members, sell your opinions and visions, communicate decisions, bring both good and bad news, and you need to do this continuously. How effective your communication is in these circumstances will determine your success as a project manager. You need to make sure that you are well understood.

You also need to be aware that people might read your e-mail much later than planned. Your message can end up in a long queue of unread e-mails, even when marked as important or urgent. Your communication by e-mail is not real time.

Yes, e-mail is convenient and can be effective, but not at all times. You need to step out of your comfort zone regularly to face your team members and stakeholders, and you need to do this right from the start until your project is closed.

Rule number 3: Be brief

Documents are an important element of your project communication mix. They support meetings, inform your team members and stakeholders, they ground your project decision making, and facilitate validation and closing processes. Project documents are a vital input for your communication, but unfortunately not all documents have the intrinsic quality to fulfil these goals. As said earlier, there is a good deal of complaint about those project documents that nobody ever appears to read. Those types of documents do not support or facilitate anything. They serve as an alibi for a so-called quality approach but usually only represent a one way ticket for the file cabinet. These documents are experienced by most people as a waste of time and are responsible for misperceiving project management as a bureaucratic activity. Then what kind of intrinsic elements make up good project documents?

One of the most important things is to safeguard the readability of your documents. Making project documentation is not a championship in writing the most number of pages. A long document saying nothing is much easier to write than a short document saying it all in a few lines. Most of these long project documents are unstructured, missing good conclusions, and contain too much gray zone. They also tend to get out of balance in terms of content, including too much content on introductions and less complicated topics, while lacking good content on the more complex and rather important issues. That makes these documents not only hard to read but incomplete at the same time. Why do we need so much paper to bring insignificant content? Now put yourself in your customer's position for a minute. Is it so surprising that these kinds of documents aren't read thoroughly? Would you like to read a fifty-page document lacking finer points and conclusions?

You should also take into consideration that all software projects generate a significant quantity of project documentation of all kinds. That means that your customer should review a large number of documents throughout the complete project lifecycle. They need to go through this on top of their daily jobs. So, do not expect that they will read all your flowery prose. For all these good reasons, you need to keep it short.

Coming to the essence requires real effort. Most project stakeholders review project documents assiduous for actions and conclusions but usually find unsolicited analysis, backgrounds, and arguments. Now what can we do?

First of all, you need to create awareness for this issue among all team members contributing to project documents. Specifying a recommended maximum number of pages for each type of document will help. Predefine the structure of the documents, including sections for actions, issues, and conclusions, and make sure that customer-facing documents do not include too much jargon and long technical descriptions. Communicate in the language that your customers use to communicate. And last but not least, do include graphical elements such as diagrams and process flow charts. These elements increase the readability significantly and will make your content much more attractive for the reader.

Rule number 4: Set clear expectations

If you want your customer's as well as team's involvement throughout the project, you need to work on setting clear expectations about who is expected to deliver what, in which manner, and when. If you want to ensure good communication in your projects, you need to advise your stakeholders in the same way about your communication approach. What do we need to explain?

- With whom to communicate
- Who will communicate
- What to communicate
- How to communicate
- When to communicate

This is sometimes also referred to as a "communication plan", commonly used by some, but a frightening idea to others. No matter how you feel about a communication plan, do not underestimate the importance of defining and explaining these communication elements. Without these beacons, the project team members' communication will be uncontrolled and unguided. At the same time, your communication strategy needs to align with your overall project lifecycle organization. For example, when can your customer expect the delivery of a document containing the requirements or design of a proposed solution? Do you organize a meeting to discuss this document? If so, who should attend? Do you need validation of this document and who is authorized to sign off? Do all documents need to be signed off or just a few? How much time does the customer have before signing off? What are the consequences when they don't sign off? What is the relation with the phase-based approach? Your customer needs quite some information before they can play your game.

Once your customer knows what to expect and how to communicate, you need to practice what you preach.

Proactive attitude makes the difference

Project success is highly dependent on your proactive abilities. Sometimes project managers behave more like spreadsheet gurus than managers. They use and maintain complex spreadsheets in which all project data is centralized. These spreadsheets include complex formulas, generating all kinds of trends and results for the project. There is nothing wrong with these spreadsheets, but by themselves these tools do not manage anything. These tools need to provide the project manager with indications and early warning signals that some things need steering or correcting. They need to trigger proactive and corrective project management action. This is what project management is all about—being proactive and correctively steering. As a project manager you need to manage your team, which requires a practical approach guided by the insights that tools like spreadsheets deliver. What can help us deploy proactive project management?

Rule number 1: Look ahead and prevent

A proactive attitude requires looking ahead instead of backwards. As a proactive project manager, you need to focus on prevention rather than detection. You need to make sure that your project reporting and tools will not explain your past failure in detail, but will help you prevent and resolve issues and problems on the horizon. The first thing that you need to do is switch your mindset from the past to the future, from problem identification to problem prevention, and from reactive to proactive.

Rule number 2: Proactive power requires interaction

Similar to communication, your proactive power requires continuous interactions with the customer and consulting teams. In projects, we face issues, risks, changes, quality, scope, and much more that can impact our time and cost performance. So when we want to reassure on time, budget, among other things, we need to manage these daily risks and issues proactively. To start with, this approach requires that we know our issues and risks. We can identify them only when interacting with the customer. Interactions such as testing, validating solutions and concepts, meetings, and evaluation moments usually reveal our project's issues and risks. It is very unlikely that you will discover issues and risks at times where the interaction level is low. Secondly, we need to make sure that we identify our challenges as early as possible.

If you want to be proactive, you always need to be one step ahead. This means when you have planned most of your customer interactions for the end-of-the-project lifecycle, your ability for proactive management will drop significantly. You will lose the same proactive power when you and your team postpone all customer interactions to the end of the project lifecycle. So, concentrating on customer interactions in the beginning and at the end of the project cycle will not give you the necessary proactive abilities. How you plan and execute your project lifecycle is the key for a proactive project manager.

Rule number 3: Measure for early warning signals

If you want to know what is on the horizon, you need to identify early warning signals of what might come. These signals do not always come to our attention by themselves. They can remain unnoticed if we do not plan for them. If you want to be proactive in your projects, you need to think really well over what you want to measure. A proactive manager reads the impact of the current progress on future activities in projects. You want to know if your current performance will cause cost and time overruns and you need to know why. So if you are using an advanced spreadsheet to measure your performance, you need to ask yourself if it tells you something about the future of your project or only informs you about the past performance of this project. Your measurement can only reveal early warning signals when you are not reporting hot air. Your measurement needs to be based on the integration of scope, schedule, and cost. So if you do not have a definition of your scope, schedule, and associated costs, you cannot expect to measure early warning signals.

Before you even start measuring, you need to have at least the following project essentials:

- The scope of work broken down in smaller units
- A timeframe planning for each of these (the same!) units of work
- Resources and approved costs against these (the same!) units of work

Only then you can start thinking of how to measure the performance. Early warning identification must be done right from the start of your project and should be carried out regularly. Starting to measure the performance when more than half of the project has been done cannot be considered as proactive.

Some project managers settle for a two-dimensional project reporting. They dive into the project data and their reports look something like this:

- Budget: 1000 000 (euro, dollar, ...)
- Project duration: 12 months

- Time spent: 6 months
- Cost spent: 400 000 (euro, dollar, ...)

After these six months, the project manager reports to the company executives and customers that they are right on track in terms of budget. They probably also report that the team is performing well, the quality is OK, and no major problems are on the horizon. What an excellent project! Or maybe not?

What this project manager forgot to do is integrate cost and time with the scope to be delivered. Let's assume that in these six months, six units were planned to be delivered. Crucial questions here are how many units have been delivered and accepted in six months with the 400 000 budget? This project will be suffering a huge time and cost overrun if only three units were delivered and accepted. You need to make sure that you are not misinforming yourself and your stakeholders with measurements not measuring appropriately. If you want to be proactive, you need to have a measurement system in place that is capable of detecting early warning signals.

Creating a guiding project culture

There is a flood of complaints about the customer involvement when speaking about less successful implementations. Some project managers also express that projects tend to take on a life of their own. In those scenarios, the project is narrowed down to the planning and execution of tasks by individuals. Both customer and consulting teams look to be disconnected from any attitudes, values, beliefs, priorities, and behavior that should be associated with this project. Driving the energy and commitment of your team to take a project from the initial idea through deployment will be a hard nut to crack with this kind of disconnection. Creating a guiding project culture merits particular attention from you as a project manager.

You need to make sure that all stakeholders and team members are aligned with:

- The project objectives
- The benefits of this specific project
- Good understanding of how you will work
- Good understanding of how you will communicate
- The vision on quality and how to achieve it
- Everybody's role and responsibilities in this project
- The change that goes along with the implementation of this project
- The risks associated with this specific project
- The scope that will be delivered
- Those parts that are considered as out of scope

That's probably stale news but you might fall into a trap when taking this for granted. Do not assume that everybody involved in this project is aligned. Aligning people and having them committed to the goals, benefits, and approach will consume a lot of your energy but it will be absolutely crucial for your success.

Culture is a set of stated and unstated, explicit and implicit beliefs and assumptions that are shared by a group that shapes and harmonizes behavior of all members.

You cannot assume that customers are committed to your plan if they are not enthusiastic for the goals and unaware about your approach. How can they support your approach if they are ignorant about the reasons and benefits for this approach? They need to know what is expected from them and how much commitment they need to plan for.

The same goes for your own internal team members. They need to be equally aligned in order to fulfill expectations. Having a good adopted and intrinsic strong implementation methodology is, without any doubt, a move in the right direction. This will allow your team members to have a strong understanding of how your company is doing implementations and why you are doing them in that way. Having this in place will save you valuable time in aligning the consulting team members about your approach as they already share these values and beliefs. What remains is a solid debrief on the specific customer case and upcoming project. If you are dreaming of more self-steering teams, you need to make sure that they share your company's values and approach.

So, you need to make sure that before you jump into the execution tasks of your project, all of the stakeholders and team members are aligned in terms of the beliefs and vision of your approach and about all crucial elements of the specific project. You need to evaluate if this alignment is strong enough to act as a solid undercarriage for your project vehicle. The road will become bumpy; a solid undercarriage will be no luxury.

The importance of closure

Closing the project proves to be a real challenge for many. At first glance, it looks easy and straightforward. After go-live and some additional support, you ask the customer to sign off for the delivery of the project, and once signed, your project is closed. Unfortunately most of us have experienced that closing usually doesn't go off that smoothly. In fact, many projects remain unclosed forever.

A first noticeable finding is that project team members do not have a closing culture. Analysts focus on the delivery of good business process descriptions and requirements capturing, developers want to show their superior technical solutions, and project managers strive for on time and on target KPIs. As a group, their key target is to deploy a new solution followed by a successful go-live. This is basically what they have on their radar. But who is responsible for and working towards closure? Closing is not so self-evident for project managers as it is for sales people. Closing is a key element in the sales cycle and being able to close a deal is the key strength for a sales manager. They are aware of this crucial process and improve themselves continuously in their closing skills. If we want to be more successful in closing our projects, we need to start to realize a closing culture within our project teams. Why we need to close, how can we facilitate the closing process, and who is responsible for closing are some crucial questions we need to find the answers for.

Having defined a project as a temporary endeavor implies closing a project. Not closing a project will transition it from a project to an operation. Unfortunately, we do not have a budget for that operation and we probably do not have a defined way of managing operations at customer sites either. This can become a true burden. If not closed, customers will continue to ask for all kinds of changes, enhancements, and various services for which the funding will be under discussion. You will end up in having a lot of meetings trying to find compromises, to determine what is still within the scope of the project and what is not, and you will need to do this for as long as the project isn't closed. Maybe your project was profitable until go-live, but at this point, your profit is starting to get squeezed dry. There are also important psychological elements attached to closing. Successful closing reinforces the feeling of success. People need successes in their professional careers to stay motivated, and success gives them the incentive to carry on striving for ultimate success in future projects. Customer team members will share the sensation of having realized something important for their company and they will share the benefits with the entire organization. And after all the hard work and effort, they are entitled to this moment of glory. When we do not close our project, other psychological effects will unfold. With no clear end to the tunnel, people will tend to think negatively about the project and will feel discouraged. Customer team members will not evangelize the benefits of their new solution; instead they will become irritated by even the smallest unavoidable issues. The chances that your consultants and developers will remain motivated for upcoming projects are minimal, especially when they already have a track of unclosed projects. For these and many more reasons, you need to continuously work on improving your project closing capabilities, just like sales people do.

Now what makes closing so difficult? Let's focus on two important elements namely:

- The existence of a closing culture
- The elements of the closing exercise

The customer organization needs to be familiar with closing and signing off. After deploying the project, if you ask your customer to sign off for closure, and this is the first moment they really need to sign off, your chances of realizing this are minimal. Signing off can make customers a bit suspicious and insecure, especially when they are unaware of the process. By applying sign-off procedures from the start of the project, those barriers will become much smaller as your customer is already familiar with closing routines.

The closing exercise itself will bring it all together. You will need to show and prove that your team delivered what was promised, the quality is up to standard, and the organization can use it with the defined benefits in their daily routines. This burden of proof requires good preparation, a strong dossier, and a good relationship with your customer. You will have the best chances for success when your dossier has already been created through a long validation cycle. Things such as approved documents describing the scope, validated change requests, confirmed test results, and signed off milestone review documents will make your case strong. At this point, you can evaluate how strong your approach was and how good your communication was throughout the project lifecycle. Can you think about a good way in which to close a project without these essential elements?

Project management essentials

Developing and implementing a smart project management practice requires profound knowledge on the discipline. The project management discipline cannot be digested in one small bite as it encompasses knowledge of various domains and disciplines. It deals with complex specialties such as scope management, cost and time management, quality management, human resources management, communications management, integration and risk management, and it can overlap with other management disciplines. This chapter does not aspire to examine all of these domains but will take you through a journey to discover some of the most essential elements in managing projects.

The project lifecycle and phases

When talking about project management and implementation methodologies, people spontaneously start talking about their phase-based approach. If you review the content pages of implementation partner's websites, you usually see diagrams illustrating a project lifecycle broken down in different phases and, when you attend commercial meetings between partners and their prospects, the explanation of the implementation approach is usually also done in terms of phases as follows.

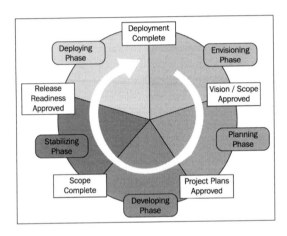

This phased-based approach of a partner is inspired by the Microsoft Solutions Framework. A project run is executed and managed by five different phases. Each phase is closed by clearly defined milestone deliveries such as approved scope and project plans, scope completely executed, approved release readiness, and a complete deployment.

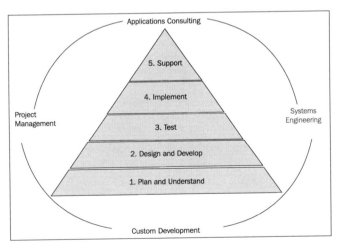

The following example shows an even more exotic variant of the phase-based approach, providing eight phases to manage the project:

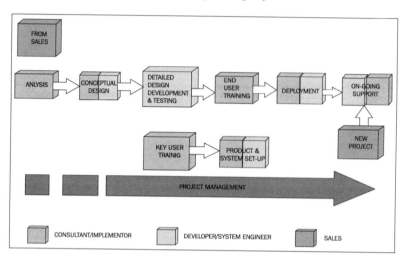

Therefore, in most partner implementation methodologies, phases are important; but do we really understand what phases are and do we respect the phase-based practice in our daily projects? Let's try and find answers.

What is a phase?

Phases represent a breakdown of the project lifecycle into smaller time units. Moving from one phase to the next, in a sequential manner, is typical for the waterfall model. The ambition of the waterfall model is to define requirements and designs quite early in the project lifecycle by means of separate phases. You can transition from one phase to another only when all the work planned for that phase has been done and all the necessary deliverables are produced and accepted. The following diagram shows the typical waterfall approach:

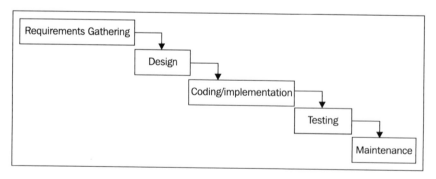

The essence of phases is that they increase the ability of management control based on the following idea: *you cannot eat a whale in one bite but it must be digested in small pieces*. The following diagrams shows two examples of a project approach.

Project A is organized in four planned phases. The activities are grouped and planned to be executed in their corresponding phase. The progress of execution will be monitored and controlled for each phase. The phases will be closed when all milestone deliverables are produced.

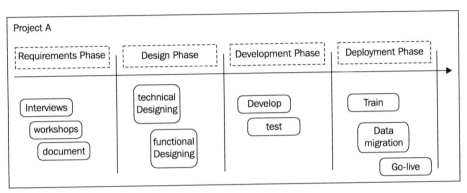

Project B is organized in one phase. All activities are planned to be executed in this phase. The phase will be closed when all deliverables have been produced. This phase will be closed along with project close out.

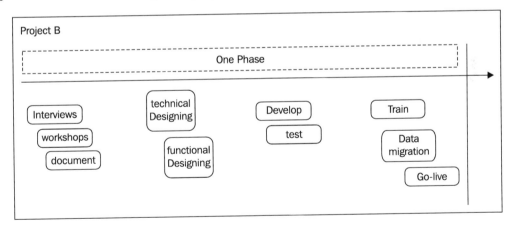

Let's assume that project A and B have exactly the same objectives, stakeholders, risks, timeframe, budget, and scope. What is the difference between project A and B? The teams will have to execute exactly the same activities in both projects, generating the same deliverables in the same timeframe and budget. The only difference is that project A is organized in four phases, while project B is executed in one and only one phase. In project A, the teams can start working on technical and functional designs only when the planned interviews, workshops, and documentation activities are finished and all deliverables are generated. This will be controlled and validated by both consulting and customer's project managers. In project B, teams might already have started developing before technical designs are ready and there are no real formal evaluation moments planned in between the activities and deliverables. So, the nature of the work is not changed, but by using phases, you control and validate the progress at defined moments. The purpose of this approach is to organize and control your timeline leading to more management control. Thus, the difference between project A and B is that in project A the ability of the project manager to really manage the progress is increased significantly, and therefore the chances of success are much higher in project A than in project B.

The following diagram shows a typical scenario that is most likely because of no controlled transition of phases in project B.

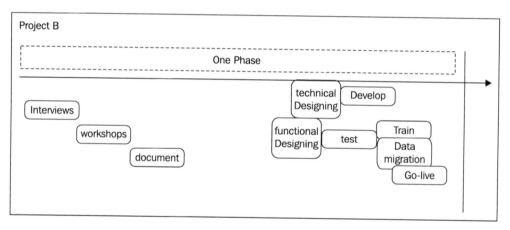

This typical scenario might unfold when not working with phases. The risk here is that activities and deliverables are systematically postponed. This causes a high concentration of to-do's at the end of the project lifecycle. This will bring on difficulties in planning and realizing a good deployment. In this scenario it is also common that no major problems have been reported until the deployment phase, which is not so surprising when most critical activities have been postponed to the end of the project lifecycle.

By the end of the project, the project manager will diagnose an increasing number of issues. Knowing that one train may hide another, it will not take long before the project manager realizes that the project is now starting a risky journey. A typical question is most likely to be: "why didn't we know about this earlier?" You can find the answer by just looking at the planning of such a project lifecycle — you are trying to eat the whale in one bite and this bite was badly planned.

Respect the phase-based approach

If your implementation methodology includes a phase-based approach, and you really support this approach, then make sure you also implement a real phase-based practice. Just having named phases on your presentation slides will not really contribute to your real-life projects. Not respecting the phase-based approach reveals itself by the following characteristics:

- Not formally closing the phases
- Initiating new phases without finishing the planned deliverables from the previous phase
- Under planned and over planned phases

If you do not close your phases formally and move to upcoming phases without finalizing the work from previous phases, you are not respecting the elementary functioning of phases. This implies losing the benefits of this approach as well. It will not only cost you the ability to track your progress phase by phase, but you will also miss a great opportunity to work on your communication and closing culture with the customer. Implementing phases provides the great benefit of bringing in a closing culture on a step–by-step basis. If you close each phase with a standard procedure, together with the customer, they will become quite familiar with closing throughout the project lifecycle. Building communication around these formal moments can only be to your advantage.

The following diagram illustrates a project lifecycle in which some phases are under planned and the others are over planned :

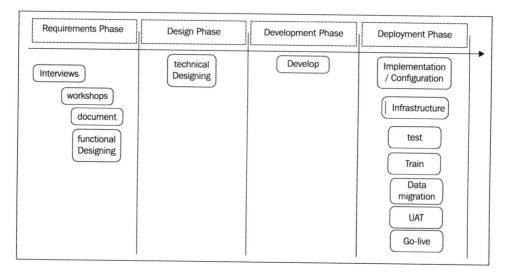

This diagram clearly shows an imbalance in the planning of activities spread over the phases. You can conclude from this diagram that this project is managed in two phases, instead of four, with an over planned deployment phase.

So, if you really want to work with a phase-based approach, you need to make sure that you respect the functioning of such an approach and you plan your phases in a balanced way. If you disregard these basic rules, then you must conclude that your implementation practice is not managed by phases.

Project management processes

Project management processes represent a logical grouping of activities, performed to produce a specified set of deliverables. Each time that you need to produce deliverables, you need to obtain validation for the goals, plan how you are going to execute, produce while simultaneous controlling this execution, and once ready, you need to close the assignment.

In the following diagram, you will find the project management processes as defined by PMBOK:

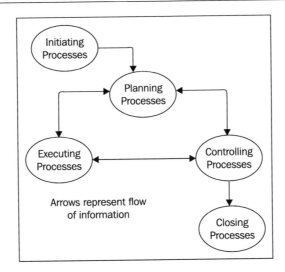

Initiating processes help you define and obtain authorization for the new project or phase. **Planning processes** help you establish the scope of the project, refine the objectives, and define the approach required to realize the objectives and deliverables of either the project or phase. The **executing process** group represents the activities performed to complete the planned deliverables. This will involve coordinating people and other resources to execute the plan. The processes required to track and review the progress and status regularly, to identify variances from plan, are gathered in the controlling process group. Once finished, each assignment, phase, or project should be formally closed by processes facilitating this closure. These processes are called the **closing process** group.

These processes are not the same as your phase breakdown of the project timeline. In fact, the project management processes occur (or should occur) in each of your phases. Depending on the phase, dominant processes will be in place. During the project preparation phases such as the diagnostic and analysis phase, initiating and planning processes can be more dominant, but this does not mean that those will be the only processes during that phase. You also need execution, controlling, and closing processes in your analysis phase.

It is important to notice that you always need to give attention to the closing processes. The closing process needs to happen in every phase or iteration. Closing is not something that you exclusively need to reserve for the end of your project lifecycle.

The diagram conveys that your planning outcome will direct the execution and controlling as a two-way traffic. How you execute will affect your planning, and the controlling can also reveal the necessity of planning changes. The same applies to the execution and controlling. Once you start executing the work necessary for producing the planned deliverables of that phase, you need to start monitoring and controlling; however, this needs to have an impact on your execution by means of corrective actions. If your monitoring has no impact on the execution, you might plough the sands.

Break it up!

If there is one thing you need to do to make you projects manageable, it will be breaking it up. You should be aware of the breakdown of your project lifecycle into smaller time units-like phases, but breaking down your scope is equally important. The best project plans are based on a good breakdown. You can find excellent project plans when buying toys for your kids (or for yourself). A good example is the *Emergency-Doctor's Car* from Lego. This includes a textbook project plan. The following image shows the best project plan in the world:

This image from the *building instruction plan* provides you with a clear definition of the scope. You will immediately know what to build and what not to build. The next image illustrates that Lego masters the skill of making rock-solid project plans. The *building instruction plan* is built up out of steps and subdeliverables. This building project will be executed in 13 steps, with each step producing clearly defined sub deliverables.

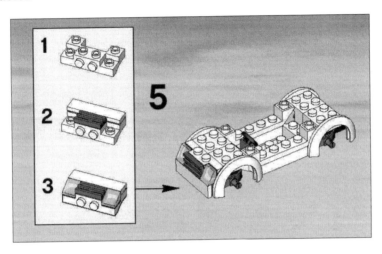

For example, in step 5 you need to produce this subdeliverable. You can start doing this only when you have finished step 4 and when subdeliverables 1, 2, and 3 have been assembled.

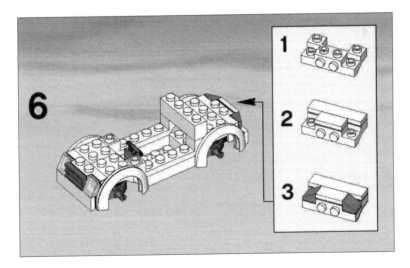

Each step has the same approach. For completing step 6, you need to have finished step 5 and produced additional subdeliverables in step 6. The *Lego building instruction plans* are excellent project plans based on the waterfall method, and the project management techniques of breakdown and the creation of subdeliverables. Were you aware that your kids have already mastered these techniques?

Most project management methodologies promote the use of **Work Breakdown Structures**, also known as **WBS**. A WBS is a fundamental project management technique, defining and organizing the total scope of a project by using a hierarchical tree structure.

In 1976, Russell D. Archibald, in his book named *Managing High-Technology Programs and Projects*, defined a WBS as a graphical portrayal of the project, exploding it in a level-by-level fashion, down to the degree of detail needed for effective planning and control. It must include all deliverable end items and the major functional tasks that must be performed.

The first two levels of the WBS define a set of planned outcomes that represent 100% of the project scope. A well-designed WBS describes planned deliverables instead of planned activities. These important deliverables are much more controllable than activities. We need to concentrate on what has been produced and not only on the effort: *activity is not achievement*. Deliverables or work that was not included in the WBS is not in scope of the project.

The following diagram illustrates a possible WBS structure for a Dynamics ERP project:

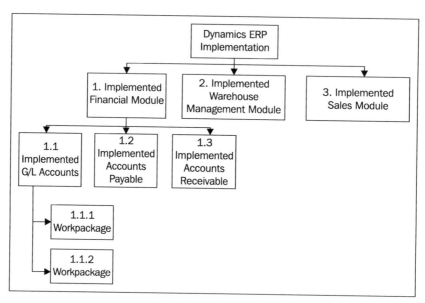

Your WBS might look like this but might be structured in a completely different way. The WBS Standardization Committee from PMI communicated the following:

> *Project managers may find themselves in many different situations and it would be inappropriate for PMI to place restrictions on their options. The WBS is a project management tool that can be used in different ways, depending upon the needs of the project manager. Therefore, there should not be arbitrary limits set on how the WBS should be created.*

A WBS represents the way that the project manager plans to manage the project. This includes planning, estimation, and controlling, all based on the WBS. In this way, the WBS is your ultimate instrument for the integration of scope, cost, and time. It is also an excellent instrument to implement a "universal project language" within your project, making the project communication more comfortable.

From estimate to follow up

We do not need to explain how important good estimates are in terms of the success of any project. Both time and cost estimates define your comfort zone within the upcoming project, and most of us, some time or the other, must have suffered from underestimated projects. Studies have identified that most of the cost overruns are caused by poor estimation skills. Furthermore, people generally tend to underestimate when asked for cost or time estimates for a new upcoming project, and we usually need to come up with estimates at times when detailed information on the project is not yet available. Nevertheless, stakeholders prefer accurate cost and time estimates in a context in which uncertainty is the only certainty. Higher accuracy demands greater effort and thus adds time and costs. And to make it complete, project estimation processes can't be bought off the shelf and there is no common industry benchmark for estimating a package implementation size. Getting close to despair? Wait, there are a lot of good estimation techniques documented and you can find plenty of literature on these matters.

The WBS as estimation instrument

One of the elements that we want to bring to your attention is one of the reasons why most of us tend to underestimate projects. Availability is a cognitive heuristic in which a decision maker relies upon knowledge that is readily available rather than examining other alternatives or procedures. In other words, people have difficulties imagining all the ways events can unfold, and out of sight equals out of mind. Therefore, we tend to assume that everything will go as we expect and this makes us overconfident in our estimation at the beginning of the project lifecycle.

Now what can we do? There are quite a few things we can try such as producing alternative scripts for how the project might unfold, drawing hierarchical diagrams of all that can go wrong, making explicit assumptions, and asking others to challenge us; we want to summon our WBS for duty. A WBS is an excellent tool in your estimation toolset and it will prevent you from assuming and forgetting too many things while estimating. The creation of the WBS will make you think of many possible events in your project. Even better is the use of template work breakdown structures. Those are work breakdown structures developed on the basis of previous projects. If you combine this with the use of project types for which you have an associated template WBS, your estimation accuracy will most certainly increase.

Another element that we want to bring to your attention is the subject of your estimation. We usually estimate the solution size or package complexity, including things such as the configuration effort to suit the requirements of business processes and the effort to produce custom objects to address the gaps in the application. In this context, we also evaluate the implementation and business complexity, but we sometimes forget to take the organizational complexity into consideration. Recent studies have identified that the implementation effort not only grows with the number of modules and submodules that are selected for the implementation, but that each user adds an organization component of costs. We need to make sure that we include all the complexity in our estimation scope. This might also be really relevant when we implement our solution in different departments of our customer's organization. The different departments might have different number of users, and they can have various experience and skills in terms of software solutions and procedures. The following diagram illustrates how you can organize your WBS in such a way that it will facilitate the estimation of the different complexities in the different departments:

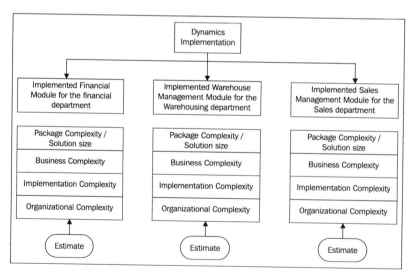

Follow up based on WBS

You can only follow up what you have planned and estimated for. Project reporting is in some cases disconnected from what was planned and estimated. The breakdown used for the estimation and initial offer can be quite different from the activities planned and controlled later on. It looks as if the estimation, planning, and monitoring live their own lives. You cannot expect great results in terms of manageability, and cost and time overruns have a high probability in those cases. The WBS is used for defining work packages and developing and tracking the cost and schedule for the project. Once you have your deliverables and work packages defined and planned, you can easily follow them up using different possible monitoring techniques.

A technique that you can consider using is the "Earned Value Concept". In their book named *Earned Value Project Management*, Quentin W. Fleming and Joel M. Koppelman describe the focus of earned value as the accurate measurement of physical performance against a detailed plan to allow for the accurate prediction of the final costs and schedule results for a given project. They also state that the WBS is an integral part of the earned value concept. The reason for this is that the earned value concept requires the integration of the technical scope of work with the time commitments and the authorized resources.

The WBS as central concept

The following diagram illustrates the benefits from the WBS in your projects:

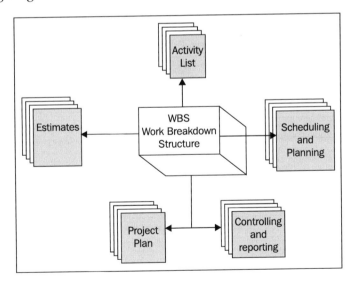

The WBS is your starting point and control point in making estimates and planning derived from activity lists. It is the necessary integration instrument for making monitoring and reporting activities possible, and it acts as a global communication instrument throughout the complete project. These are significant benefits from an easy-to-use instrument and therefore worthwhile to use in your own implementation practice.

Project management adoption

As you might know, there is no such thing as a free lunch. Adapting to a new approach including a new vision and new procedures, steps, documents, and tools, requires continuous effort and management. This section will inform you about the change in aspect of project management adoption and will inform you about the reasons why change initiatives fail.

The tireless quest for the perfect espresso

We might have something to learn from the coffee beans. When we say coffee, you might think about Illy. Founded in 1933 by Francesco Illy, illycaffè produces and sells a unique blend of high-quality coffee. Ernesto Illy revolutionized coffee growing in Brazil and elsewhere in the world. In his tireless quest for the perfect espresso, he encouraged the production of top-quality coffee and constant investment in research. *Our goal is perfect beans, zero defects, and we think we get close to that*, Mr. Illy told The New York Times in 2001. *It takes 50 beans to make a one-ounce cup of espresso*, he once said. *One bad one and I guarantee that you'll taste it. It's like one rotten egg in an omelet.*

Microsoft partners don't make coffee, they work on various projects, which is their business. If you have one big bad project, you'll definitely taste it as well. Profit goes down, your customer satisfaction deteriorates, and even more important, your employee satisfaction will not become any better. Those few failing projects are the rotten egg in your company omelette.

So, this should be your goal—perfect projects, zero defects, and trying to get as close to that as you can. This is probably obvious, but then again, not so easy. You need to make sure that all your projects are successful at all times. This is a continuous effort and involves everyone in your team. Everybody—sales, project management, consultants, developers, among others—needs to be aligned, knowledgeable, goal driven, and proactive. Your people and processes are the beans in your cup of espresso.

Embracing change

Adapting to a project management methodology doesn't come easy. Mark Twain said: "I'm all for progress, it's change I don't like." It requires continuous and true effort of a large team. Besides the continuous effort, there is also the element of change and as we know change isn't easy. It requires people to alter their current ways of working and adapt to new procedures and tools. You will need to prepare for stiff resistance by starting with the essentials like executive buy in. Without executive and management support, your change program will be doomed to fail. Therefore, the executive team must confirm a need and a compelling reason to adapt to a new or enhanced approach. They need to have a strong desire to resolve known business pain points and they must share and communicate the importance of adapting to the new procedures with the entire organization. John Kotter, in his book titled *Our Iceberg is melting*, describes ten reasons why change initiatives do not succeed:

- Underestimating the need for a clear vision of the desired change
- Failing to build a substantial coalition
- Failing to clearly communicate the vision
- Not generating a sense of urgency tied to improved performance
- Not building a plan for short-term wins
- Failing to lead and coach changes in business behavior
- Failure of managers to operate in and above day-to-day execution
- Not practicing what you preach
- Permitting roadblocks against the vision
- Failing to anchor changes in business culture

This should not hold you back from starting your change initiative because the rewards are great, and your business, customers, and employees will all benefit from quality-improving initiatives. But you should be aware that implementing change successfully requires great efforts.

The indispensable organizational benefits

In the previous section, we discovered that we will encounter many traps on our journey to adopt a rock-solid project management approach. The change process involved will require continuous and significant effort of a complete organization. Let's concentrate now on reaping the fruits. What benefits are in it for us? Why do we plan for all this effort?

A core competency for your company

By successfully adapting to an intrinsic strong implementation methodology, it becomes a core competency for your company. This implies that your company excels in understanding the needs of your customers, managing projects on time and within the budget, and designing and developing solutions that exceed customer expectations. This will allow your company to position uniquely in the market, while providing unique benefits to your customers in a way that will be difficult for your competitors to imitate.

Profitable projects

Projects are unique and temporary endeavors, facing continuous risks and lots of uncertainties. Effective and well thought-out project management is a necessity for realizing and maintaining project profits—an economical necessity for companies making their earnings through the delivery of project services. According to independent study companies such as Gartner, the companies that have developed their implementation methodology, to a level of making it a core competency for their company are rewarded with the following benefits:

- Top performing partners execute deals at a faster pace with new customers, with average implementation times for new deals.

- Top performing partners maintain the perception of high quality in the services they deliver, and at the same time, make more money.

- Top performing partners strive for repeatable service delivery, enjoying lower project backlogs with favorable utilization rates.

Satisfied customers and happy employees

In services companies, employees are a crucial asset. That's why human resources departments invest time in recruiting the right employees, with regards to their knowledge and their commitment for the company. Happy employees are usually more motivated, and the extent to which they align their motivation with the company's goals is linked to your customers' satisfaction. Every employee needs to experience success in the daily job. Queuing unclosed and unsuccessful projects is a burden gnawing employees' motivation. It goes without saying that customers' satisfaction is also directly connected to your projects' success. A solid and effective project management practice will significantly increase your project success, which is proven and illustrated by many independent consulting surveys and reports. Your customers and employees will be much happier when your company develops an implementation methodology to such a level that it is a core competency.

Summary

In this chapter, we went through the emerging and changing project management profession. We discovered that some basic and essential project management techniques can easily make a great difference in our project management practice. Smart planned project lifecycles and phases, along with respecting the phase-based approach and simple techniques such as the WBS, will bring instant value to your project services chain. We also learned that by safeguarding the four pillars of project success, a solid undercarriage for your project vehicle is guaranteed—a perfect insurance for bumpy roads. Do not be mislead by the skeptics' criticism of project management. We learned that their case is not strong enough to bring down the need for project management. However, we must consider and treat the implementation of a new methodology as an organizational change management initiative.

In the next chapter, we will learn and experience how Microsoft Dynamics Sure Step will empower you to sell new implementation projects and how it will efficiently prepare you for the upcoming project.

References

- Russel D. Archibald. (2003). *Managing High-Technology Programs and Projects*. John Wiley & Sons; 3rd edition

- Kotter, J. (2006). *Our Iceberg is melting*. St. Martin's Press; 1st edition

- Flemming, Q.W., Koppelman, J.M. *Earned Value Project Management*. Project Management Institute; 2nd edition

4
Selling with Sure Step

In the previous chapters, we reviewed the general methodology concepts, including the notion of full lifecycle methodologies for business solutions. In a nutshell, a customer lifecycle methodology begins with the solution discovery phase, continues with the solution delivery phases, and goes on through to the operation phase and any future upgrades of the solution. Microsoft Dynamics Sure Step Methodology is an excellent example of a customer lifecycle methodology, and includes guidance in all of these areas.

In Chapter 2 we went deeper into the solution discovery phase. We talked about the service provider embracing solution selling in this phase, and the benefits they would gain from this systematic approach. For the customer, we saw how this phase helps them with their due diligence process, and why this phase is not only critical for the selection of a solution that matches the requirements and vision of their organization, but also sets the stage for a quality delivery of the envisioned solution.

This chapter builds on those concepts, and gets into specifics of the solution discovery phase of the Sure Step Methodology, known as the Diagnostic phase. We will cover the following topics in this chapter:

- An overview of the Sure Step Diagnostic phase
- How solution selling guidance in the Diagnostic phase leads to a repeatable process for the sellers, including a detailed look at the Sure Step Decision Accelerator offerings
- Applying the solution selling process to an existing customer
- How the Diagnostic phase supports the customer's due diligence process
- Guidance in the Sure Step 2010 Diagnostic phase for industry and cross-industry solutions

The Sure Step Diagnostic phase

The Sure Step Diagnostic phase is the first phase of the Sure Step methodology and constitutes the pre-implementation phase of the methodology. The Diagnostic phase has been architected to achieve dual objectives:

- To provide a consistent and repeatable process for the seller to accelerate and close their sales cycles

- To afford a thorough process for the customer to help them select the right solution to meet their needs

Besides these objectives, an additional gain can be achieved from the proper execution of the prescribed steps in the Diagnostic phase. Following the key steps and guidance in this phase ensures that both parties arrive at a common understanding of the business needs and the envisioned solution to meet them, thereby setting the stage for a quality delivery of the envisioned solution.

The Sure Step Diagnostic phase flow comprises Activities and Decision Accelerator Offerings. In Sure Step, an **Activity** is a specific action or step in the flow. An Activity may result in a deliverable as the output of the step, or it could be a prescribed step in the process that leads to an outcome further down the line. In contrast to an Activity, a **Decision Accelerator (DA)** Offering is a "mini" project in itself, and each DA offering may require multiple actions to achieve its stated objective. We will go into more details on DA offerings in the next section.

It is important to remember that the intent of Sure Step is to help both the seller and the customer to select the right solution, so keeping with that ideology, Sure Step is not intended to be a lead generation tool for the seller. Sure Step begins at the *Prospect* stage of the Microsoft Solution Selling Process, meaning that it does not get into marketing, campaigns, and other activities to generate awareness for a solution, or to profile a particular market segment for prospective customers. Sure Step functions in the opportunity management stages, so it begins after a lead has been identified, and provides guidance for assisting in solution selection and assisting the seller in closing the sale for that solution.

The concept of Decision Accelerator (DA) Offerings

The Decision Accelerator offering is a focused set of actions, designed to engage the customer and provide the desired information to them within a short engagement, so that the customer can move forward to the next stage of their decision making process. For the seller, the Decision Accelerator offerings are designed to help them accelerate or shorten the sales cycle to bring it to a successful closure. For the customer, these offerings are rapid engagements, designed to help them search for the answers they need to get to the next step of their decision making process.

Because the DA offering itself may include multiple actions, it could have a flow or a series of steps of its own. The DA offering may start with a kickoff or initiation of the mini engagement, and progresses through prescribed actions to produce the stated deliverable or deliverables and to achieve the desired outcome. The DA offering typically ends with the presentation of the results to the customer, and a close-out of the mini project.

Each DA has a specific purpose, and each of them can be executed individually or in combination with each other. This flexibility is one of the unique characteristics of the DA offering, although not every characteristic is required. The sales team can work with their customer to decide which of the DA offerings are applicable to the given engagement. They can also decide to execute the DA offerings individually, or together as a combined engagement.

A repeatable process for the sales teams

With its alignment to Microsoft Solution Selling Process (MSSP), the Diagnostic phase innately supports the solution provider's sales cycle, providing guidance and activities that lead the seller through a prescriptive selling cycle. You may recall that MSSP, which you were introduced to in *Chapter 2, Solution Selling and Driving Due Diligence*, was created to enable Microsoft's internal and partner sales mechanisms. As we discussed, MSSP is based on the solution selling concepts, a philosophy that helps the solution provider and their buyer to forge a trusting relationship between them, while facilitating a working relationship between the two parties to craft a common solution vision for the mutual benefit of each other.

The following diagram shows the Sure Step Diagnostic phase flow and alignment of the seller with the MSSP. The flow shown in the diagram specifically depicts how the sales cycle for a prospect, that is, a new customer is supported. Sure Step Diagnostic phase also has a similar flow for existing customers, which will be discussed in a later section. The flow includes six Decision Accelerators for the prospect (we will discuss the seventh DA for the existing customer in the later section).

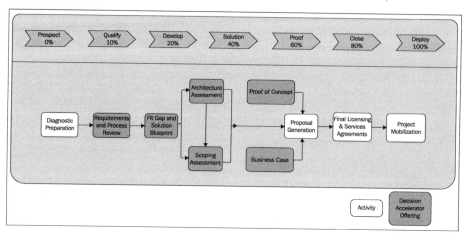

Just as with MSSP, the Sure Step Diagnostic phase is broken down into seven stages of the sales cycle. For the seller, these stages correspond to the probability that the sale will be completed. The Activities and Decision Accelerator Offerings are then aligned to these stages in a manner so as to accelerate the sales cycle to bring it to a close. The final stage in this process is a lead-in to the solution delivery, or the Implementation phase and the corresponding activities of Sure Step.

- **Prospect – 0%** through **Qualify – 10%**:
- **Diagnostic Preparation** Activity
- **Qualify – 10%** through **Develop – 20%**:
- **Requirements and Process Review** Decision Accelerator Offering
- **Solution – 40%**:
- **Fit Gap and Solution Blueprint** Decision Accelerator Offering
- **Architecture Assessment** Decision Accelerator Offering
- **Scoping Assessment** Decision Accelerator Offering
- **Proof – 60%**:
- **Proof of Concept** Decision Accelerator Offering
- **Business Case** Decision Accelerator Offering
- **Proof – 60%** through **Close – 80%**:
- **Proposal Generation** Activity

- **Final Licensing & Services Agreement** Activity
- **Deploy – 100%**:
- **Project Mobilization** Activity

Starting the discovery process with solution positioning

- The Sure Step Diagnostic phase begins with the Diagnostic Preparation activity, which provides the sales teams with key information on positioning the solution to the customer. Along with the guidance on positioning the solutions for select industries and their corresponding sub-industries, the solution capabilities for the Microsoft Dynamics ERP and CRM solutions are also covered in this section.

- As seen in the previous diagram, the Diagnostic Preparation activity is situated across the 0% — Prospect and 10% — Qualify stages of the selling cycle in Sure Step. At the 0% — Prospect stage, the customer is looking for more information on the potential solutions in the marketplace, and they may or may not have a complete grasp of the needs of their organization for the new solution. The positioning content can then help the seller start the initial dialog with their customer around the general business needs that the Microsoft Dynamics solutions are designed to solve. The content could be used as preparation by the seller for face-to-face meetings with their prospective customers, as part of a script for a telephone conversation with the customer, or for a prospectus or introductory letter to the customer that may set the stage for a future meeting.

The positioning content can also be used by the sales teams to respond to high-level questions on a customer's **Request for Information (RFI)** or **Request for Proposal (RFP)**. Most of this positioning information is available on product websites, but it has been brought together in Sure Step as a quick reference for the sales teams.

Positioning guidance and solutions for the industry is another important area covered in this activity. In the Sure Step 2010 release, the methodology has been expanded beyond coverage of general Microsoft Dynamics solutions usage to a specific application of the solution, for an initial subset of industries. The topic of industry solutions will be covered in more detail in an ensuing section.

Sure Step also provides links to other Microsoft tools such as the Microsoft Dynamics Business Solutions Roadmap and the Industry Playbook, to help us position the right modules of the solution in this activity. The Microsoft Dynamics Business Solutions Roadmap tool is designed to determine the right modules of the core Microsoft Dynamics products, along with the corresponding number of seats that a customer may need for their organization. The Industry Playbook tool, on the other hand, addresses the **Independent Software Vendor (ISV)** solutions for Microsoft Dynamics for given industries and their sub-industries.

The next screenshot shows the general positioning guidance for the Microsoft Dynamics solutions, including links to the Microsoft Dynamics Business Solutions Roadmap tool:

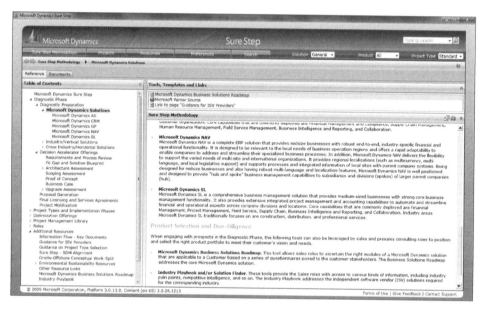

As the sales team moves towards the 10% — Qualify stage, they will need to gauge if the customer organization has already defined a selection process, and appointed resources to evaluate solution fit and alternatives, as well as ascertain if the customer has a high-level budget allocation to acquire the solution in the near term. They will also want to ensure that the customer's evaluation is a fair one, meaning that it is not already weighted towards a particular competitor and they are just going through the motions to appease corporate standards or rules. When the qualification has been accomplished, the sales teams can begin making use of the Decision Accelerator offerings to help the customer envision their future solution.

The following sections explain the usage of Decision Accelerator offerings for the sales cycles of the selling organization. A later section expands on this usage, and provides the customer's perspectives for their usage.

The first step to envisioning the future state

The first Decision Accelerator offering in Sure Step is the Requirements and Process Review offering that is designed to help the customer determine the business requirements for their future state, as well as visualize their "to-be" process flows for the associated organizational functions.

The first part of this DA offering enables the seller to ascertain the customer's requirements, with detailed, role-tailored questionnaire templates specific to the ERP or CRM solution that the customer is exploring. The role-tailored aspect of these questions in these templates allows the seller to address the functional requirements of the specific groups in the organization, such as accounting managers, marketing personnel, inventory manager, product planner, or production manager. This is a key enabler of solution selling in that the seller is able to engage the prospective customer in a manner that resonates with them. Instead of approaching the customer and leading with product features and functionality and potentially turning them off, the seller now has the ability to engage the customer in a meaningful discussion on their day-to-day functions and job responsibilities, allowing them to unearth the customer's pain points and other valuable information such as current system limitations and other inhibitors of their performance.

A good solution seller and/or a services sales executive should be able to parlay these questions to develop a relationship with the customer. Depending on the size and scope of the prospective engagement, the sales team may also involve a solution architect, senior consultant, or project manager in these discussions, to provide real-life credibility and experiences to the customer. Going through the questions in a methodical fashion, the sellers document the findings from these customer sessions, and they in turn become the basis for the business requirements of the solution.

The following is a screenshot from Sure Step of the contents of the Role-Tailored Questionnaire for Microsoft Dynamics AX. The AX questionnaire includes questions to initiate dialog with the executives of the organization, such as the President or CEO, through to individual roles such as Accounting Manager, Accounts Payable Coordinator, and Materials Manager, among others.

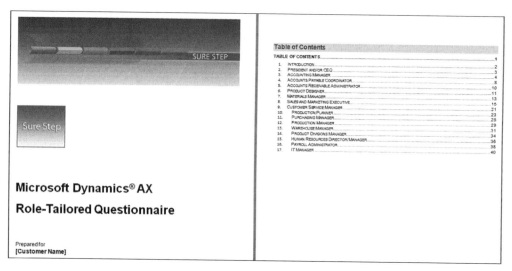

While the questionnaires assist with the requirements part of this offering, this DA also provides access to specific business process maps to enable the process objective of the offering. The business process maps constitute the standard processes when using the solution features, and they can be used as a starting point to envision the future state workflows of the customer organization.

From the service provider's perspective, they are helping the customer through their needs analysis in this exercise. While the templates included in Sure Step for this offering, including the Questionnaires and Process Maps, are distinctively fashioned along the lines of the corresponding Microsoft Dynamics product, it is not a stretch for the customer organization to take this output and use it as the basis for other solution evaluations. In doing so, there is also the potential that the customer decides to go down the path of an alternative solution other than Microsoft Dynamics. Keeping that in mind, it is important for the service provider to expect fair compensation for their services. This is one of the keys to positioning this mini-engagement as a DA offering — the service provider is putting forward experienced resources from their organization to enable the customer to envision the future state of their organization, and document the requirements for a solution to meet this vision. In the strict sense of the engagement, the services rendered are akin to business consulting, even if there is a bias towards a given solution.

As such, the service provider can legitimately position their services for customer compensation. Of course, the service provider may also choose to view the engagement as a business investment, and provide all or part of the services pro bono; however, it is in their best interests to do so only when they see it as fair competition, and that they have been afforded an equal shot at winning the customer's business as their competitors have.

It also bears mention that the Requirements and Process Review does not always have to be executed, and there are circumstances such as when the customer has already independently executed a thorough analysis of their needs and documented them into a Request for Proposal (RFP). However, in the cases that a customer already has an RFP in place, it is possible that another competitor or vendor assisted the customer in developing the requirements, in which case you may have to execute the Requirements and Process Review DA, at least to an extent. This discussion is elaborated in the *Other usage scenarios for the Decision Accelerators* section.

Identifying the right solution

After the requirements for the new solution have been identified and documented, the next step in the process is to ascertain how well the proposed solution fits for these requirements, and how it aligns with the vision of the customer organization. The Sure Step Fit Gap and Solution Blueprint Decision Accelerator offering has been architected to serve that purpose. This also aligns well with a major tenet of the Microsoft Solution Selling Process (MSSP) to make yourself equal before you make yourself different.

Fit Gap analysis is an important exercise that the customer and sales teams should perform in the solution evaluation phase. The premise of the analysis is to go through each of the requirements defined for the new solution and determine if they can be met by the proposed solution. To do so, the first step entails that the sales team translate the business requirements gathered in the previous exercise into solution requirements. As noted in the previous section, it is also possible that the sales team gets involved after an RFP or **Request for Quote (RFQ)** has been generated, in which case, it becomes even more important to be able to translate the general business needs into specific solution requirements.

Functional solution architects and/or experienced functional consultants are typically involved in breaking down a larger business need into smaller solution requirements. An example of this may be when the customer indicates that an overhaul of their **Sales and Operations Planning (S&OP)** process is one of their business needs. S&OP involves many areas, including sales planning and forecasting, supply and inventory planning, among others. While this is an extreme example, it just goes to show that a business need may be a bigger objective, but a solution requirement will need to be more compartmentalized to ensure that the solution delivery team can truly map the degree of the requirement to the solution.

If a requirement can be achieved either by the out of the box solution features or by configuring the standard solution, the requirement is considered as a *fit* to the proposed solution. It is also possible that minor change in the current process or workflow of the customer organization could lead to a fit with the solution. However, if the base solution needs to be customized, or in other words, some code needs to be written to achieve the requirement, that requirement is considered as a *gap* to the proposed solution.

It is also important to understand what constitutes the *solution*. Typically, the Fit Gap analysis is conducted with the base Microsoft Dynamics solution. If, however, add-on Independent Software Vendor (ISV) solutions for the Microsoft Dynamics solution are expected to be part of the overall solution, the term *solution* should encompass the base Microsoft Dynamics solution as well as the corresponding ISV solutions. Accordingly, a requirement will be considered a *fit* if it can be met by the combined solution, without the need for any additional custom code components.

The percentage of the requirements that fit with the overall solution to the total number of requirements deemed necessary for the new solution is expressed as the **Degree of Fit** of the proposed solution.

Number of Requirements that fit the proposed solution =

Requirements met by the standard features of the solution + Requirements met by a configuration of the solution + Requirements met by a workflow/process change in the customer organization

Degree of Fit of the proposed solution (expressed as a percentage) =

Number of requirements that fit the proposed solution/Total number of requirements for the new solution

The point about a simple change in the customer's business process or workflow to meet a given requirement cannot be overemphasized. In practice, this option is often not given consideration; instead, you can see the service provider coming up with expensive customization designs or add-on solutions as alternatives. But the first step should always be to examine the current workflow of the customer organization. We need to find answers to questions, such as are they presently going through the steps because of limitations in their current systems, or perhaps because of a creative workaround that was set up sometime in the past and is no longer necessary, or any other minor reason that a simple shift in a procedure could result in the company using the standard feature of the solution to achieve their goals? If our answer to the questions is yes, it is preferable for both parties to consider workflow change as the alternative, not only from the perspective of lower delivery costs for the solution, but also from a long-term perspective—the more the customer can use standard features of a solution, the easier it will be for them to maintain the customizations as well as to upgrade to future releases of the solution whenever they decide to do so. In the long run, this results in a lower value for the **Total Cost of Ownership (TCO)** for the proposed solution for the customer. If the seller is truly practicing the solution selling ideology, they will also work towards lowering the TCO for the customer, and not towards increasing the scope of the solution via customizations. Additionally, the service provider should always strive to architect the simplest solution to meet a customer's needs, thereby lowering the overall risk profile of the proposed solution. This should also be a point of consideration for the seller in moving away from complex customizations wherever feasible.

Coming back to the Fit Gap analysis, the output of the exercise is to determine the Degree of Fit of the proposed solution to the customer's requirements. However, what value for the Degree of Fit the solution should have for it to be acceptable is a contextual question. Some organizations may require a minimum of 75% Degree of Fit for lower TCO objectives. Others may be fine with a lower value for the Degree of Fit due to the specific nature of their business that precludes them from using out-of-the-box functionality to meet their needs, and could be evaluating if they should be developing their own application or if it would feasible to start with an existing code base and expand it to meet their needs.

The following screenshot shows a sample output from Sure Step of a Fit Gap analysis for a Microsoft Dynamics CRM engagement. This is just a simple screenshot with five requirements being mapped to the categories, but it shows the pictorial depiction of the Degree of Fit for the customer to the CRM solution.

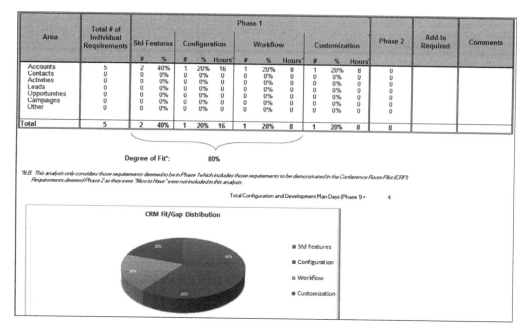

Upon completion of the Fit Gap analysis, the second part of the Fit Gap and Solution Blueprint Decision Accelerator offering is to develop the solution blueprint. The solution blueprint is a document that communicates the service provider's conceptual design of their proposed solution to meet the customer's requirements. The document should include the seller's understanding of the customer's business needs along with the overall solution, including any add-on solutions, customizations required, and integration components that are deemed necessary to meet the customer's future state vision.

Determining the infrastructure implications

The acquisition of a packaged application for the business solution includes the following three components:

- Software costs (and any associated maintenance costs)
- Services or implementation costs for the delivery of the solution
- Hardware or infrastructure costs

The Sure Step Architecture Assessment Decision Accelerator offering deals primarily with the third component of the business solution acquisition costs. It bears mention that infrastructure costs are incurred regardless of whether the solution will be on-premise, that is, physically located on one of the customer's sites, if the solution is hosted by a third-party provider, or it is an online solution. The requirements will definitely vary depending on whether the solution is on-premise, hosted, or online—for example, the former will require more hardware or server components, while the latter two may have higher bandwidth and latency needs.

Given the understanding of the customer's requirements and the proposed solution blueprint to meet the customer's needs, the sales team is able to develop the conceptual architecture of the solution in this exercise. This exercise, which is typically carried out by technical solution architects or technical application consultants, includes developing the high-level hardware and infrastructure plan. Besides the business requirements from the previous activity and the solution blueprint, other inputs considered for this activity include projected transaction volume, key user scenarios, and any other benchmarking activities. The infrastructure and hardware recommendations that result from this exercise are then used by the customer to obtain the estimate for the infrastructure to support their business solution.

The Architecture Assessment DA offering also provides deeper offerings to help the customer in other areas such as performance projections and benchmarking, and high-availability and disaster recovery planning. A customer could have a concern in a specific area of their business that generates high usage or traffic patterns of the solution. Or due to the mission-critical aspect of the solution, they may require that the infrastructure plan encompass failover mechanisms to minimize or eliminate downtime. The customers may also want the plan to include disaster recovery, in order to ensure that their data is protected appropriately and can be recovered in the event of failure. For such situations, the Architecture Assessment DA offering has more technical sub-offerings, including the Proof of Concept Benchmark DA and the High Availability Disaster Recovery DA. Both of these offerings are performed by very senior and experienced technical resources, and can be used to provide the customer with the desired answers and allay any concerns about the operation of the system.

Estimating the delivery costs, approach, plans, and roles

The Sure Step Scoping Assessment Decision Accelerator offering deals with the second component of the business solution acquisition costs noted in the previous section—the services or implementation costs for the delivery of the solution. But this offering provides far more than just the costs—the decision point for the overall approach to delivering the solution, resulting in the development of a high-level schedule and the delivery team structure.

The first step in executing the Scoping Assessment Decision Accelerator engagement is to determine the overall solution rollout approach. In this exercise, the solution delivery team and the customer work together to determine whether the solution can be rolled out in smaller, manageable releases, or if the entire functionality is desired at the time of solution go-live. Rolling out the solution in multiple releases is known as a **phased** approach to solution delivery, wherein select solution functionality is enabled in individual releases, with each release building on the prior one. The alternative to a phased approach is delivering the full solution in a single release, which is often referred to as the **big-bang** approach to the solution delivery. A key point to bear in mind is: the reader should not confuse the phased approach with, say, the phases of a waterfall solution delivery method. The waterfall phases break down an overall project or release into smaller segments, while the phased approach is a technique to break down the overall engagement into multiple projects or releases.

The larger the scope of the project, and/or greater the reach of the solution within the customer organization, the more desirable is a phased approach over a big-bang approach. The following are the supporting reasons:

- A phased approach enables the customer organization to start using the solution much sooner, facilitating a smoother adoption of the system. As the scope for each release is limited, the delivery team can promote that part of the solution quicker to production, thus enabling users to start working with the system earlier than they would have with the big-bang approach.

- Solution testing can also be more manageable as the limited scope may mean a more focused applicability of the solution and fewer workflows that are impacted.

- Customers can also start to benefit from the solution sooner, by selecting those requirements that are important to them but could be easier or quicker to solve with the new solution.

- For complex solutions, customers can also earn valuable support for the project from early adoption of the system, resulting in a quick win for the delivery team, which, in sales/consulting jargon, is often referred to as "going after the low-hanging fruit".

- From an overall risk management perspective, the phased approach is often seen as the less risky strategy for all the reasons noted here.

Of course a phased approach is not always the best one. Sometimes, the customer organization will need all the features enabled before they can begin using the system. In that case, the big-bang approach may be the only alternative. But the big-bang approach also has other advantages:

- If the same user base will be using the addition functionality, they will not need to be retrained at every release.

- Solution testing will encompass all likely scenarios, so the customer organization can find out, once and for all, whether or not the overall solution will meet their needs. This could also potentially reduce overall testing costs. In a phased approach, you test the scenarios for the first release, and then potentially retest those scenarios in concert with the others when testing for the second release.

- "Throw-away" interfaces or integration code does not have to be created in instances where part of the system being used may necessitate external sources to be temporarily connected to the new system.

Regardless of whether the overall solution can be rolled out using a phased or a big-bang approach, the customer and solution delivery teams also need to select the delivery approach for the individual releases. Solution delivery has two distinct approaches — waterfall and agile.

- **Waterfall**: A sequential process that depicts a linear flow of activities from one phase to another, culminating with the solution being promoted to production and then into operation.

- **Agile**: An iterative solution development method that promotes a collaborative process between the resources that own and specify the requirements for the solution with the resources responsible for the development and rollout of the solution.

Just as with the overall phased or big-bang approaches, there is no right or wrong with either of the solution delivery approaches; it is just a matter of organizational preference. Some organizations prefer the structure of the waterfall approach, as it clearly breaks down the activities in each phase leading to the deployment of the solution. Others prefer to let the requirements of the solution evolve during the development activities, which is a characteristic of the agile approach. The Microsoft Dynamics Sure Step methodology supports both approaches by offering Standard, Enterprise, Rapid, and Agile workflows (plus an Upgrade workflow for existing customer deployments). We will cover this aspect in more detail in the next chapter that is focused on solution delivery.

The next step for the sales and solution delivery team, in the execution of the Scoping Assessment Decision Accelerator offering, is to work with the customer and understand their solution priorities using the solution blueprint as the input. To do so, the delivery team will need to identify the inherent constraints, as well as any imposed constraints for the project. Inherent constraints are often imposed by the system—for example, a system will need a certain logical configuration order, such as starting with the chart of accounts, and then moving to the general ledger of an ERP system. Imposed constraints, on the other hand, are typically external constraints—for example, the customer may have licensed specific software that is up for renewal, which the customer does not desire to do, and would prefer that the corresponding module of the new solution is enabled before the license of the third-party software expires. Understanding these constraints allows the solution delivery team to come up with a schedule that meets the customer's objectives for the new solution.

The next step in the execution of the Scoping Assessment Decision Accelerator offering is to determine the effort required for the solution deployment activities. This includes the solution setup, configuration and development, the environment setup, and the user training needs, among other things. Many organizations develop costing spreadsheets and databases to support them in these tasks, and typically populate the spreadsheets based on their experiences on similar past projects. Other organizations use Estimator tools that include base values for enabling specific functionality. These base values may have been garnered from past history, but typically they constitute the average value from the experiences of several consultants over multiple projects. As such, these Estimator tools provide a consistent, repeatable framework for estimating the solution delivery efforts. Of course, the Estimator tools would also provide a means to override a given estimate, say to add an uplift that may be needed in riskier engagements.

The Sure Step methodology includes two such robust Estimator tools for the Microsoft Dynamics AX and Microsoft Dynamics CRM solutions. The output from this estimation exercise produces the overall effort for the solution deployment in the desired time unit, such as hours or days. This effort can then be translated into the solution delivery costs, by associating the corresponding resource rates for each of the tasks. The next screenshot shows a section of the Sure Step Microsoft Dynamics AX Estimator tool:

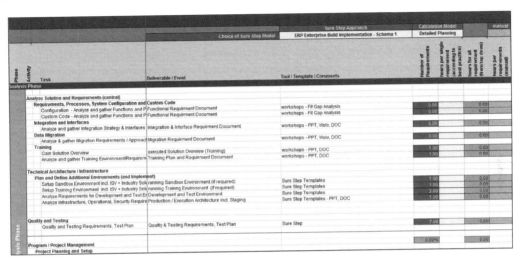

Armed with the information on the overall solution rollout approach, the individual release delivery approach, the inherent and imposed constraints, and the effort needed for the solution deployment activities, the sales and delivery teams can determine the solution rollout schedule in the next step.

Reducing the risk perception

While the Sure Step Requirements and Process Review, Fit Gap and Solution Blueprint, Architecture Assessment, and Scoping Assessment Decision Accelerator offerings are designed to help the customer envision their future solution and the costs associated with delivering that solution, the Proof of Concept DA is provided to allay any potential concerns for the customer in specific areas of the solution, while continuing the theme of solution envisioning as well.

The Proof of Concept Decision Accelerator offering requires the utilization of solution delivery resources to set up, configure, and customize the solution to a specific subset of the customer's requirements. As the customer has not yet acquired the software licenses, the delivery team will typically build their own demo environment to execute this solution setup, such as in a Virtual PC (VPC) program that virtualizes a standard PC and its hardware. After the solution setup has been completed, the delivery team will set up a solution demonstration in a conference room setting, where the customer's business and technical decision makers will be able to preview and criticize the solution features.

The Proof of Concept DA is an appropriate offering in instances such as when the customer, after going through the Requirements and Process Review, Fit Gap and Solution Blueprint, Architecture Assessment, and Scoping Assessment DA offerings, is fairly comfortable with the Microsoft Dynamics solution but still has concerns in specific areas. There are two key points here. The first is that the customer is fairly certain that the proposed Microsoft Dynamics solution will meet their needs, and the second is that the sales team identifies those specific areas where the customer is looking for additional proof points. These are important points to bear in mind because the Proof of Concept exercise should be a time-bound, limited scope engagement exercise that helps the customer with the final decision point before moving forward with the system acquisition. From the service provider's perspective, these points become crucially important if the Proof of Concept DA is positioned as an unpaid engagement, as resources who may otherwise be working on billable customer engagements are being called upon to work on this prospective customer's requirements.

The Proof of Concept DA can also become the starting point should the customer decide to move forward with the proposed solution. If the due diligence done by the delivery and customer teams includes configuration of the system, and/or custom code is written to meet a specific requirement, these should be carried through to the implementation of the system. This is another aspect where having a customer lifecycle methodology such as Sure Step allows the teams to build upon the work from the previous phases, even if that previous phase happens to occur during the sales cycle.

Another point about the Proof of Concept engagement is the potential that the project scope or solution vision may be altered after the output of this exercise. It is quite possible that the customer team may think of additional usages, or request a different solution to meet their requirement. In these cases, the sales team will need to go back and update the solution blueprint and corresponding delivery estimates, and perhaps even redesign the proposed system architecture.

Estimating the Return on Investment (ROI)

The Sure Step Business Case Decision Accelerator offering is designed to provide Return on Investment (ROI) analysis for the solution that can help the customer executives understand the value proposition for the solution and justify their investment. The Business Case DA determines the quantifiable business value for the given investment, as well as the Total Cost of Ownership (TCO) for their new system.

Going back to the discussion in Chapter 2, determining the impact of the solution on the customer organization and articulating the value is a very important activity for the customer and sales teams. When there is a value associated with the solution, it becomes a lot easier to drive executive support, which is critical for the project. Also, having clearly defined value projections will help motivate the teams through inevitable struggles during the course of the implementation of the solution. In some situations, companies are hesitant to share certain financial information, but given the investment they are about to make in terms of money, resources, and time, it behooves them to go through this exercise so that they can clearly understand the potential for organizational gains with the new system.

In the Business Case DA, the customer and service provider teams work together to determine the direct and indirect benefits associated with the proposed solution. Direct benefits have measurable impact on the budgets or costs. Examples of direct benefits resulting from the new system include:

- Increased inventory turns and the resulting lower inventory costs
- Reduction in personnel needed to accomplish a task
- Increased orders processed through the system during a given period
- Reduced returns due to wrong shipments

Indirect benefits, on the other hand, are not easily quantifiable. They may need observation and projection of estimated impact. Still, these are important factors to account for. Examples of indirect benefits from the new system include:

- Productivity increases gained from better visibility
- Reduced administrative overhead costs
- Reduced communication costs
- Increased customer retention

The Business Case DA also pulls together all the costs associated with the acquisition of the solution, with which the customer gains an understanding of the TCO for their new system. TCO cost elements include solution acquisition costs, operating costs, and long-term costs.

As mentioned earlier, the solution acquisition includes three components—software costs (and any associated maintenance costs), services or implementation costs for the delivery of the solution, and hardware or infrastructure costs. The software costs come directly from the licensing agreements. The Scoping Assessment DA produces the cost estimates for the services delivery, while the Architecture Assessment DA produces the inputs to determine the hardware or infrastructure costs.

Operating costs include costs involved in training and retraining the personnel in the customer organization, their resources involved in the testing of the solution, and other costs such as insurance, electricity, and other physical infrastructure needs. Long-term costs, on the other hand, may include costs for periodic solution reviews, and costs for solution upgrades and scaling.

The benefits and costs form the basis for the determination of the Return on Investment for the solution. Sure Step provides an effective tool for ROI calculations, which has been developed by an independent analyst firm, Nucleus Research. The standardized tool provides a systematic way to capture the benefits and costs, which in turn allows the teams to project the expected ROI, payback period, and/ or **Net Present Value (NPV)** for the investment. Separate ROI tools are provided for the analysis of ERP and CRM solutions. The following screenshot shows the report section of the Nucleus Research ROI Tool for Microsoft Dynamics AX:

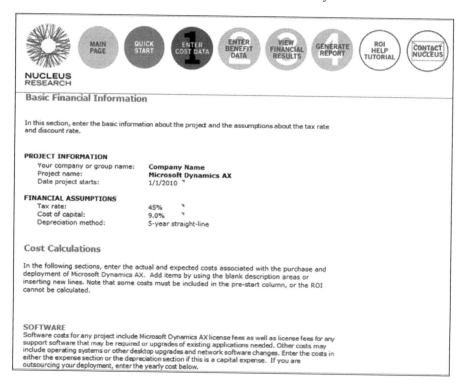

The service provider executes the above steps of the Business Case DA to develop the financial results and report. The financial results include insights into risk assessment areas such as capital recovery and variance potential. These results are then provided to the customer's business executives and calibrated as needed.

Besides the financial analysis noted previously, the Business Case DA also helps the organization determine **Key Performance Indicators (KPIs)** and **Conditions of Satisfaction (COS)** for the new solution. Establishing the KPIs and COS is an important exercise for the long-term health of the initiative, as they provide a means to track on-going progress of the engagement, and eventually the success (or failure) of the solution. Hand-in-hand with establishing the KPIs is the need to determine the baseline metrics for these KPIs, which will help the teams understand where they were at the start of the engagement and what they have achieved with the new solution.

Developing the project charter

The Sure Step Proposal Generation activity summarizes the conclusions drawn from the Decision Accelerator offerings and the preceding Diagnostic activities into a project charter for the customer. The project charter includes the high-level project scope, solution delivery approach, workflow, timelines, activities, and dependencies. It also includes the roles that will be involved in the solution delivery, both from the service provider and customer teams, and their corresponding skills requirements.

The proposal generation activity begins with summarizing the high-level scope. For this, the sales team will review the outputs of the Requirements and Process Review Decision Accelerator offering and the Fit Gap and Solution Blueprint DA offerings. Based on the requirements that were identified, defined, and documented in these exercises, the project charter will define the scope, including the business needs and functional requirements for the new solution, and the to-be business processes.

The project charter will also include non-functional requirements and any other technology requirements such as integrations and interfaces to external systems. Any performance needs such as system response, latency, system downtime, and failover requirements, will also be noted in the proposal. For this, the team will summarize the findings of the Architecture Assessment DA offering.

The project charter should also discuss the solution delivery approach that was ascertained in the Scoping Assessment DA offering. This includes deciding whether we will go ahead with multiple releases or one single release. It also involves deciding on the suitable implementation approach for each of the releases—waterfall or agile.

The project charter should be accompanied by a high-level project plan. While the overall implementation approach will be covered in the project charter, the high-level timeline, activities, and dependencies for the solution delivery will be noted in the project plan.

Another aspect covered in the project charter is an assessment of the proposed roles and responsibilities, and the project team skills and requirements. The starting point for this assessment can be the output of the Scoping Assessment DA offering. The project plan should then specify the next level of detail, including denoting in which activity and when the corresponding roles will be involved in the implementation. An overall project governance model should also be defined in the project charter, especially for longer engagements that involve multiple releases. The governance model should clearly articulate the project management and key roles for each of the releases. The model should also define the structure to bubble up communications and issues at a program level, such as the formation of a steering committee that will include key business stakeholders from a cross-section of the customer organization as well as key stakeholders from the delivery team.

The project charter can also include project communication plans and schedules, including the timing and information structure for project statuses, from individual release resource teams through to the steering committee.

The assumptions, scope delimitations, and risks identified for the engagement are key areas that should be highlighted in the project charter. It is important to list any assumptions that went into the definition of the solution, along with the requirements that are clearly out of the scope of the engagement, in order to avoid any misconceptions or misunderstandings. The project charter should also note the identified risks and attempt to identify and outline a mitigation strategy for each of them. Any dependencies owned by the customer and outside of direct project control should also be clearly highlighted.

The Proposal Generation activity is typically performed in the Proof stage of the Microsoft Solution Selling Process and traditionally follows Proof of Concept and/or Business Case activities. The sales team looks to influence the solution decision of the customer in this activity, and strives to obtain verbal approval from the customer. Upon receiving a verbal approval of their proposal, the sales team can proceed with the development of a budgetary estimate and the creation of the **Statement of Work (SoW)**.

Closing the sales cycle

The Sure Step Final Licensing & Services Agreement activity builds on the Proposal Generation activity to formalize the agreements between the customer and the selling parties. The selling parties could be multiple entities or, in some instances, one single entity. From a software licensing and on-going software maintenance standpoint, it could include Microsoft, Microsoft Partners, and Independent Software Vendors (ISVs) for add-on solutions to the core Microsoft Dynamics solutions. Similarly, it could also include multiple parties on the services delivery side, including Microsoft-Certified Implementation Partners and **Microsoft Consulting Services (MCS)**.

A typical first step in this exercise is to provide the customer with a budgetary estimate for the services delivery. The budgetary estimate essentially summarizes the results of the Scoping Assessment Decision Accelerator offering, and includes any rate discounts that may have been proposed between the service provider and the customer. If the customer has been actively involved throughout the Diagnostic phase activities, the budgetary estimate should not come as a surprise to them. However, the service provider can expect some level of dialog on rate discussions and timeframes, which is the reason for providing the customer with an estimate, as it facilitates open communications through negotiations towards finalizing a formal agreement.

After a satisfactory round of negotiations for both parties, the service provider initiates the Statement of Work as the formal agreement to commence implementation of the solution. The SOW builds off the project charter and project plan documents initiated in the Proposal Generation activity. It is a formal legal agreement for services that will need to be signed off by the customer and the service provider, so it will include many of the components of the project charter, including the project scope, any requirements not in-scope, assumptions, risk factors, approach, timeline, and resources. The SOW will also include legal terms and conditions both from a services delivery and a payment schedule perspective.

The Statement of Work itself can take different approaches. The most common approach is the Time and Material (T&M) format, where the customer is expected to render their payments for all services and expenses generated during the course of the solution implementation at agreed upon intervals. Project managers from both parties are responsible for ensuring that the project stays within scope and budget, with change order controls and processes typically in place to manage deviations. The larger the scope and length of the engagement, the more likely it is that the parties will agree to the T&M format, which will allow for a lower risk profile, especially for the service provider.

The following is a screenshot from Sure Step of the contents of the Statement of Work for the Standard project type. The SOW has been provided as a template for organizations using Sure Step to customize to their specific needs, including necessary legal references.

The other approach, which is being seen more frequently in tighter economic times, is a Fixed Scope engagement. In this approach, the customer and service provider agree to a very strict definition of the requirements in scope up front, and the service provider is then responsible for delivering all the requirements for the agreed fee. This approach is typically more risky for the service provider, especially in the larger engagements. The scope of the engagement typically goes through some levels of modifications during the course of the implementation. This typically results in the service providers building a risk quotient into their fee structure, to ensure that they are covered to an extent in mitigating circumstances. It bears mention that Sure Step includes guidance and templates to manage the inevitable scope modifications—this is covered in the Proposal Management sections of the Project Management discipline.

Besides the Statement of Work, the other component that is provided to the customer is the Software License and Maintenance agreements. As mentioned earlier, this could be only for Microsoft Dynamics, or it could include any associated ISV solutions.

The third component for a business solution delivery is the hardware and infrastructure requirements. These are typically addressed by the customer's procurement group, based on the recommendations made from the Architecture Assessment DA offering.

Initiating the delivery cycle

The final activity in the Sure Step Diagnostic phase is the Project Mobilization activity, which is the precursor to the start of the solution implementation. This is a critical activity for the sales and consulting teams, especially in instances where the resources involved in the sales cycle are different from those who will deliver the solution.

The Project Mobilization activity takes place after the customer has signed off the Statement of Work. It ensures that there is a clear knowledge transfer of the customer's requirements and the envisioned solution between the sales resources and the delivery resources. In this activity, the services delivery managers also lock-in the consulting resources who will execute the implementation of the solution. If the resources need any additional training before the start of the implementation, the managers are responsible for making sure that the training is scheduled and executed without affecting the start of the solution delivery.

Other usage scenarios for the decision accelerators

In the previous sections, we discussed the positioning and usage of each of the Sure Step Decision Accelerator offerings at length. Each of the offerings has been designed to serve a specific purpose, and they build on each other to help the customer envision their future solution. As noted before, the DA offerings are each independent and optional, so only those that are required for a customer engagement need to be used. That being said, there are three critical DA offerings that should be executed in some shape or form to ensure that the solution meets the vision and requirements. The three DA offerings are the Fit Gap and Solution Blueprint DA, Architecture Assessment DA, and Scoping Assessment DA.

The first DA, Requirements and Process Review, is important only if the customer does not have a full grasp of the requirements for the new solution or the future processes with the new solution. However, these days many customers start their business solution selection process with a Request for Proposal (RFP). If the RFP encompasses a thorough composition of the organization's requirements and future processes, the seller can begin with the Fit Gap exercise to determine if the requirements fit well with their solution. However, as noted earlier, even if a customer already has an RFP in place, it is possible that another competitor or vendor assisted the customer in developing the requirements. In that case you may have to execute the Requirements and Process Review DA, at least to an extent.

Determining the Degree of Fit of the solution is of critical importance, as is determining the solution blueprint, the future infrastructure, and the approach, timeline, and costs to deliver the proposed solution. This is why the Fit Gap and Solution Blueprint DA, Architecture Assessment DA, and Scoping Assessment DA are deemed as critical DA offerings. If, after executing these offerings, the customer is convinced that they have the right solution to meet their needs, the sales team may be able to go straight to the Final Licensing and Services Agreements activity and skip the other DA offerings.

For smaller deals, questions often arise from sellers about whether or not the Sure Step Decision Accelerator offerings are still applicable. Irrespective of whether the DA offerings are positioned as paid offerings, they are still applicable because they reduce the risk factor for a solution of this importance for the customer, as well as for the service provider, who ensures that they have documented and accounted for all the requirements in their proposal. It is important to remember that the duration for each of the DA offerings is dictated by the selling and customer teams. So, for smaller engagements, it still behooves the service provider to at least utilize the templates provided in Sure Step and go through the steps in an abridged manner if needed. This will ensure that they are not making any erroneous assumptions, and they are also clearly communicating to the customer their understanding of the requirements and the vision of the solution. Going through this process also reduces the risk of underestimating the deal, as during this process the sales teams may unearth points that they may not have considered. Therefore, at a very minimum, the sales teams should use the Sure Step templates to document their assumptions and solution vision, and make them known to the customer. Another option may be to combine the three offerings and execute them as a series of steps, resulting in the documentation noted above.

Solution selling to a current customer

In the previous section, we covered the Sure Step Diagnostic phase guidance for a new or prospective customer. The Diagnostic phase also supports the process for selling solutions to an existing customer, which is the topic of discussion in this section.

The following diagram shows the flow of activities and Decision Accelerator offerings for an existing customer. The flow is very similar to the one for a prospect, with the only difference being the Upgrade Assessment DA offering replacing the Requirements and Process Review DA.

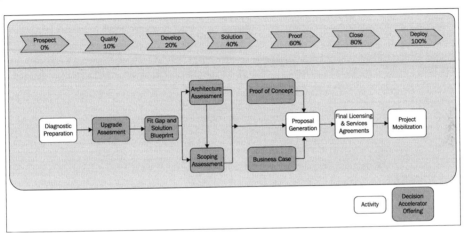

Much like the flow for a prospect, the flow for the existing customer begins with the Diagnostic Preparation. In this case, however, the sales team uses the guidance to explain the capabilities and features of the new version of the corresponding Microsoft Dynamics solution. When the customer expresses interest in moving their existing solution to the current version of the solution, the next step is the Upgrade Assessment DA offering.

Assessing the upgrade requirements

The services delivery team has two primary objectives when conducting the Upgrade Assessment DA. First, the delivery team assesses the current solution to determine the impact of the proposed upgrade. Second, they determine the optimal approach to upgrade the solution to the current version.

The Upgrade Assessment DA begins with the solution delivery team meeting with the customer, to understand the requirements for the upgrade. The solution delivery team is usually comprised of solution and/or service sales executives, as well as solution architects and senior application consultants to provide real-life perspectives to the customer.

Sure Step provides product-specific questionnaires that can be leveraged for the Upgrade Assessment exercise. The following screenshot shows two examples of the table of contents of these upgrade questionnaires — one for Microsoft Dynamics AX and the other for Microsoft Dynamics GP:

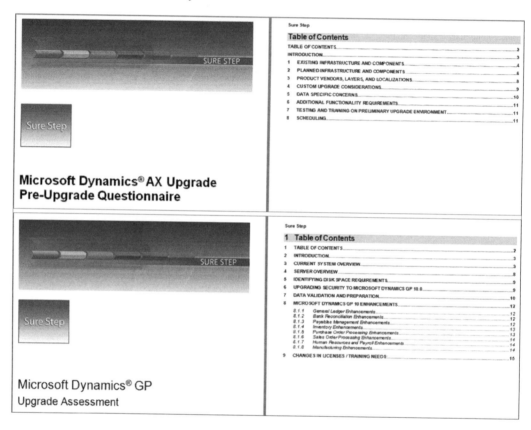

In the next step, the solution architect and/or application consultants review the configurations, customizations, integrations, physical infrastructure, and system architecture of the customer's existing solution. The team then proceeds to highlight those requirements that can be met by the new feature enhancements, and determine if there are any customizations that may no longer be necessary in the new product version. The team also reviews the customizations that will need to be promoted to the upgraded solution, and identifies any associated complexities and risks involved in upgrading the solution. Finally, the team will clearly delineate those requirements that require the implementation of new functionality. For the new functionality, the delivery team can avail of the corresponding product questionnaires from the Requirements and Process Review DA offering.

The last step in the Upgrade Assessment DA offering is to agree upon the delivery approach for the upgrade. If no new functionality is deemed necessary as part of the upgrade, the solution can use the Technical Upgrade project type guidance, workflow, and templates. On the other hand, if a new functionality is deemed necessary, it is recommended to use a phased approach in which the first release is a Technical Upgrade to bring the solution to the current product version, then the ensuing release or releases implement the new functionality using the other Sure Step project types (Rapid, Standard, Enterprise, or Agile).

Applying the other Decision Accelerators on upgrade engagements

If the upgrade is strictly to promote the solution to a current, supported release of the product, the solution delivery team can skip the Fit Gap and Solution Blueprint exercise and go to the Architecture Assessment DA offering to determine the new hardware and infrastructure requirements, and the Scoping Assessment DA offering to estimate the effort for the upgrade. The team may also choose to combine all these offerings, and just use the templates and tools from the other offerings to provide the final report and estimates to the customer.

If the upgrade is going to introduce a new functionality, depending on the magnitude of the new requirements, the customer and sales teams may deem it necessary to execute or combine the Fit Gap and Solution Blueprint, Architecture Assessment, and Scoping Assessment DA offerings. This ensures that a proper blueprint, system architecture, and overall release approach is collectively discussed and agreed upon by both parties.

In both cases, the Proof of Concept DA and Business Case DA offerings may not be necessary, although depending on the scope of the new functionality being introduced in the upgrade, the customer and sales teams may decide to use the Business Case tools to ensure that the project justification is established.

After the completion of the necessary DA offerings, the sales team can then proceed to the Proposal Generation activity to establish the Project Charter and Project Plan. The next step is then to complete the sale in the Final Licensing and Services Agreement activity, including agreeing upon the new terms of the product licenses and the Statement of Work for the solution upgrade. Finally, the delivery team is mobilized in the Project Mobilization activity, to ensure that the upgrade engagement is kicked off smoothly.

Supporting the customer's buying cycle

As we noted at the start of this chapter, the Sure Step Diagnostic phase is designed to help the seller and the buyer. In the previous section, we covered the applicability of the phase to the seller; in this section, we will talk about how the customer's due diligence efforts are enabled with a thorough process for selecting the right solution to meet their vision and requirements.

In *Chapter 2, Solution Selling and Driving Due Diligence*, we discussed the stages that correspond to the customer's buying cycle. The next diagram shows how the same Sure Step Diagnostic phase activities and decision accelerator offerings that we applied to the solution selling process also align with the phases of the customer's buying cycle.

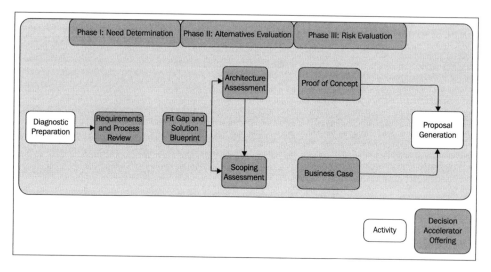

- **Phase I: Need Determination**
- **Diagnostic Preparation** Activity
- **Requirements and Process Review** Decision Accelerator Offering
- **Phase II: Alternatives Evaluation**
- **Fit Gap and Solution Blueprint** Decision Accelerator Offering
- **Architecture Assessment** Decision Accelerator Offering
- **Scoping Assessment** Decision Accelerator Offering
- **Phase III: Risk Evaluation**
- **Proof of Concept** Decision Accelerator Offering
- **Business Case** Decision Accelerator Offering
- **Proposal Generation** Activity

Let's first begin by addressing the application of the Decision Accelerator offerings to a customer's perspective. From a seller's perspective, the term *offering* can be viewed as a sellable unit. But the term Decision Accelerator, on the other hand, extends beyond the seller to the customer, as the intent of these units is to help them get expedient answers to their questions and move their decision making process forward in a logical and structured manner. So in that context, the Decision Accelerator offerings term is very much applicable to the customer as well.

The following sections will discuss the alignment of the activities and Decision Accelerator offerings to the customer's buying cycle. If the reader has not already done so, they are encouraged to review the previous sections to understand the constructs of the Decision Accelerator offerings, as that is not repeated in this section.

Defining the organizational needs

The buyer starts their needs determination phase by both understanding the organizational pain points and gathering information on solutions available in the marketplace. The latter need can be addressed by the guidance provided in the Diagnostic Preparation activity. Guidance provided on core Microsoft Dynamics solutions, as well as links to additional information sources such as websites, can help the customer understand the capabilities of the solution at a high level. If the customer's organization operates in an industry covered by Sure Step, they can also gain additional information on how the solution relates to their specific industry needs.

While the guidance in the Diagnostic Preparation activity provides the customer with the external awareness of available solutions, the Sure Step Requirements and Process Review Decision Accelerator offering facilitates the customer's understanding of their own internal needs. Using the role-tailored questionnaire templates in this offering, Subject Matter Experts (SMEs) from the customer team can work through "a-day-in-the-life-of" scenarios for each of the roles, so that they can quantify the departmental and organizational needs from a user perspective, rather than from only a product perspective.

Customers can also use the detailed process maps as a starting point to begin visualizing the organization's workflow with the new solution. Again, this helps the customer describe their needs from a user's perspective. Ultimately the success or failure of a solution is determined by how applicable or pertinent it is to the user, so this point cannot be overemphasized.

The documentation of the requirements and to-be processes forms the basis for the future solution vision. Depending on how they are developed, the customer organization can leverage these documents to conduct a thorough evaluation of the solution alternatives and select the best solution to meet their needs.

Determining the right solution

After the needs are determined, the buyer begins evaluations of the solution alternatives. This is where the Sure Step Fit Gap and Solution Blueprint, Architecture Assessment, and Scoping Assessment Decision Accelerator offerings can help the customer determine if the Microsoft Dynamics solution is the right one for them.

As discussed in the earlier section, the Fit Gap and Solution Blueprint DA offerings begin by determining the Degree of Fit of the solution to each of the requirements. Some customers may desire a higher value of the Degree of Fit so as to minimize customizations, while others may be operating in a specialized environment that necessitates a fairly customized solution and as such they may be comfortable with a lower value of the Degree of Fit. However, in both the scenarios the customer will want to ensure that their Total Cost of Ownership (TCO) for the solution is acceptable.

Following the determination of the solution fit, the customer SMEs will work with the solution provider to develop the blueprint for the future solution. The solution blueprint is typically presented to the customer's executive or business sponsor. As such, the document should be written in business language, and should clearly explain how the business needs or pains will be met or resolved by the proposed solution.

Armed with the solution blueprint, the buyer then obtains other key information for evaluating if the solution meets their cost criteria. The Architecture Assessment DA will provide the customer the proposed hardware and architecture, with which the customer's procurement department can determine the physical infrastructure costs. Should the customer have any concerns on performance, scalability, and reliability of the solution, they can also request more technical validation from the service provider by requesting more detailed analysis in the corresponding areas.

Finally, the Scoping Assessment DA provides the customer business sponsor with the effort estimate and the associated costs for the solution delivery. This DA also provides the customer with the understanding of the overall approach to delivering the solution, including timelines and projected resources, roles, and responsibilities.

Understanding and mitigating risks

In the last phase of their buying cycle, the customer will want assurances that the projected solution benefits far outweigh the associated risks. The Sure Step Proof of Concept Decision Accelerator offering can help allay any specific concerns for the customer's SMEs or departmental leads around a certain area of the solution. The solution delivery team will set up, configure, and customize the solution, and will use customer data where possible, to show that the application of the solution matches to the customer's requirements. Any solution efforts executed in this offering are then carried over to the implementation and become the starting point for the solution delivery.

The Sure Step Business Case Decision Accelerator offering also helps the customer in this phase of their buying cycle, but more from the perspective of managing the executive and organizational buy-in for the solution. Using an independent analyst-developed ROI tool, this offering can help the customer team justify the acquisition of the solution to other key stakeholders in the organization such as the CEO, CFO, or the Board of Directors. This can be a key step to counter organizational politics, and it can also be very important during the inevitable ebbs and flows of a solution delivery cycle.

Finally, the Sure Step Proposal Generation activity provides the customer sponsor and customer project manager with the overall project charter and project plan, ensuring that they have clear documentation of what has been agreed upon between the buyer and the seller, to avoid any assumptions or misunderstandings down the line. The project charter will also identify the risks associated with the solution delivery, and should outline a mitigation strategy for each of them. The project charter developed by the solution provider may also note any dependencies or assumptions owned by the customer—the customer should ensure that they have the necessary resources in place so that these dependencies do not become impediments to the delivery team.

Approach for upgrading existing solutions

Similar to the evaluation process for a new solution, the Sure Step Diagnostic Phase also supports the due diligence process for a current customer looking to upgrade their solution. The following is a very similar flow to the new solution evaluation, with the only difference being that the Upgrade Assessment DA offering now replaces the Requirements and Process Review DA.

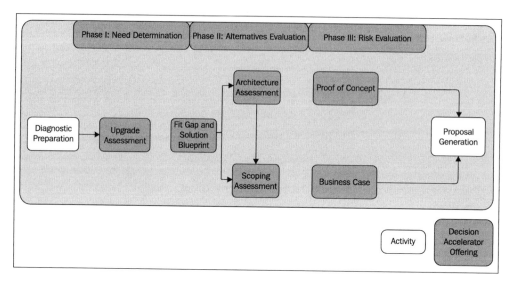

As discussed in the earlier section, the Sure Step Upgrade Assessment Decision Accelerator offering captures the business needs for the customer to change or enhance their current solution, as well as determines the best approach to upgrade to the latest version of the solution. If the current solution includes customizations that may no longer be deemed necessary because of new features, the delivery team will identify this. They will also evaluate the complexity for the overall upgrade, as well as the release process for the upgrade.

The Upgrade Assessment DA exercise findings will also dictate the degree to which the customer should undertake the Fit Gap and Solution Blueprint, Architecture Assessment, Scoping Assessment, Proof of Concept and Business Case Decision Accelerator offerings. Depending upon the magnitude of new functionality desired, the customer sponsor and SMEs can decide to skip or combine the offerings as necessary. Regardless of how the DA offerings are utilized, the project charter and project plan should be developed for the customer in the Proposal Generation activity.

Positioning the solutions for specific industries

As noted earlier, the notion of industry and vertical solutions was introduced in Sure Step 2010, with guidance provided for solution positioning and delivery. From a positioning standpoint, Sure Step provides guidance on the business pain points for the customers in the given industry and vertical, along with the Microsoft Dynamics solution capabilities that align to the customer needs.

The December 2009 release of Sure Step 2010 introduced solution coverage in three areas—two industries and one horizontal or cross-industry. Industry solutions describe the core Microsoft Dynamics solutions applied to the specific industry along with their verticals and subverticals. On the other hand, the cross-industry solutions describe a solution or composite of multiple Microsoft solutions surrounding the core Microsoft Dynamics solution. The cross-industry solutions can certainly be adapted to a particular industry or vertical as well, but the guidance provided in Sure Step is at the general cross-industry solution level.

The highlighted areas in the next screenshot illustrate the navigation to the industry solutions content in Sure Step 2010. The screenshot also shows a new content filter called **Solution** that was introduced to enable this guidance.

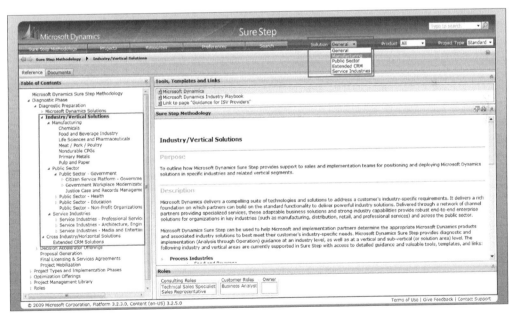

Following is the solutions coverage provided in Sure Step 2010:

- **Industry/Vertical Solutions**
  - ○ Manufacturing industry and the corresponding verticals
  - ○ Public sector industry and the corresponding verticals

- **Cross Industry/Horizontal Solutions**
  - ○ Extended CRM or xRM Solutions

In addition to the above industries, content for the service industry and verticals was also introduced in the first Content Pack (CP1) for Sure Step 2010, and is shown in this updated screenshot. This section was written before the release of CP1 and does not include coverage of the Service industry content; however, the last chapter in this book does introduce the service industry content.

Manufacturing industry

The manufacturing industry is broadly classified on the basis of the means by which the goods are manufactured into two areas—process manufacturing and discrete manufacturing. Process manufacturing represents a branch of manufacturing wherein the production of the goods is achieved through formulas and recipes, resulting in the "processed" items or **Stock Keeping Units (SKUs)**. In contrast, the production process in discrete manufacturing industries is achieved through the specification of bills of materials and routings, resulting in components, subassemblies, and/or assembly SKUs.

Solution capabilities aligned to the discrete manufacturing verticals are supported by core Microsoft Dynamics solutions, including Microsoft Dynamics AX and Microsoft Dynamics NAV. As such, the coverage of the discrete manufacturing verticals has been embedded within the standard solution content in Sure Step. Examples of content available to support the due diligence and solution selling activities for discrete manufacturing customers include the Requirements and Process Review Decision Accelerator offering, which we discussed in the earlier section. The *Role-Tailored Questionnaire for Microsoft Dynamics AX* has specific questions related to the discrete production process addressed to the production planner and production manager, while the *Requirements and Process Review Questionnaire for Microsoft Dynamics NAV* addresses the production planner and shop supervisor. Business process maps detailing the discrete production process are also provided, including the "Production Process Flow for Microsoft Dynamics AX" and the "Manufacturing Process Flow for Microsoft Dynamics NAV".

In the Microsoft Dynamics AX 2009 release, additional product features were introduced to address the needs of customers in the process manufacturing verticals. Accordingly, Sure Step 2010 included guidance for the corresponding process manufacturing verticals aligned to the AX solution.

The process manufacturing industries coverage in Sure Step 2010 includes seven verticals. Guidance is provided either at the industry level or at the corresponding vertical level as applicable.

- Food and beverage
- Chemicals
- Life sciences and pharmaceuticals
- Non-durable consumer packaged goods
- Primary metals
- Pulp and paper
- Meat, pork, and poultry

It bears mention that the content may be expanded in the future to include additional Microsoft Dynamics ERP solutions such as Microsoft Dynamics NAV. Therefore, although the existing Sure Step positioning content is based on the Microsoft Dynamics AX solution, the service provider can certainly leverage the business requirements and solution visioning content to additional Microsoft Dynamics ERP solutions such as Microsoft Dynamics NAV, if needed.

For each of the verticals noted in the previous list, Sure Step includes guidance on specific business needs such as catch weight and recipe-based units of measure for the food and beverage vertical or centralized quality control and compliance support for the life sciences and pharmaceuticals vertical. This guidance is then supported by how the Microsoft Dynamics AX solution capabilities meet these requirements.

Sure Step provides process maps to support the manufacturing verticals, and this includes the process manufacturing verticals noted above. The next screenshot is an example of the details provided in the process maps, from a discrete manufacturing and a process manufacturing standpoint.

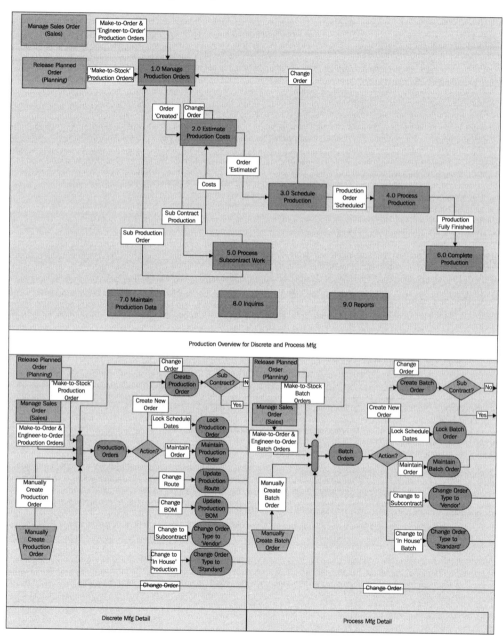

Sure Step also provides questionnaires for the process manufacturing verticals that help determine whether the customer's needs align to a process (batch) manufacturing flow. It can also help determine if the customer's flow is more aligned to discrete processes, or if they have mixed-mode (both process and discrete). Additional content and guidance is available in the Decision Accelerator offerings and activities in the Sure Step Diagnostic phase for the manufacturing verticals. If the general Microsoft Dynamics AX solution content is applicable to the process manufacturing vertical, Sure Step may also include "supplement" templates, indicating that the users should avail of both the core template and the corresponding supplement while executing the steps in the flow.

The Public Sector industry

The public sector industry refers to the operations and businesses controlled and operated by the state or government. The public sector industry spans a vast area that encompasses several sub-industries and verticals. The industry is characterized by very specific business needs at the vertical level, as well as regulatory variations at the country level.

Accordingly, the public sector guidance in Sure Step 2010 is broken down into the following sub-industries and verticals:

- **Government**
    - Citizen service platform — government service center
    - Government workplace modernization
    - Justice case and records management

- **Health**
    - Shared services
    - Health case and records management

- **Education**
    - Student inquiry and recruitment
    - Student enrolment and admission
    - Student management
    - Educational case management

- **Non-profit organizations**

While the Sure Step 2010 release provides guidance on organizational needs for these sub-industries' verticals, the solution capability alignment is based only on the Microsoft Dynamics CRM solution. However, future releases are expected to expand the content in this area, which includes showing how the capabilities of the Microsoft Dynamics ERP solutions would meet the corresponding requirements of the public sector customers.

The positioning guidance for the public sector is provided at the industry level or at the corresponding vertical level as applicable. This includes business process questionnaires oriented to specific public sector solution areas, Fit Gap Analysis worksheets for select solution areas, addendums for architecture assessment considerations, scoping guidance addendums for the scoping assessment offerings, and sample presentation slide decks for Proof of Concept offerings.

One of the examples is a questionnaire in the Requirements and Process Review Decision Accelerator offering that is catered to the economic development needs of a government organization. The next screenshot shows the table of contents for this questionnaire.

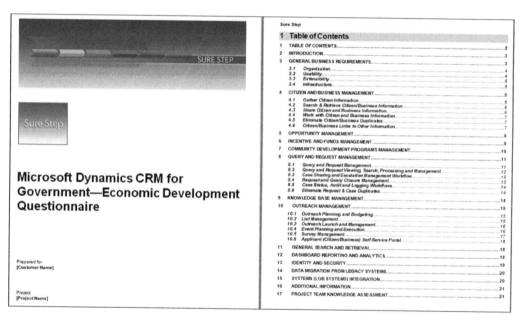

In the ensuing section, we will discuss a use case of the Decision Accelerator offerings to help a public sector customer with their due diligence.

Decision Accelerator use case for a local government council

This case study illustrates an example where a combination of Decision Accelerator offerings was executed by the service provider to help the customer through their decision-making process. The customer, a local government council in Australia with 300 employees and a six-person IT team, provides government services for a municipality of approximately 40,000 residents. The council was using a proprietary application to manage service requests, but the process and solution poorly addressed the needs of the constituents.

To attain the service benchmarks outlined in their strategic plan, the council determined that they needed to replace the existing customer access request system. They needed a solution to improve constituent satisfaction by reducing call waiting periods. They needed a solution that would help their people to answer more constituent requests at the first point of contact. They also wanted to give their constituents more choices for contacting the council. Finally, the solution was also expected to provide an integrated view of each constituent with tools that were easy to use, enabling more consistent service by the council system users and helping them to resolve requests quickly.

An initial investigation into off-the-shelf systems to solve their needs resulted in a dead-end for the council. Spurred by a solution demo witnessed by the council members, the council decided to get Microsoft involved in shaping up a comprehensive government service center solution.

Following an initial qualification activity, the sales executives formed a pre-sales delivery team constituted of Microsoft and Microsoft partner resources. The team was tasked with understanding the needs of the council to develop and present the envisioned solution.

The pre-sales delivery team presented a plan to the customer that included the execution of three Decision Accelerator offerings, the Fit Gap and Solution Blueprint, Proof of Concept, and Scoping Assessment, as shown in the following diagram:

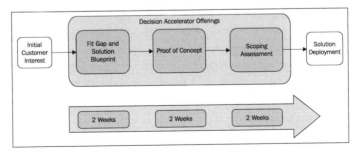

The council accepted the plan and agreed to fund the exercise. The pre-sales delivery team executed each DA offering over the duration of a couple of weeks and used one or two resources for each DA. One DA naturally flowed to the next DA in the process, which further enhanced the council members' confidence in the process.

The delivery team took the time to understand the council's requirements, developed an envisioned solution, built and demonstrated a proof-of-concept solution, and finally delivered an assessment and plan to structure the solution delivery. The process exceeded the council's expectations, leading to the following remark from one of the members:

Usually in local government we get handed a product and told to work our processes around that. It can mean changing the way people work, which is time and money. So it was refreshing working with Microsoft because they did it the other way around. They asked us what our processes were and they worked to that, tweaking their product to make it fit. They really listened to the business and let us dictate. And the result is a solution that's ideal for local government.

This case illustrates the effectiveness of a thorough Diagnostic process resulting in a win-win for both the customer and the service provider. It also shows the flexibility of the Decision Accelerator offering structure in Sure Step, which allows the account teams to select which offerings to employ and in which order to execute them. Remember that the people closest to the customer are the best ones to dictate the right process to meet the customer's needs. As such, they should also be the ones to decide what process to follow to meet their objectives. Having a flexible, yet consistent and repeatable process allows the field teams to do just that!

Extended CRM or xRM solutions

xRM, or xRM, refers to the usage of Microsoft Dynamics CRM as a platform, and any other external applications integrated to it, for the purpose of managing transactional relationships. Essentially, the **X** in xRM represents the corresponding business practice that is enabled by the solution. Examples of relationship management solution extensions include **Healthcare Relationship Management (HRM)**, **Media Relationship Management (MRM)**, **Student Relationship Management (SRM)**, and so on. The fact that an xRM solution can be extended to multiple industries or verticals is also the reason that the content in Sure Step is positioned in the "cross-industry" area.

The flexibility of the Microsoft Dynamics CRM platform components enables it to be leveraged in a wide variety of ways by many different organizations. The product enables the rapid creation and deployment of numerous relational **Line of Business (LOB)** applications on a single platform with shared resources and technologies, giving users a consistent experience across the LOB applications with technologies that are already familiar to them. These applications are highly scalable and can be rapidly adapted to fit the unique needs of users and the business, while minimizing the total cost of ownership.

In the Diagnostic Preparation activity, Sure Step 2010 includes key benefits for positioning the xRM solutions, which are noted here:

- The familiar Microsoft Office-type user interface, which drives user familiarity and solution adoption
- Predefined patterns for security organizational management
- Embedded capability for user-driven reporting and analysis
- Declarative data modeling, with instant web service data operations
- Known performance and availability metrics for the platform
- Ease of extensibility and integration using standard Microsoft .NET technologies
- Scalable delivery using multitenancy and scale-out provisioning

Additional content is also provided in several of the Decision Accelerator offerings. Examples include a specific Fit Gap worksheet for xRM and a business case report template catered to the justification of the xRM solutions for customers.

The overall guidance and artifacts provided for xRM is also expected to be refreshed with additional content in an upcoming Sure Step release aligned with the Microsoft Dynamics CRM 2011 product release.

Future industry and cross-industry solutions

Upcoming releases of Sure Step are expected to expand the industry and cross-industry content. At the time of writing this book, the Sure Step team was close to releasing a Content Pack called CP1 for the Sure Step 2010 release. The content pack was projected to include content on the service industries and corresponding verticals. Planning for a second Content Pack, CP2, had also begun by then. This pack was projected to cover the retail industry and verticals. Revamped manufacturing content is also projected for an upcoming release of Sure Step.

Customer service solutions, featuring Microsoft Dynamics CRM and CRM's Call Center functionality, integrated with other Microsoft solutions such as Microsoft SharePoint, Microsoft Exchange, Microsoft Office Communications Server, among others, are projected to be covered under cross-industry/horizontal solutions in a future release of Sure Step. Additional solutions in this area may include CRM Online with the **Microsoft Business Productivity Online Suite (BPOS)**.

Summary

In this chapter, we focused on the Diagnostic phase of Sure Step. We discussed how this phase has been designed for a dual purpose — to assist the seller to position the solutions and close the sale and to help the customer conduct their due diligence process and select the right solution to meet their needs. We covered the usage of the Decision Accelerator offerings for a prospective customer and an existing customer. We also discussed the positioning of industry/vertical and cross-industry/horizontal solutions with Sure Step 2010.

The Diagnostic phase is one of the important phases. If the due diligence activities are not executed properly, the implementation process may suffer and the customer's satisfaction will be low. In this chapter, we introduced several key concepts around this, summarized here as a quick reference.

- **Prospect for general Microsoft Dynamics solutions**: Start with the general Microsoft Dynamics positioning guidance. Leverage the Decision Accelerator Offerings, beginning with the Requirements and Process Review DA. The three key DA offerings to consider after that are the Fit Gap and Solution Blueprint DA, the Architecture Assessment DA, and the Scoping Assessment DA.

- **Prospects in specific industries**: Start with the specific industry/vertical positioning guidance for manufacturing, public sector, and service industry customers, or the Extended CRM guidance for customers looking for xRM cross-industry solutions. Leverage the DA offerings, including the Requirements and Process Review DA, the Fit Gap and Solution Blueprint DA, the Architecture Assessment DA, and the Scoping Assessment DA.

- **Existing customer**: Leverage the general Microsoft Dynamics positioning guidance as needed. Start with the Upgrade Assessment DA to ascertain the right approach to upgrade the existing solution to the current product release. If new functionality is to be introduced during the upgrade process, leverage the other DA offerings, including the Fit Gap and Solution Blueprint DA, the Architecture Assessment DA, and the Scoping Assessment DA.

In the next and ensuing chapters, we will get into solution delivery approaches, along with the guidance, workflows, templates, and tools provided in Sure Step for implementations.

References

Microsoft Case Studies: http://www.microsoft.com/casestudies/

5
Implementing with Sure Step

In the previous chapter, we discussed how Sure Step enables the customer's due diligence process and the partner's selling cycle in the Diagnostic phase. We also discovered that by carrying out the prescribed activities of the Diagnostic phase, one of the outcomes is that both the customer and the service provider arrive at a common understanding of the business needs and a vision of the required solution, thereby setting the stage for a quality delivery of the envisioned solution.

This chapter builds upon our learning of the customer situation, and discusses how Sure Step can assist the service provider in delivering the envisioned solution on time, in scope, and on budget. In this chapter you will discover:

- The implementation approaches in Sure Step, including the notion of phases and cross phases
- The waterfall-based implementation project types, including Rapid, Standard, and Enterprise project types
- How to set up Solution Rollout Programs
- A detailed description of each of the Sure Step waterfall implementation phases
- The Agile Implementation project type

Implementation approaches in Sure Step

The Sure Step methodology provides two distinct implementation approaches for solution delivery—waterfall and agile—as introduced in the previous chapter. The **Waterfall approach** to solution delivery is a sequential process that depicts a linear flow of activities from one phase to another, culminating with the solution being promoted to production and then into operation. In contrast, the **Agile approach** represents an iterative solution development method that promotes a collaborative process between the resources that own and specify the requirements for the solution and the resources responsible for the development and rollout of the solution.

The notion of phases and cross phases

Keeping with the principles of the waterfall approach, Sure Step provides waterfall-based project types that group the activities across five vertical implementation phases—analysis, design, development, deployment, and operation. These phases and their activities are detailed later in this chapter. Sure Step also groups its activities into *horizontal swim lanes*, or *cross-phase processes* as they are called in Sure Step, which we will discuss in more detail in this section.

Cross-phase processes are a key aspect of Sure Step because they allow the logical grouping of related activities that span multiple phases of a project, highlighting the activity flow for a specific aspect of the implementation effort. Cross-phase processes highlight the dependencies between the activities in the grouping, as well as interdependencies with other cross phases. The grouping can also provide a role view or pivot for the users of the methodology, such as depicting the series of activities that will be lead by the Project Manager, the Trainer, or the Developer.

The Agile project type groups its activities into Sprint cycles. The **Sprint cycles'** activities encompass the analysis and planning for the solution, the solution design, and the development of the solution. Following development, the Agile project type leverages the Deployment and Operation phases of the waterfall-based approach, to aid the rollout of the solution in a consistent fashion. We will discuss the usage of phases and cross phases in the Agile project type in a later section.

The following diagram shows how the phases and cross-phase processes are manifested in the Sure Step waterfall-based project types.

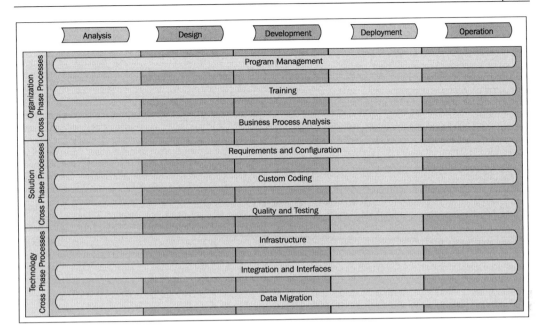

Sure Step aligns the activities into nine cross-phase processes that are grouped into three areas—**Organization**, **Solution**, and **Technology**.

- The three Organization cross phases are:
    - **Program Management**
    - **Training**
    - **Business Process Analysis**

- The Solution cross phases are:
    - **Requirements and Configuration**
    - **Custom Coding**
    - **Quality and Testing**

- The Technology cross phases are:
    - **Infrastructure**
    - **Integration and Interfaces**
    - **Data Migration**

Each cross phase can include multiple activities; however, depending on the project type, a cross-phase process may or may not be used. For example, in the Rapid project type, the Custom Coding or Integration and Interfaces cross phases have no activities called out, as the Rapid project type is catered to out of the box solution delivery. This is explained in more detail in the upcoming section.

Waterfall-based implementation project types

To address the scale and complexity of the customer's implementation engagements, Sure Step offers the users the choice of three waterfall-based implementation project types and one waterfall-based upgrade project type. The focus of this section will be on the three waterfall-based implementation project types—Rapid, Standard, and Enterprise. The Upgrade project type provided by Sure Step will be covered in a later chapter.

The Rapid project type

The Rapid project type represents the simplest delivery approach among the Sure Step waterfall-based project types. The Rapid project type is designed for out-of-the-box implementations of the Microsoft Dynamics solution, which essentially entail zero or minimal customizations of the standard solution.

The Rapid project type prescribes fourteen activities to solution "Go-Live", and as such, it is positioned in Sure Step as a lean or accelerated delivery approach. The relatively low number of activities, of course, doesn't directly translate to fewer implementation hours, but it does imply a minimalistic approach that requires extreme discipline and hard work from the customer and consulting teams. This is because such a lean approach does not factor in any time for missteps—it has no leeway in the budgeting and resourcing structure of the project.

The following is a screenshot of the **Rapid Project Type**, including the activities shown in the left navigation tree:

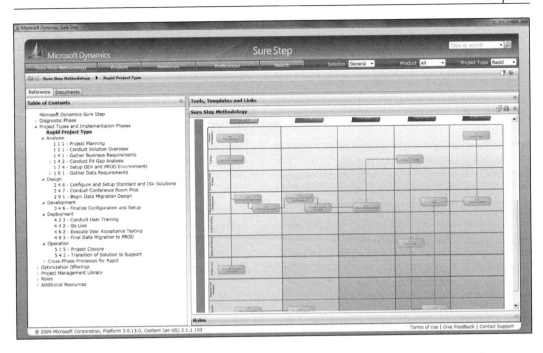

Before selecting the Rapid approach, it also very important that in the Diagnostic phase, the service provider and customer determine that the standard Microsoft Dynamics has a high degree of solution fit with the customer's requirements, and that no major customizations or add-on Independent Software Vendor (ISV) solutions are needed to complement the standard solution. If proper due diligence is carried out to determine that a high degree of fit exists, the Rapid project type can indeed live up to its name and provide a rapid delivery of the solution. It could be a recipe for disaster if one of the two parties—the consulting or customer teams—willfully chooses this project type even though they are aware of additional rigor being needed in developing the solution.

The following are the ideal conditions for the usage of the Rapid project type:

- A very high degree of fit exists between the customer's requirements and the selected Microsoft Dynamics product's features. The general rule of thumb is to look for about 90% degree of fit or higher to justify the usage of a Rapid project type.

- No customizations or minimal customizations will be needed to meet the customer's requirements, nor does the solution include any ISV solutions. It is important that if there requirements that are classified as "gaps" with the prescribed solution, they will require only simple custom code development efforts.

- Business process analysis is not in the scope of the Rapid engagement. A "rapid" engagement necessitates that the customer undertakes this effort, and is not a requirement for the consulting team.

- Integration or interfaces to third-party sources is outside the scope of the engagement. Developing code for integrating to outside sources can be fraught with factors outside the delivery team's control. For that reason, going with a minimalistic approach is not recommended if the solution requires integrations and interface development.

- The migration of data from legacy or third-party systems to the envisioned solution is straightforward or outside the scope of the engagement. Just like integrations to third-party sources, extracting data from outside sources introduces factors beyond the control of the delivery team, and hence is not recommended.

From a general customer profile standpoint, the Rapid project type is typically used in small-to-medium sized businesses deploying Microsoft Dynamics solutions. The typical number of users for the solution in these companies is small—up to 25. The usage scenarios for the solution could include companies moving away from homegrown legacy systems or smaller systems that no longer support their growth. These customers must have gone through the selection process in the Diagnostic phase to determine a good fit with the Microsoft Dynamics solution, and would be looking for the solution to go into production with a limited amount of functionality in a relatively short timeframe so as to quickly realize value from the solution.

Also, the customers that fit the Rapid project type profile may have a relatively small number of users, both on the business and IT side, with prior experience in implementing or using ERP/CRM solutions or solutions that encompass a high swath of the organization. The relative inexperience in this area requires that the customers choose a good partner who understands their vision and can deliver the solution to meet it. For the customer, it is also judicious to lean towards a more out of the box solution deployment. Hence it is preferable to choose the Rapid project type, so that they can start with a more straightforward solution and gain the experience before jumping into complex solution scenarios.

While the typical usage of the Rapid project type is for smaller businesses, it is important to note that this project type should not be considered as limited to the size of the customer. When you look past organizational size and look at usage patterns and needs, you may find other use cases for this project type. For example, the Rapid project type could also be applicable in multisite deployments, where the solution has already been developed and delivered to the first site and a very similar solution is being delivered to additional sites.

The Standard project type

The Sure Step Standard project type is suitable for a majority of Microsoft Dynamics projects, and hence the most widely used. This project type includes activities in all nine cross phases, to support customizations, integrations, and interfaces, as well as business process analysis. As such, the Standard project type can be used on typical medium scale, single-site implementations.

The next screenshot is of the **Standard Project Type** in Sure Step. Included in the screenshot is a partial view of the activities shown in the left navigation tree, indicating additional severity in each of the cross phases.

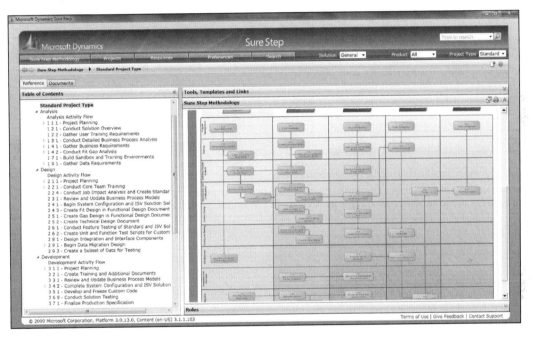

The Standard project type is best suited for medium-to-large sized businesses that find a fairly high degree of fit of their solution requirements with the corresponding Microsoft Dynamics solution. The rule of thumb on the degree of fit is around 70-80%, but more importantly the required customizations should not be overly complex, in which case, the Enterprise project type may afford a more rigorous approach to managing the custom code development process.

The usage scenarios for the Standard project type include the following:

- The customer's requirements can be met to a fairly high degree (about 70-80% fit) by the selected Microsoft Dynamics solution, which may or may not include an Independent Software Vendor (ISV) solution in addition to the core Microsoft Dynamics solution. The activities in the Standard project type provide more prescriptive guidance for the setup of the ISV solution in conjunction with the Microsoft Dynamics solution by service provider, and hence the Standard project type is more suitable than the Rapid project type.

- Business process analysis activities are included. One of the most widely used features of Sure Step is the extensive business process maps included. These process maps afford customers and service providers an excellent starting point to map their future workflows from the standpoint of using the standard Microsoft Dynamics solution functionality. Not only do the process maps allow the customers' end users to understand in a graphical manner how the solution functionality is designed to operate, but they also allow them to visualize how their current processes could fit into the new system and if there are opportunities to make simple tweaks in their processes to alleviate the need for complex customizations. The importance of this cannot be minimized for the long-term outlook and Total Cost of Ownership (TCO) of the solution.

- **Organizational Change Management (OCM)** is identified as a key discipline for the customer engagement, though the need is not as stringent as it would be for large-scale engagements.

- Custom code development is needed for the requirements classified as "gaps", with the prescribed solution being simple to complex, but not overly complex, as stated earlier. For highly complex customizations, the additional rigor in the Enterprise project type may be better for the customer and service provider.

- Custom code development may encompass integration or interfaces to third-party sources, as well as migration of data from legacy or third-party systems to the envisioned solution. Again, it is suggested not to make these coding efforts overly complex.

The Standard project type customer profile is the one with a fairly decent number of system users—typically up to 250. With a higher number of users from a cross-section of the organization, the solution not only needs to account for varied requirements in each of the business units, but it also needs to handle interdependencies across these units. As such, moderate-to-complex customizations can be expected to retrofit the standard solution to the customer's workflows. The solution will also likely need to interface to a few subsystems, both from a data integration standpoint and from a reporting and business intelligence system or data warehousing standpoint.

The customers in the medium-to-large segment also typically have a reasonable number of experienced business and IT users who have used and/or deployed other non-legacy business solutions. Averages in this segment may be up to twenty years of full-time experience on the business side, and ten years on the IT side, with ERP/CRM and general business solutions. For the customer, it is important that these users are an integral part of the team that is helping to fashion the overall solution requirements, in selecting the solution that best corresponds to their needs, and in delivering the solution, including configurations and all the way through to user acceptance testing. It is easy for these users to be wrapped in their day-to-day activities and not have time for the project, and as such it is the responsibility of the management of the customer organization to ensure that these users get some sort of a relief from their daily tasks to be able to participate and have meaningful contributions to the solution delivery engagement.

The usage of the Standard project type can also be extended beyond the medium-sized organizations to large enterprises. For example, a large multisite organization, looking for a common solution across its organization, may look to deliver a similar solution that has already been deployed in a pilot site. While the pilot site solution may have been developed using the more robust Enterprise project type, future rollouts of the solution to ensuing sites could use the Standard project type. Such usage scenarios of solution rollouts are described in a later section.

The Enterprise project type

The Enterprise project type is the most rigorous of all the Sure Step project types. Designed for large complex scenarios, the **Enterprise project type** is characterized by deep program management activities, requiring focus and discipline from the customer and service provider throughout the length of the engagement. Large-scale engagements are typified by complex requirements and solution scenarios that necessitate a thorough approach for governance and oversight in all disciplines, including project management, solution configuration and setup, custom code development, and testing. To cater to these types of usage scenarios, the Enterprise project type is provided.

The following is a screenshot of the **Enterprise Project Type** in Sure Step. Included in the left navigation tree view in the screenshot is a partial view of the activities in the Analysis phase, which highlights the depth and diligence that is prescribed for project governance alone.

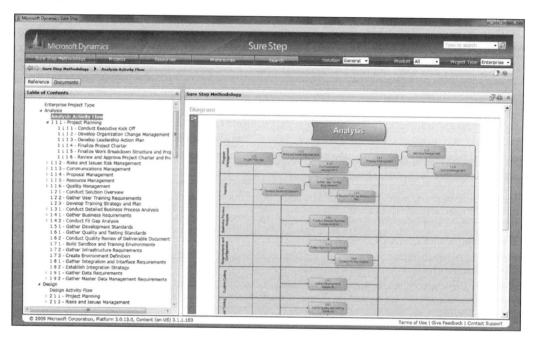

The typical usage scenarios for the Enterprise project type include the following:

- The requirements for the solution include complex customization and/or multiple ISV solutions in addition to the core Microsoft Dynamics solution. In large engagements, especially multisite projects, it is not atypical to see multiple development teams spread out in different continents, building on specific requirements for the same solution. It is critical that these teams are all "working with the same sheet of music" so to speak, meaning that they are all working towards the same goal. To ensure that there is tight coordination between the teams and each of the teams understands the interdependencies, the Enterprise project type is used.

- The custom code development efforts may include complex integration or interfaces to third-party sources, as well as migration of data from legacy or third-party systems to the envisioned solution. Again, the diligence provided by the Enterprise project type is needed here to ensure that risks are identified up front, as well as that mitigation scenarios are also developed to alleviate the risks, if needed.

- Due to the far reach of the solution, a concerted effort for Organizational Change Management (OCM) is needed for the customer. The Enterprise project type prescribes activities for OCM experts to plan up front, and develop strategies and techniques for managing the projected change across the organization.

- In concert with the OCM activities are the deep Business Process Analysis activities that allow the service provider and customer organization to discuss and document the future or to-be workflows for the customer. The activities and templates provided in Sure Step facilitate this for enterprise-scale customers.

- Large scale engagements also require the installation and management of multiple environments for developing the solution. This not only requires a bigger investment in the hardware for the project, but it also requires activities for planning, setting up, maintaining, and transitioning these environments, including clear documentation for the teams that will be supporting these environments after the handoff, as prescribed in the Enterprise project type.

- Multisite engagements, especially ones where a common, consistent solution is desired across the organization, also need a rigorous set of solution configuration and development activities advocated by the Enterprise project type. The development of the solution for these organizations can get even more complicated when each location also has a set of unique needs that need to be considered over and above the common list of requirements across the organization. The unique needs may stem from local country laws, accounting and reporting regulations pertaining to the local country, or from specific requirements of the local marketplaces.

The profile of the organization requiring the usage of the Enterprise project type is one with a very high number of system users — 250 users and above. Depending on the number of locations that the solution is to be deployed at, coordinating across all the users requires a well-planned and thought out approach that is provided by this project type. This includes activities for gathering the requirements across the locations, training the super-users and end users for each location, as well as a thorough user acceptance testing of the solution at each site prior to deployment.

The organizations in this segment are also characterized by a large number of experienced users in the business and IT groups. Due to the size and reach of the solution, the customer organizations typically appoint selected resources from this experienced group as dedicated resources for the length of the solution delivery engagement. In effect, these resources are extensions of the implementation team, and these power users typically become the lead internal "go-to" persons to support other users after the solution becomes operational.

Setting up a program for solution rollout

In the previous sections, we have discussed the different options for implementing Microsoft Dynamics solutions using Sure Step. Sure Step has three waterfall project types (Rapid, Standard, and Enterprise), along with one Agile project type (Agile). These types guide the implementers through solution development and rollout of a single release, or to a single location of an organization. However, these project types can also be used in concert with each other, on phased solution rollouts or on multisite engagements, and this will be the focus of our discussion in this section.

Phased solution rollouts

In the previous chapter, we introduced the notion of the phased approach to solution delivery. This approach, not to be confused with the phases within a waterfall project type, refers to the rollout of the solution to the customer organization in multiple releases. The phased solution delivery approach is executed in practice by selecting and enabling an initial subset of solution functionality in the first release and then building on that with the help of additional features in subsequent releases. The alternative to a phased approach is delivering the full solution in a single release, also referred to as the big-bang approach to solution delivery, which we have already covered in the previous sections.

The Sure Step project types can be used together to facilitate the phased solution rollout. Essentially, each release is treated as a subproject, and the corresponding complexity of the requirements being enabled in each release will dictate the appropriate usage of the corresponding project type. The general concept of the phased solution rollout is depicted here:

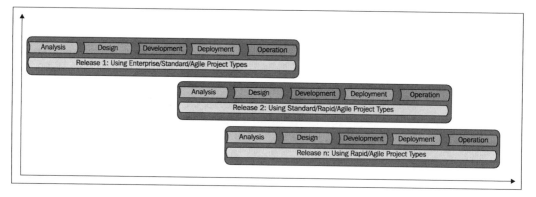

Following this concept, the next diagram shows an example of its usage for an ERP solution implementation. In this diagram, **Release 1** of the phased approach uses the **Standard Project Type** to enable the **Finance Operations** of the customer. This is followed by **Release 2**, using the **Rapid Project Type**, to deliver the **Inventory Control and Order Fulfillment** functionality. The last release, **Release 3**, uses the **Agile Project Type** to deploy **Advance Planning and Scheduling** functionality.

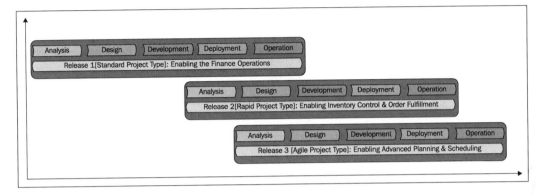

Multisite engagements

As you move into the larger organizational domains, the ERP/CRM solution requirements often transcend multiple locations for the customer. Multisite engagements can include both multiple sites in a single country and multiple locations around the world. The latter, of course, introduces far more complexity with country-specific requirements such as taxation and accounting rules. But in a majority of the cases, the customer's overarching objective is to deploy a common solution across all the sites.

To enable the development of a common solution across multiple locations, Sure Step provides the **Core-Site Build Option** with its Enterprise project type. In this approach, the service provider works with the customer to conduct Requirements Gathering Workshops, involving key Subject Matter Experts (SMEs) and Business Leads from all the relevant locations of the organization. The output of these workshops is a combined **Functional Requirements Document (FRD)** for the enterprise, which forms the basis for the "Core Build".

The Core Build can be viewed as a "common denominator solution". In the classic 80-20 rule, the Core Build will include functionality to support about 80% of the requirements of the enterprise. However, the Core Build is just a developed solution, meaning that it cannot be rolled out by itself. The Core Build is always deployed in conjunction with a **Site Build** that constitutes the functionality to meet the remaining 20% specific requirements of the corresponding site. The actual rollout at a given site can be staggered in time, or they can be rolled out with overlap—the timing itself is very topical and depends on the specific requirements being enabled for the enterprise.

The next diagram shows the Core-Site Build concept. The diagram shows one Core Build and subsequent Site Builds (**Site 1 Build, Site 2 Build, Site n Build**) and corresponding Site Rollouts (**Site 1 Rollout, Site 2 Rollout, Site n Rollout**).

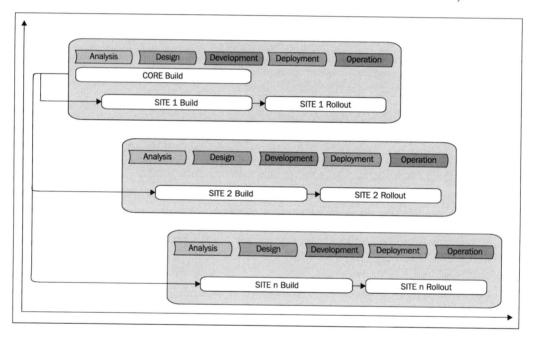

In some cases, the customer may also have diverse set of companies within their portfolio, each of which has a very unique set of requirements, and so it is better to treat each of the sites as its own project. For these multisite instances, the Sure Step project types can be used in tandem, similar to the approach undertaken in the phased approach. An example of this scenario is shown in the next diagram. The diagram shows individual Site Builds and corresponding Site Rollouts (**Site 1 Build-Rollout, Site 2 Build-Rollout, Site n Build-Rollout**).

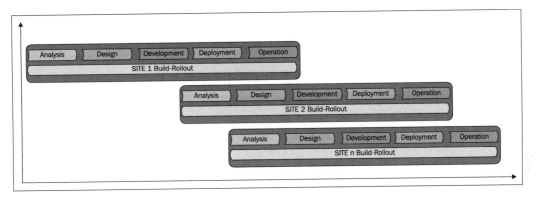

The Sure Step waterfall implementation phases

The previous sections provided an overall look at the different delivery options provided in Sure Step, including the different project types for single releases along with the ability to combine the project types for phased or multisite deployments. Given this background, it is a good idea to dive deeper into each of the implementation phases, to get specific use cases and real-life scenarios for the content and templates provided in the methodology. We will look into it in the following sections of the chapter.

The Analysis phase

Most of us know what an Analysis phase is, and we usually explain it as the execution of activities to demystify the customer's requirements and business processes in greater detail—the "What in detail" so to speak. Is that all ?

The start of the project

By kicking off the Analysis phase, we start with the real implementation of the project. A good start will set the tone for our further implementation. The question, *What is the purpose is for the Analysis phase*, is usually responded to with the following answer: *To further analyze and document the customer's requirements*. Sounds right; or is it?

Start your engines

This answer is quite incomplete as it neglects the important function of starting the project. This is where we start our engines, set our course, and take off. In aviation, the departure is known as complex and critical. This is not really different in software implementation projects—the beginning is always crucial. In the Analysis phase, we are not only investigating and documenting customer requirements and processes, but we are also kicking off risk and issue management, scope management, change management, cost and time management, communication management, and quality and resource management. It is here that we set the tone for our project culture and communication for this specific assignment. So, we need to understand that much more needs to be done than just investigating requirements and processes, and we need to plan for much more.

Expect some delays

In the Diagnostic phase, we worked hard to get a signed contract from our customer, the formal go for our project. The truth is that many things can occur after delivering and defending our proposal. The ideal case for us would be the customer accepting and signing our proposal immediately and giving us a go ahead to start our implementation project. If we are lucky, events might unfold in this way, but alternative scenarios are no exception either. The customer decision making process might consume significant time in terms of duration. It can take weeks, or even months, before we get the approval. In tough economic times, the investment decision can also be postponed until the upcoming fiscal year, causing even more delay. Once we receive the formal nod from the customer by means of an approved contract, we are still not certain that the implementation project can start overnight. The execution of implementing activities needs to be strategically and carefully planned, so it might take some extra time after the contract agreement before we can really start. We need to consider this time (dis)connection between the Diagnostic and Analysis phase when setting out our flight plan for the Analysis phase.

A chance to establish the project culture

In *Chapter 3, Managing Projects*, we discussed the importance of establishing a guiding project culture for our specific projects. In fact, we defined it as one of the four pillars of project success. Connecting both customer and consulting teams to our values, beliefs, priorities, and behavior associated with this project is crucially important for our success. Before we jump into the execution tasks of our project, we need to align all stakeholders and team members with our approach and all crucial elements of this project. We need to practice what we preach, right from the start of our implementation project. Now, when does the implementation project start? The answer is, it starts right now in the Analysis phase.

A look back

Before we define and discuss our next steps, let's have a look back on where we are now. The following diagram describes the flow from decision accelerators to the final proposal. This diagram includes only three important decision accelerators: Requirements and Process Review, Fit Gap and Solution Blueprint, and Scoping Assessment. A diagnostic phase could also include the other decision accelerators, but as stated before, you can deploy decision accelerators as desired. The diagram categorizes two types of tools and templates—working and key deliverables. Working deliverables are those tools and templates that serve as the toolbox for your consultants, helping them to increase their efficiency and quality. They can pick any instrument from the box whenever they need it. Sometimes, they need to use many of these tools, while in other cases, they will need only a few. Key deliverables are a subset of the customer-facing deliverables. These are documents that we will deliver to our customer as the final output of the engagement. It is important to see that these documents will support our communication and formalize the customer's validation of the described topics.

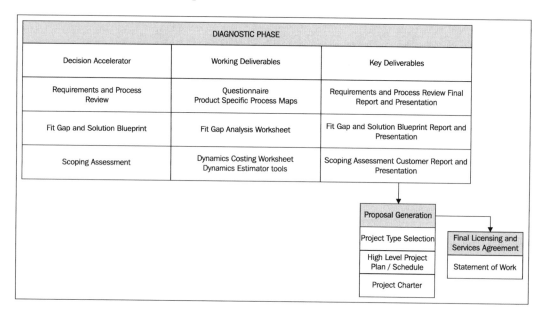

When speaking about aligning people with our vision and approach and creating a guiding project culture, we need to realize that by executing Decision Accelerators, we did produce valuable tools and rich information. In fact, everything we need to jump start our guiding project culture has been compiled in the project charter—a key deliverable from the Proposal Generation activity.

A good project charter is priceless

In Sure Step, the project charter is generated during the Proposal Generation activities—a key activity in the proof stage of Microsoft's Solution Sales Process (MSSP). The conclusions drawn in the preceding diagnostic activities become inputs to this Proposal Generation activity, where the key tasks involve drawing conclusions and packaging the available information and documentation.

The Sure Step project charter answers the basic and necessary questions about the project:

- Why?: What are the business objectives, key success factors, and project objectives? What is value proposition addressed by the project? Why is it being sponsored?

- What?: What are the major deliverables? What is in scope and what is out of scope?

- Who?: Who will be involved and what will be their responsibilities within the project? How will they be organized? Who are the key stakeholders?

- When?: What is the project schedule and when will the milestones and deliverables be complete?

- How?: How will the teams engage? How do we address change, issues, and risks? How we will execute, manage, and control the project?

The following screenshot is the Table of Contents of the Sure Step project charter and clearly illustrates that all of the diagnostic conclusions are gathered here:

So, can you think about a better instrument to align all stakeholders and team members in terms of the vision of our approach and about all crucial elements of this project? The value of a project charter is priceless as it compiles all relevant project information on what, who, how, and when into one document functioning as a rock-solid guideline for all stakeholders governing the entire engagement.

Project planning sessions

We discussed earlier that there might be a time gap between the end of the Diagnostic phase and the start of the Analysis phase. Therefore, we might need to revise and update our project schedule and project charter at the beginning of the Analysis phase. The following illustration illustrates the finalization of the Diagnostic output in the planning sessions in the beginning of the Analysis phase:

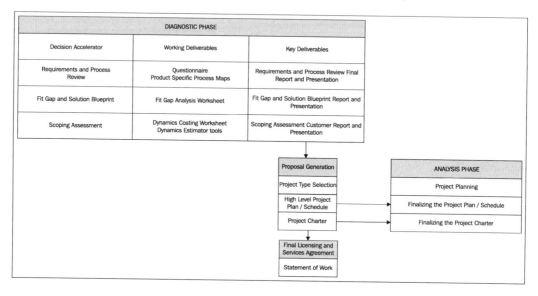

Project planning sessions are conducted as joint exercises with the customer. The session agendas include an overview of the project, timeframes, deliverables, the establishment of the project structure, risk and stakeholder analysis, as well as planning for communication, change control, resources, and quality.

Kick-off your communication culture

We all know the concept of kick-off meetings, but do we undervalue the importance of it? We sometimes tend to deliver our kick-off meetings as an operation, namely by redelivering the exact same content repeatedly. We typically introduce our company, ourselves, and the consulting team, and we ask the customer to do the same.
Then we talk about our phases, the time and budget constraints, and the product we are about to implement. And finally we try to close this meeting in a positive atmosphere. This kick-off meeting content is then identically redelivered in all of our projects. But is this good enough? To answer that question, we need to consider the following two important things:

- Projects are unique by definition.
- There might be a time gap between the end of the Diagnostic phase and the start of the Analysis phase.

Unique projects require unique kick-off meetings. What makes each project unique? Let's list some important differentiators:

- Stakeholders and the organizational context and complexity
- Stakeholders' objectives and expectations
- Business and project objectives
- Critical success factors
- Areas and requirements within scope
- Areas and requirements out of scope
- Customer and consulting implementation teams
- Budget and time constraints

These elements are always different in our implementation projects and therefore we need to address them during our kick-off meetings. By doing so, our kick-off meetings will include the necessary elements to make them unique. We need to bridge our kick-off content with the unique character of each implementation project. This means kick-off meetings cannot be executed in an operational way. Kick-offs need to be tailored to each specific project and presented in the context of the customer's unique organization.

This is exactly why Sure Step recommends the following agenda topics for the kick-off meeting:

- Introduction
- Project definition and objectives
- Key deliverables
- Success criteria

- Project approach
- Project team and organization
- Roles and responsibilities
- Training and testing
- Controlling, reporting, and sign-off
- Communication
- Project scope
- Q&A session to provide an opportunity for the customer, stakeholders, and team members to express any concerns or worries

Wrapping up

Yes, preparing for this kind of kick-off meeting will consume some time, especially when you need to create this content for the very first time, grasping for information in various documents and places. Take a look back at the agenda points. Where can we find this information? Yes, you are right; the project charter compiles all this information into one document. A solid project charter, generated through diagnostic activities, is your jump start for unique and effective kick-off meetings. This is why Sure Step lists the following preconditions for the kick-off meeting:

- Initial project planning is in place
- Project stakeholders are identified
- The project charter is established
- The project is ready for execution

We can now further complete our diagram by adding the kick-off meeting. The following diagram illustrates how the generated information from diagnostic activities is compiled in the project charter and reused as input for the kick-off meeting.

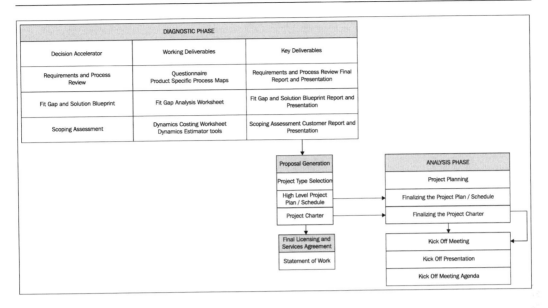

A value-oriented kick-off meeting is key to align all the stakeholders at the start of the implementation project. In the time period between the end of the Diagnostics phase, the signing of contract, and the start of the Analysis phase, many scenarios might unfold. At the consulting site, the team involved with the diagnostic activities for a specific project is likely to be released by now and already planned and active on other engagements. At the customer site, key users may have switched departments or left the company. New managers or department heads can be employed, bringing new visions and priorities with them. Business procedures and requirements might have been reviewed and altered because of new arising business opportunities. Many new scenarios are possible when facing a longer period between the end of the Diagnostic and the start of the Analysis phase.

Then what is our mission now? During the kick-off meeting, we need to verify and validate if we still have the consensus and support for what has been stated in the project charter. This is absolutely crucial for starting a successful engagement. Do we still have the same stakeholders? Do they still support the project objectives and priorities? Do we still have a consensus around what is in and out of scope? Are the new consulting team members aligned with the diagnostic conclusions? Do they have questions about the scope and business processes? Is it clear what documents need to be signed off, who needs to sign off, and what signing off really means? We also need to present and review the planning and set out our next steps including what is expected from whom.

So, the kick-off meeting is not just a small coming together to present ourselves and the company, it needs to be more than that. We not only need to align people on the what, how, and when, but also need to hunt for existing issues and changes that have occurred since the end of the Diagnostic phase.

To train or not to train?

One of the first activities that you might consider to plan for after the kick-off meeting is training. Training is not only an excellent vehicle to educate people, but it is also a great instrument to manage perception. In Sure Step, training is one of the cross-phase processes, facilitating a better project lifecycle planning. Phases should not be exclusively reserved for their core activities but need to contain a good mix of all cross-phase activities. In this vision, training should not exclusively be reserved for the Deployment phase. Why would we consider planning for training in the Analysis phase? How can we benefit from this? Our goals for training in the Analysis phase are important. The following are some of the ideal goals we should have in mind:

- Creating awareness for the new solution
- Introducing the functional architecture and standard concepts of in-scope functional areas
- Introducing the applications' vocabulary
- Creating a mutual understanding of processes and functionality within customer and consultancy teams
- Facilitating perception and organizational change
- Improving efficiency and quality of the upcoming analysis workshops

If executing training during the Analysis phase realizes even a small portion of these objectives, it would still be worthwhile. Do we then need to plan for training the complete end-user team about their new solution? The answer is simple, and it is *no*. We do not want to educate the end users at this moment in the project lifecycle, as this would be far too early and not effective. Research clearly shows that by the go-live time, the end users would have forgotten most of it and our training investment would not generate any return. What we want to plan for are small training sessions for well-targeted groups. We want our key user team to understand the functional outlines of our solution, related to their expertise domains. Therefore, we need to demonstrate and throw light on standardized functionality and flows for the applicable functional areas to a selected audience. It might unfold discussions, but this is exactly what our aim is—good customer interaction, feedback, and active listening can provide us with a wealth of information.

At this point, we might already find some opportunity to demonstrate that it is possible to execute existing processes in a slightly different sequence or manner, yet still achieve the same or better results. You got it right, we should start managing perceptions right here before our core analysis activities. Organizational change management is not something that you initiate just before go-live; it should be omnipresent in your project lifecycle planning. You might ask what possible risks are associated with this training. The biggest risk is to address the wrong audience. This training, which is referred to as "Conduct Solutions Overview" in the Sure Step jargon, is unsuitable for the real end-users as they have only one objective—they seek for answers on how this new solution will address their detailed daily work. In this Solutions Overview training, they will not find those answers leading to potential frustrations and negativity. And as you know, bad news travels fast. That is the reason we need to manage these sessions well and we need to communicate effectively to our customer for whom these sessions are intended.

The following diagram illustrates the continuation of the activity flow after the kick-off meeting:

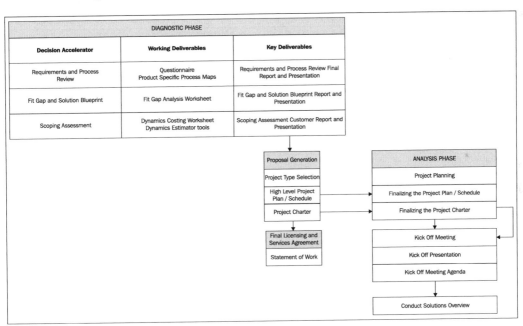

The uncontrolled Analysis phase

Project management status reporting usually does not disclose many problems during the Analysis phase. When we ask our application consultants about the status during the analysis activities, they usually reply that all is going well. Most project managers do not perceive this phase as an intricate situation and we entrust the success of this phase to the competence of the involved business analysts. We reassure ourselves that when we deploy highly skilled and experienced business analysts and application consultants for the business process analysis workshops, we do not need to worry about too many unexpected troubles. It also appears that most project managers are not too concerned about the deliverables in this phase either. We just need to have a written document describing and explaining the customer's needs in terms of desired functionalities for their business processes. It now looks as if the only one challenged during the Analysis phase is the business analyst, while the project manager is only facing a nice little job, namely planning the workshops and gathering some feedback during the workshop activities. If this were to be true, then we would not need a project manager during this phase. Let's take a closer look and find out what the real challenge is for the project manager in this phase.

We have already discovered in the previous sections that we need to plan for more than just the pure analysis activities and that the Analysis phase represents the start of the implementation project. This will challenge the project manager to kick-off the project culture and approach and this involves a bit more than just planning a few interview sessions. But even if we would ignore this, the real analysis activities are also demanding good project management. If we limit our responsibilities to planning of workshops, asking our applications consultants how it goes and then wait for the final document deliverable, we are giving away all control. The first control element that we lose is progress reporting. If we can report the progress only in terms of the final document deliverable, there is not much we can really do except to waiting for this final document and figure out the progress in terms of percentage complete. Now we all know how accurate that is. The second control element that we will be missing is the quality control. If we are waiting for this final document deliverable, we can assess the quality only once it is ready; but by then it may be too late to initiate corrective actions. Most project managers may not even read the complete analysis document deliverable as they lack sufficient time to go through all the details. Giving up on progress and quality tracking capabilities in your first phase of the project lifecycle is not a wise thing to do and it will set the tone for the rest of our project. If we do not give attention to these important aspects here, we most likely will not do it later either. Unfortunately, there is something else that can go out of sight: setting priorities for the analysis activities, scope management, issue and risk management are endangered when deploying passive project management during the Analysis phase. These elements are covered in the next section, where we will list and discuss some real-life analysis scenarios.

Real-life analysis scenarios

In an uncontrolled Analysis phase, we can recognize the following typical scenarios.

Back to square one

To come straight to the point: application consultants starting afresh analyzing everything all over again—how recognizable is that? Quite a few application consultants start their core analysis activity, totally disconnected from diagnostic results and without guidance on the priorities of the to-be analyzed scope. Can we predict the outcome of such a scenario? The outcome is probably an analysis document covering a lot of detailed information on less important topics, and at the same time, lacking good information on the more important and complex areas. In many cases, customers also get frustrated because they had to supply the same information all over again. It looks like we are back to square one and that our earlier executed "pre-study analysis" activities didn't make much difference. Customers will not understand why we charged for it and complain about lost effort. Act surprised!

Scope creep sneaking in

Most of us know all about changing scope. It is one of most popular reasons reported as cause for project failure. Knowing all about this threat, we prepare for it. Armed with change requests, we combat the scope creep monster from the first moment we identify it. At least that is what we tell ourselves. The problem is that most of us identify scope creep only in the later stage in the project lifecycle, when we come out of development activities and engage with testing activities, or even worse, when we are preparing for go-live. Unfortunately, our chances to win the battle at this stage are minimal.

We need to be aware that scope creep is likely to slip inside furtively during the Analysis phase especially when our analysts are disconnected from good diagnostic results. During these workshops, our analyst team will meet with several department heads, key users, and business analysts, among others. They will all have their views on what should be automated and how. They might give new information about existing requirements or even formulate complete new requirements at this stage. If our analyst does not identify or report this now, our scope creep monster will start growing and become a giant at the later stage.

No issues, no risks

Passive project management during the Analysis phase will not provide the analyst team with much guidance on their responsibility, specifically not when speaking about issues and risks. During the Analysis phase, project managers frequently ask their consultant team about how things are going and only rarely they will report issues and risks. In most cases, everything is reported to be under control. This is because the application consultants do not feel responsible for identifying issues and risks at this stage. Risk and issue identification at this stage is commonly seen by the analyst team as a responsibility for the project manager. The problem is that the project manager is not engaged in all workshops and interviews, and lacks the needed information for this issue and risk identification. As a consequence, not many (if any) risks and issues are reported during this phase and that is a missed opportunity. One thing is certain: there will be issues and risks to be faced in the Analysis phase, but if they are not identified and reported here, we will face the consequences later in the project lifecycle.

We can summarize by stating that there are more than enough reasons why project managers should take control over the Analysis phase. There is much more to be done than the core analysis activities, and even the management of these analysis activities requires a solid approach and a clear vision from the project manager. In the next sections, we will discuss how Sure Step can help us.

Analyze what?

To know what needs our full and what might require less of our attention, we need to look back at our diagnostic results. The following diagram illustrates the connection with the diagnostic results:

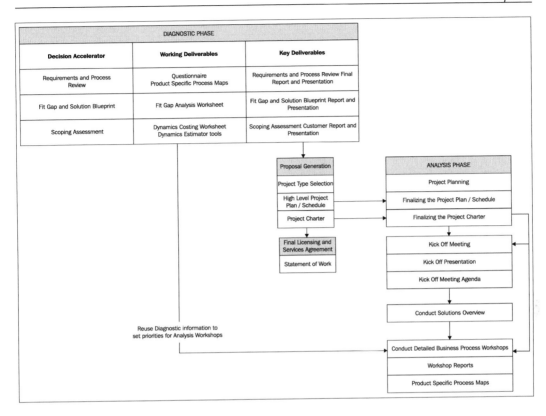

Consultants can prepare for the Business Process Workshops by reviewing diagnostic conclusions and reusing diagnostic instruments and deliverables. The project charter should provide a complete picture on in and out of scope, business priorities, key success factors, and known issues and risks. Business-specific process maps represent an excellent jump start for the Analysis phase if these were modeled during the Diagnostic phase. They visualize already identified bottlenecks and complex areas within the overall customer business context and will clearly provide a guideline for the consultant team to plan the analysis activity. The analysis team will also benefit from the Fit/Gap Analysis Worksheet providing very valuable input in terms of:

- Requirements linked to business processes
- Requirements prioritized
- Requirements categorized in terms of standard feature, configuration, customization, workflow, and ISV solution

The following illustrates how the Fit/Gap Worksheet can act as input instrument for the Business Process Workshops:

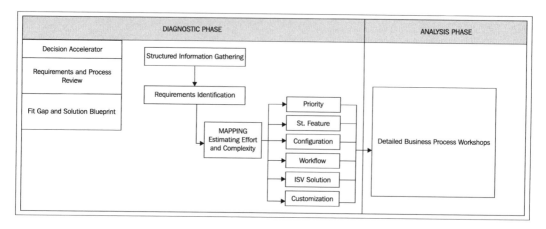

With given prioritized requirements, including estimated effort and complexity ranking by means of categories, an application consultant can plan and prioritize the available analysis time much better, leading to more efficient and quality-driven analysis engagements in less time.

Go for interim analysis deliverables

If we want to follow up on the progress and quality of our application consultants during the Analysis phase, we should plan for intermediate deliverables. Produce a simple document, such as a workshop report, because it can make quite a difference. As a project manager, you need to instruct your teams that a workshop report needs to be produced after each workshop. It contains standardized sections, so that all application consultants will use the same format in documenting the workshop results. This makes it much more convenient for project managers to follow up as every document can be read in the same way. Once a planned workshop is finished, a workshop report needs to be made available by the consultant. A lacking workshop report will be questioned by the project manager and might lead to corrective actions. Workshop reports generated after the workshops themselves, and not long after the sessions, will prevent the additional risk that important information will be forgotten.

A great additional benefit of working with standardized intermediate document deliverables for analysis activities is the possibility to direct the desired output in terms of structure and quality. It will also set clear expectations to the consultants for the delivery.

The following screenshot shows one page from the workshop report:

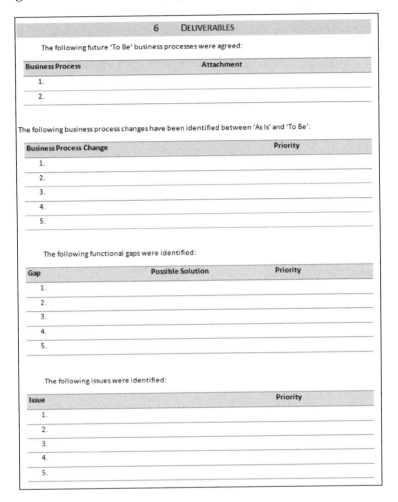

This page makes it very clear that application consultants should not just record what the customer stakeholders tell them during the workshops, but they are also responsible for generating conclusions, for linking the information with the diagnostic scope, for identifying issues, and for motivating process changes in order to avoid superfluous customization. As a project manager, you can now organize your follow up by asking two questions:

- Do we have a workshop report by the end of the workshop?
- Is section 6 filled in by the application consult in a quality way?

This approach represents a vast difference from the "waiting for the final deliverable" approach.

Managing scope creep during the Analysis phase by means of Fit/Gap Analysis

One of the consequences of an unmanaged Analysis phase, as discussed in the previous section, is the scope creep sneaking in feature. During the Analysis phase activities, new information about existing requirements becomes available, casting the original request in new light, or even new requirements can be formulated. These cases are unavoidable, even with a solid implementation methodology. Not identifying these changes in scope affects all stakeholders in terms of duration, cost, quality, and expectations, making identification our real challenge. The diagram here introduces the Fit/Gap assessment as a valuable instrument during the Analysis phase:

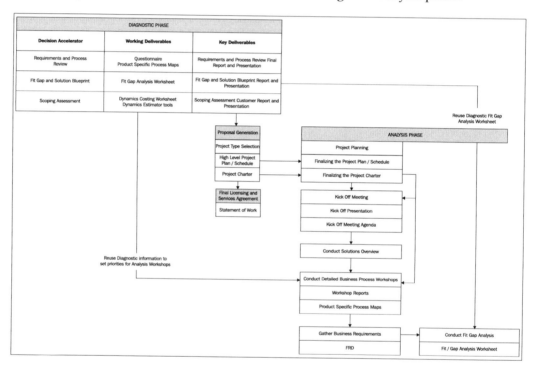

Once all business processes and requirements investigation has been tied up, it is time to document all findings and conclusions in a Functional Requirements Document (FRD), providing a complete description of the requirements for the new solution. Now that we have all the scope defined to the level of detail required, we can reassess the Fit/Gap situation.

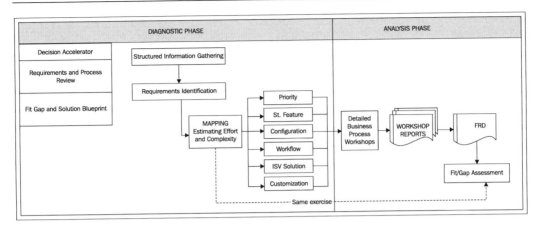

Sure Step advocates the benefits of reassessing the Fit/Gap situation once requirements are captured in the Analysis phase. It prevents scope creep from sneaking in unnoticed, it reinforces the knowledge on the envisioned solution for all stakeholders, and it provides warning signals to the project manager to address a number of topics. If our assessment revealed new requirements, changes, and other important scope challenges, we need to embrace this precious information. It proves that our consultant team was very attentive for the scope impact on both project and business, and we are triggered for some good project management action, our real job. Act now! What can we do then? We should at least communicate about these identified areas. What is the opinion of the consulting team, how does the customer team feel about it, what is the impact, can we find alternative business processes and solutions, and so on. We should not panic about these cases, nor ignore them. These cases are omnipresent in projects, and identifying them in the Analysis phase is a step in the right direction. What is recommended to resolve them? As projects are unique, your approach and solution for these challenges will be unique as well. You will probably need a recipe with various ingredients such as business process changes, rejecting a number of new unimportant demands, and accepting some real scope changes. Your recipe needs to taste well in this context. It needs to be aligned with the objectives, budget, time, and cost constraints, while being accepted by a substantial coalition of stakeholders.

Did we just mention scope changes? Sure Step makes it clear that scope changes and their management cannot be uniquely reserved for the final phases of the project lifecycle. Addressing scope changes in Sure Step is an element of "proposal management". Sure Step literally states: *Proposal Management is an activity that needs to be executed within all cross phases of the project implementation lifecycle.* Thus we can start making Change Requests from the Analysis phase. This means that the customer organization will be familiarized with this process quite early in the project lifecycle. A **Change Request** is an effective instrument to keep scope creep under control, but it needs to be handled with care. This instrument will lose all its impact when operated in only one phase and overabundant. Sometimes we tend to think that the change request is there to resolve not only all of the scope issues but also all quality issues. When clear quality issues are injudiciously and shamelessly filed as change requests and every scope issue is transferred into a change request, we are creating a mountain of paperwork. Best practice tells us that in these scenarios, the scope change issue will remain unresolved as customers will not sign off for these changes. Act surprised! Expert use of the change request implies a well-balanced use spread over the complete project lifecycle as suggested by Sure Step.

We can now further complete our diagram of the Analysis phase:

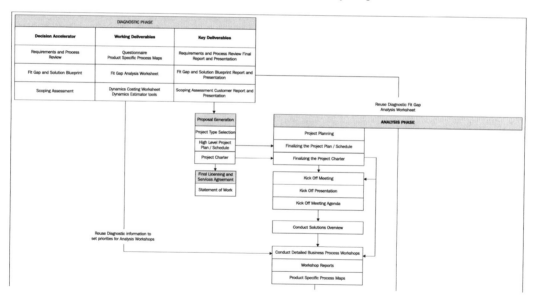

Do not forget about data migration

Focused on the functional solution, data migration is often handled as a second-class issue. We love designing functional solutions, bridging business processes and software functionality, and are so focused on it that anything else vanishes without a trace. Not really smart, as non-functional requirements can be a hard row to hoe, consuming considerable resources and creating quite some risks. Most of us have already experienced how data migration challenges can impact project duration and even go-live decisions. That's why Sure Step addresses data migration. Topics such as condition of existing data, data cleansing, amount of historical data to be migrated, identification of existing data sources, and master data management need to be tackled right from the start. They need to ensure that these topics are addressed in the analysis workshops.

Interact with the infrastructure department

Good project lifecycle planning requires a good mix of cross-phase processes in each and every phase. We have already seen that the Analysis phase is not exclusively reserved for the core analysis activities but that it also needs active project management and strong communications, training, and attention to data migration topics. It is also recommended to start interacting with the infrastructure stakeholders to build the sandbox and training environments. These environments are needed to allow customer training and familiarization with the core Microsoft Dynamics product, prior to any configuration or customization, and it provides an excellent opportunity to build up relationships and communications with the customer infrastructure people. The earlier we start to engage with them, the more time we have to prepare them for the turn-key moment.

The Design phase

Solution designing is a crucial activity in any software project. Even when not much customization is involved, we still need to envision the "HOW" of the project.

Do we really need a Design phase?

"Do we really need a separate phase for designing the solution?" is an often-heard question. Some claim to initiate solution designing during the Analysis phase; others include it in the Development phase, or even "when convenient". From a waterfall perspective, you can plan your design activities in one or more phases as long as you execute what you planned for in a specific phase. So, there is no real waterfall reason for a specific Design phase. However, phases represent a breakdown in time, in order to plan and manage our project lifecycle better. That's why Sure Step plans for a separate Design phase with dominant solution designing processes. After capturing the scope baseline, we can now concentrate on further developing our solution concept during a well-managed timeframe. Most of us are familiar with the "what" and "how" rule of thumb: during the Diagnostic and Analysis phase we concentrate on the *what* aspect, whereas during the design phase we develop the *how* aspect of our project. This indicates what the dominant processes will be during those phases, but don't get mislead: project management and cross-phase processes have taught us that we need to plan for more in a phase than the core activities only.

The risk of a passive Design phase

The core activities of both Diagnostic and Analysis phases involve customer interaction by nature. Pre-sales activities such as requirements and business process assessments, proof of concept demonstrations, workshops, and interviews, among others require customer interactions. This is not so obvious during design and development activities. Design activities are commonly envisioned and narrowed down to documenting the *how*. This means designing equals writing documents on the *how* aspect, with the only planned customer interaction being the validation of the document. Combining this with the same passive vision on the Development phase will jeopardize our project success significantly, as we are factually locking out the customer from the project until the real deployment activities and postponing many of implementation activities. Do we really want to take that risk?

All activity in the Sure Step Design phase

Start singing Sure Step's praises because it will release us from a passive Design phase. The real implementation activities start right here during the Design phase! Sure Step tells us not to wait until the end of the Development phase before initiating implementation activities. We need to maintain our contact with the customer organization by frequently interacting with the stakeholders. We need to raise the awareness and knowledge level of our stakeholders on the project and solution, stimulate organizational change, and continue risk and issue identification and management. There is so much to be done, and yes, we will also document some *HOWs*, but without limiting ourselves to this.

We are implementing a standard package solution

Now let's think about this for a minute. What does it say? It means that we are not delivering a pure development project. A bulk load of requirements can be fulfilled by installing standard features, configuring, or ISV solutions. Then why do we sometimes initiate the implementation only after finalizing the development activities? Some standard functionality will be dependent on the customized functionality, and these requirements cannot be implemented immediately, but this does not apply to all. One of the key advantages of a package solution is that we can deliver quite quickly compared to customized solutions. We need to take advantage of this by initiating the implementation as soon as possible. There is really no reason for postponing, we will benefit from the early delivery of even small parts of the solution.

From requirements to design

During the Diagnostic phase, we gathered high-quality information, broken down into requirements, and mapped with our standard solution by categorizing into standard feature, configuration, customization, ISV solution, and workflow. We refined this understanding during the Analysis phase and rechecked it again with our standard product. This means we can start the Design phase based on structured information that will guide us on what to do next: implement and document.

Document and implement

The following diagram shows what to implement and document:

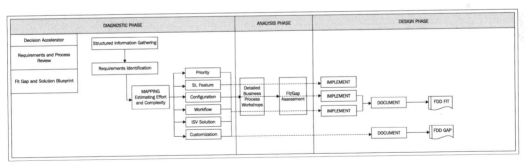

Coming out of the Diagnostic and Analysis phases, Sure Step does not bring in only the information, but also priorities, guidelines, conclusions, and a profound understanding of the to-be implemented solution. Standard features from the standard or ISV solution can be immediately implemented, along with the straightforward configuration requirements. Our implementation team must now start the engines and boost this project into warp drive. Some of the functionalities will have to wait to be installed or configured as they might depend on the customized functionalities. Do not panic about that; we can finalize the implementation later. The good news is that we have delivered part of the solution already, and the first customer complaining about that is still to be found!

Documentation is also part of the game. It is important to have a documented solution design, but we needn't include everything. We do not document the standard features but will concentrate on configuration settings and customized functionality. We use **Functional Design Documents (FDD)** to document our configuration and customization outlines. The configuration settings are to be documented in the FDD-FIT, while the customization is documented in the FDD-GAP.

Sure Step also provides a **Technical Design Document (TDD)**, as well as a **Solution Design Document (SDD)**. The TDD is a translation of the FDD-GAP in technical terms. The goal of this document is to define and document the technical details of each system modification or enhancement. This can be an essential component for the upcoming development activities when we are, for instance, working with junior developers or even in an offshore development context.

The purpose of the Solution Design Document is to allow the business decision makers and other stakeholders to obtain a clear view of the proposed solution design in business language. This can be a required document in companies with a high organizational complexity. Where the FDD documents are beneficial in all waterfall project types, the SDD is typically used in an Enterprise project type.

The application consultant will work hand-in-hand with the appropriate key user to implement and document. That's why at this stage, we should provide our key user with some training and coaching on the product's features and functions. This will not only bring our key user to the next level in knowledge of the product, but will also avoid misunderstandings and generate more commitment from the key user. Working closely with the key user will improve the collaboration for both teams, which is absolutely necessary for success.

Initiate testing

Once we have implemented features and functions, we can unleash the power of a critical success factor in every project—testing. Testing will allow us to interact with the key users, identify issues, work and steer the perception, and update business process models. Initiating testing at this stage will also enable our key users to prepare for, organize, and take control over the user tests scheduled in the upcoming project phases. They can start their envisioning process of using the new solution right here. They will understand what testing involves and increase their product knowledge. Well-informed and committed key users are vitally important for project success, but we cannot expect that key users will reach our level of knowledge overnight. We need to make sure that they can build up their knowledge and understanding in small pieces so that they will be ready when needed. That's why we start here by initiating tests and test scripts in the Design phase. We will start with testing features and functions that we implemented together with the key user reinforced by the available Sure Step test scripts. After that, the key user can continue to prepare test scripts for upcoming tests.

Because of the starting of testing activities, we will have issues coming in as well. Again, embrace this, as it is an excellent opportunity to communicate and work around these issues and to plan for corrective actions. This is exactly what we want: revealing the issues so that we can overcome them instead of saving them for a later stage by not identifying them.

Interact with the infrastructure department

Installing and configuring the core product and organizing tests will also involve elements of the infrastructure, namely the test environment. This is a good opportunity to continue to interact with the infrastructure stakeholders. What is needed for all this? What do we need to do to convert the training into a real test environment? We can work hand–in–hand with the infrastructure people, allowing them to get a better understanding of the infrastructural consequences of this new product; the interaction might reveal some new issues or risks as well. As you know, that is exactly what we want as it will allow corrective actions.

Don't give up on data migration

We need to continue our work on data migration that we started in the Analysis phase, by designing the migration process and mapping the fields to be migrated between existing legacy systems and the Microsoft Dynamics application. Because we initiate tests in the Design phase, we can create a subset of data for testing here as well.

Start planning the deployment

A good project manager sees beyond today and knows that a well-organized Deployment phase is needed for a successful go-live. This project manager also knows that the success of the deployment depends on the commitment of the user organization. At the same time, we need to understand that our deployment activities will lay a heavy burden on that organization. Training, user acceptance tests, performance tests, and infrastructure readiness will demand a lot of their time and effort. We need to inform our customer about this and ask for their commitment and planning, and we need to do this well in advance. The Design phase is well chosen to initiate this. By now both teams have a very good understanding of what is to come, so we should tackle this right here. Sure Step provides us with a deployment plan that outlines the processes and activities that need to occur during the deployment phase of the project. It will ask for the customers' understanding and commitment for these activities. This is more than just scheduling the deployment. The Deployment plan must be an input for your communication around topics such as deployment scope, deployment strategy, deployment resources, training and testing organization, and the deployment schedule. Our goal is to get the customer's buy-in for the deployment activities. The bottom line is not just a document, but communication, communication, and again communication.

The Development phase

This is what software companies probably know best: development. It leans most against our business ecosystem of information technology (IT) and therefore we are on home ground. Nothing new under the sun then; or is there?

Developers only?

The Development phase is quite often organized as a "developers only" period in time, not infrequently facilitated in the same philosophy. This is where the application consultant's load is reduced significantly, where our development team takes over and they might even retreat into full isolation at the service provider's premises. Is this the best strategy? It is beyond doubt that the development activities will have a prominent place during this phase. And yes, developers might need to work undisturbed for a while, permitting maximum concentration. But as we have learned from the other phases' organization, there is more to take into consideration.

We need to keep our eyes open for the project lifecycle planning and ensure that enough customer interaction and involvement are included as planned. We need to secure our communication levels with all stakeholders and maintain the collaboration between application consultants and key users. Last but not least, we also need to continue to further prepare the customer's infrastructure department for deployment. To conclude, the development force will play a crucial role in this phase but they should not be the only players in this ball game.

Develop and freeze custom code

The requirements mapped as customization during the Fit-Gap exercises and designed in FDD-Gap and TDD documents are developed at this stage. This not only includes the functional requirements, addressing requested functionalities for the solution, but also non-functional requirements such as data migration and interface requirements. The development team needs to start by reviewing the solution and technical design documents after which they initiate the real development. They should engage in respect to all quality and documentation standards that were approved. In larger development teams, it is also essential that the development work is coordinated by a lead developer. The produced deliverables pass through multiple iterations of unit and function testing. Once successfully passed, the code is frozen to denote that it is not open to modifications any longer. Further modification can be made only if issues are found during data acceptance, process, or integration testing. Do not forget to update the design documentation when the delivered customization differs from the envisioned one.

Complete the testing

Once the customized functionality deliverables are being produced, we can further complete the testing that was initiated in the Design phase. We can now engage by testing more and more full processes, bringing it to the level of full solution testing. You got it right—testing is a cross-phase process allowing us to continue interacting and communicating with our customer throughout the complete project lifecycle. It is now time of engage the integration and data acceptance testing. By now, our key users should be quite familiar with the testing procedures and they are continuously increasing their knowledge of the solution. They will fine-tune the test scripts, and can start working on the user acceptance test script necessary to drive the user organization through these tests in the Deployment phase. Thanks to our continued testing effort and collaboration with the user organization, we will collect issues and questions and we will detect uncertainties and sensitivities within the key user team. It is imperative to work with this information! We need to tackle this right here, ensuring an optimal Deployment phase.

The following diagram illustrates how far we have progressed from the Design into the Development phase:

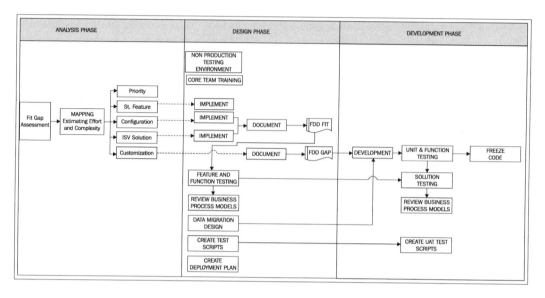

We can also continue the collaboration on the development of test scripts, which we started in the Design phase. Together with the key users, we can now prepare the user acceptance test scripts that will guide the **user acceptance testing (UAT)** during the Deployment phase. UAT is the culmination of all the previous testing activities. Although previous test scripts can be leveraged, it is important that the UAT scripts focus on the main functions that system users perform.

Last call for changes

In any project, requests for changes are always on the horizon, no matter how well we have defined our scope and how well we have worked on the organizational change management. In the discussed lifecycle planning of Sure Step, we tried to keep interacting with the customer organization, to identify issues, risks, and requests for changes in all phases. This gives us the benefit of identifying them early, staggered throughout the project. In this way, we can manage proactively and prevent issues from becoming a true burden in the Deployment phase. In the Development phase, we will still retrieve and manage change requests, but by now, we need to be aware that after this phase, we need to bring the changes to a lower level and our end-user organization needs to be aware about this. It is our responsibility as a project manager to sensitize our customer counterparts about this. Another communication challenge!

Can process models still change?

The answer to this question is Yes. Because of our planned activities and interactions in the Development phase, we will receive feedback from both customers and consulting stakeholders. Our developers may have critical comments, the application consultants can throw up important insight, and our customer can also raise questions. A typical interaction that can generate this kind of feedback is testing, and as we have discussed, the testing activity is continued during the Development phase. Based on this feedback, we might need to bring in some changes to our solution design or persuade our customer to implement business process changes. Review and update of business process models is a continuous process that should be iterated throughout the project lifecycle, with reviews and updates in Design and Development phases.

Start finalizing

It is entirely clear that Sure Step evangelizes good project lifecycle planning and this is again emphasized in the planned activities and deliverables of the Development phase. We have already seen that this phase is not exclusively reserved for the core development activities. Thoughtful readers will also discover that we need to start finalizing the lion's share of the implementation activities during the Development phase. This means that by the end of this phase, we have delivered the bulk part of our deliverables, which will allow us to concentrate on the pure deployment activities in the Deployment phase.

Finalize system configuration and ISV solution setup

During the Design phase, we started to install and configure the standard feature and ISV functionalities, matching to our customer's requirements. We can now complete this configuration effort as customized functionality will become available during this phase. This means we can now also implement and configure the customized features and, at the same time, bring the testing to the solution testing level as discussed in the previous section. The solution testing will inevitably cause configuration changes and, after this process, we can freeze our configuration settings for the new solution.

Finalize design updates

Because of identified issues, changes, and updated business process models, we must update our appropriate design documentation as well.

Hand over non-production environments

The purpose of this task is to hand over the non-production environments to the customer's infrastructure team and ensure their readiness to accept and support them. This will allow us to interact with the infrastructure resources and build up their knowledge around infrastructure topics for the new solution.

The following diagram will complete our overview picture of the Development phase:

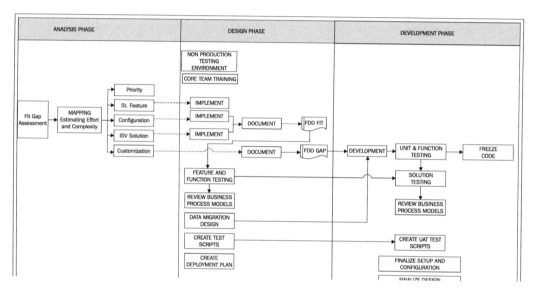

At the end of the Development phase, we can checkmark the following as complete:

- Customized development
- Solution testing
- Configuration and setup of standard and ISV solution
- Design documentation
- Test script creation

This will allow us to fully concentrate on deployment activities in the Deployment phase. What a five-star project lifecycle planning!

The Deployment phase

Some consider the Deployment phase as the tail end of the project lifecycle, while for others, it seems that they still need to start most of the implementation activities in this phase by starting the configuration and testing of the product. Then what have they done up until now? Deployment is a critical process in delivering a successful project. It involves preparing the transition to the operational use of a brand new solution for the entire company. That's quite something!

Let's discover the critical activities for this phase.

What is critical for a successful deployment?

There is no question that infrastructure and solution readiness are the basis of a good deployment, but they only represent "half way there". The other half, even the bigger half, is the organizational readiness of the customer. Is there a supporting coalition within the user organization for this new solution? Can the key user organization see and appreciate the benefits of this new solution and can they balance this with the efforts and difficulties that they experienced? Can they put the existing criticism and resistance into perspective? Can they envision the next steps and challenges? These are all important questions that any project manager must reflect on during the transition to deployment. The answers on these questions will guide us on how to organize the Deployment phase and where to put the emphasis. This must be our focus point during deployment.

Trainers, evangelists for change

Adequate training is one of the most important steps in a successful implementation. Making the users much more efficient in their daily jobs is a key objective that you will find in any business solution implementation project. For that reason only, users need to have strong knowledge of and insights into the product. But effective training will not only empower the users with the necessary knowledge on how to use this system in their daily company procedures, it will also orient their perception and trust in something that is new to them. For a majority of users, this can be their first encounter with this brand-new solution and you get only a single chance to make a good first impression. For all these good reasons, we need to plan sufficient training and resist the temptation to reduce this to a minimal level in order to cut costs.

Conduct end-user training

Sure Step envisions the end-user training during deployment as short, directed sessions that begin with a broad overview and narrow successively to the end users' defined job tasks. Training scenarios must be role-based so that each user can work through the specific activities and tasks required by their daily job. It may be necessary to start each session with a Business Process ("to-be") training session, to ensure that all end users have adequate knowledge of the new processes.

A critical success factor is that the final task-oriented training is scheduled as close to the deployment as possible, in order to prevent knowledge erosion.

Compose the trainer team

This training can be conducted by customer key users, trainers, or consultants of the consulting implementation team, or by an external third-party training vendor. It will most likely be a mixture as finding one trainer to do it all will not be so easy. Involving key users in the delivery of training for their departments is a wise thing to do. Key users know the end users much better, have strong knowledge on the business processes, and are strongly connected to the product and reinforced by their management. As such, they can evangelize the new solution and its inevitable change much better than any outside trainers. However, we need to make sure they have the proper product knowledge and a well-organized approach.

That's why we need to provide them with a train-the-trainer session beforehand. Some areas in our solution might require high-level expertise of the trainer and therefore it might be necessary to deploy specialized trainers from the consulting or from learning organizations.

What about the data?

By now, all data migration design, development, and testing is finalized. We will need the data migration execution for training, testing, and deployment reasons. The end-user training will need test data that simulates true use-case scenarios. The user acceptance tests also need actual transactions, from a day identified by the customer, and which would provide a good sample of their business. So, for both activities we need to migrate data which, in a way, will prepare us as well for the final data migration to the production environment supporting the deployment.

Sure Step recommends that the final migration is done in two steps:

- **Initial migration of data into production**:

  The initial migration of data into production is performed to avoid overloading the systems and is typically done a week before the actual go-live. This data typically includes static data.

- **Final data migration into production**:

  The final data migration is preferably done over the weekend prior to go-live. As most of the initial data is loaded a week before go-live, the final data load will take into account the data entered into the system after the initial data load. This concept expedites the migration process and eliminates last-minute glitches that can jeopardize the cutover.

The go-live as the user acceptance test

You might not believe it, but in some cases, go-live procedures are initiated without a prior user acceptance test. The most common excuse is "we told the customer to test, but they didn't". You might even find cases where the UAT time was used to compensate time and budget overloads of previous phases. In a scenario lacking a UAT, the go-live will function as a user acceptance test and the results of that go-live are highly predictable.

Do not forget the important goals that a UAT fulfils:

- Validating that the new solution supports the company's operational processes as envisioned through the requirements process
- Gaining the necessary confidence in the system by mitigating the risk of failure
- A last chance of identifying issues that had a lucky escape during previous test cycles
- Motivating the go-live decision
- Obtaining system sign-off
- Generating results that will support the project closure process

Your continued key user interaction will now pay off

We have learned through the sections on the previous phases how important it is to schedule interactions with the key users in all implementation phases. The cross-phase processes and the planning of these throughout the project lifecycle is a crucial element within Sure Step. When it comes to UAT, we will really reap the benefits of this strategy. Our key users were connected with the product throughout the complete project lifecycle. They built up their knowledge and perception of our product, in small steps, by being involved, trained, and coached in each phase. Being involved with testing in the previous phases has lead to an understanding of the process and importance of testing. By now, they are really ready to support you in the organization and execution of UAT.

Can you imagine key users who were disconnected after the analysis for months and are only getting some training now? Just asking a user organization to perform UAT on a system that they barely know doesn't make much sense.

Early planning and commitment making the difference

UAT represents a serious loading on the resource planning of the customer organization. A substantial number of the customer's employees need to free up time for both training and user acceptance testing. Nevertheless, this company is still in operational mode and so their absence needs to be carefully planned.....in advance! It is also critical that the customer is really committed to investing in this effort and therefore they also need to be motivated in advance. Without early planning and real commitment, we will run into trouble and the "no time—will do it later" excuse will smack our ears. The good news is that we did create the deployment plan in collaboration with the customer already in the Design phase. At least when we did it the Sure Step way!

The focus of the user acceptance test

UAT must focus on testing the complete end-to-end system to ensure that the new solution meets the customer business requirements. The focus of the test scenarios is the daily routines of the users in the different departments, supporting the operational use after go-live. We are not testing one requirement after the other, but real-life business processes based on real-life data.

Document and analyze the results

The testing results need to be compiled, analyzed, and subsequently compared to the test criteria. Sure Step provides efficient UAT test script worksheets and templates. These tools are made product specific, including even role-based versions. They also can contain some preconfigured testing scenarios.

The following screenshot gives an example of a product-specific UAT test worksheet, including product-specific test content.

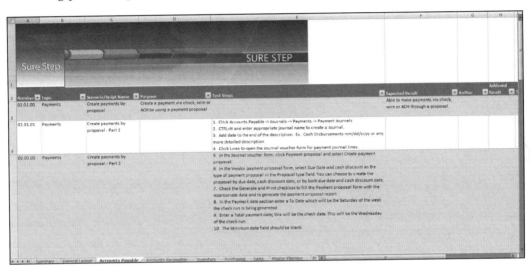

Execute performance tests

Many variables can interact to impact system performance. There may be a large number of users, a large number of transactions, improperly configured infrastructure or environment variables, or many other elements that can impact the performance. We need to scrutinize performance before and after the go-live. Therefore, scheduling performance tests at this stage is no luxury.

Infrastructure readiness

At this stage, we need to ensure that we will be able to run our new solution in a stable and performing environment during and after the go-live. That's why we need to continue our infrastructure effort during the Deployment phase by building and configuring the production and disaster recovery environments.

The following table lists the possible Environments that can be initialized:

Environment	Initialized	Description
Sandbox	Analysis Phase	An environment that allows the project team members and users to test functionality, try what-if scenarios, and demo standard out of the box features to the customer
Training	Analysis Phase	An environment setup with functionality being deployed, customer data and customer business scenario exercises for conducting Solutions Overview, Core Team, Train-the-Trainer (TTT) and End User Training
Testing	Design Phase	For the execution of Test Scripts during Integration testing, Data Acceptance Testing, Performance Testing and User Acceptance Testing. Depending on the complexity of the engagement, separate environments may be necessary for Performance and User Acceptance Testing (UAT).
Development	Development Phase	For the setup, configuration and customization of the Microsoft Dynamics solution. Depending on the number of development teams involved, more than one DEV environment may be needed
Staging		To transition setup, configurations and custom code from Development or Testing environments to Production. Other usages of this environment may include the following: for executing UAT, for running a Conference Room Pilot, or for Parallel Testing - to compare results from the existing system with the Microsoft Dynamics solution.
Production	Deployment Phase	The Final LIVE environment that runs the customer's Microsoft Dynamics solution in production mode

Check and cross check

Flight attendants, please prepare for cross-check. Are you familiar with these words? A cross-check is a procedure performed by flight attendants before a plane pushes away from the gate, and again when the plane lands. This procedure of checking the doors for having been armed with emergency escape slides is only one of the series of checks to ensure that a plane can taxi, depart, and land safely. This ensures safety and a quality service as expected by the customers.

When we prepare for go-live, we should execute some checks as well. Delays and crashes will not make a great impression in our business either. That's why we need to assess final system readiness and ensure that all necessary steps and deliverables are in place. The Sure Step Go-Live Checklist can be a valuable instrument to help us complete that procedure in collaboration with the customer.

Ready to take off

The go-live initiates the successful processing of daily business transactions and activities in the new system. It took time, effort, sweat, tears, meetings, e-mails, interactions, and especially a lot of hard and intelligent work to get to this point. This is our take-off both for the customer organization and the consulting team. A precious moment, but not without danger if badly planned. As with any departure, we need to stay focused and need to prepare for some potential turbulence. To make the go-live cutover successful, we need to plan and document our cutover procedures. We even might need to run the cutover process as a dress rehearsal. The Go-Live Cutover Plan provided by Sure Step can help us in doing so. Reusing the deployment plan with a separate section on the cutover processes might be valuable as well.

And once in the sky, clap your hands and pop those corks because this really is an achievement! Celebrating this special moment together with your customer is not only fun, but it reinforces the feeling of success for both teams. Well deserved, enjoy!

The Operation phase

Pack your bags? Not really. The go-live broadcasted our project live in the air but our show is not over yet. The go-live is not the end of the project. It is time now for some on-board services.

Provide post-go-live support

After the go-live cutover moment, critical challenges unfold for the end-user organization. They now really need to give up on their old and familiar routines and adapt to new procedures and software features and functions—not an easy moment for them and they need our support. Imagine somebody stepping into your office and providing you a brand new computer stuffed with unfamiliar programs. How would that feel? Just knowing that experts are there to address their questions and concerns is a comfortable thought and will avoid any cases of panic. Quality onsite support will also allow us to advise the key users on how to address specific issues and the support role in general. A good key user team will also filter various support requests. During the longer duration of the post go-live support, the consulting organization can also switch from onsite to remote support, making the consultants available through live meeting, phone, or e-mail communications. This step requires a mature key user organization that is able to control the bulk part of the support requests—another good reason for investing time and effort in the key users throughout the complete project lifecycle.

Assuming that you will no longer collect issues and changes at this stage is like backing the wrong horse. The first days or even weeks of operational use of the new system will produce a lot of issues and change requests. These should be managed by using the same process as in the previous phases. However, we need to be perceptive of the fact that a vast amount of the complaints, issues, and change requests might be caused by resistance, fear, and other challenges of change. That's why we might consider additional communication and training to assist the customer through the reality of change.

Some things to do

The off-the-shelf benefit of having an Operation phase in the methodology is that it enables us to communicate some important things to our customer before and during the project. It makes clear that we will stay after the go-live because we still have some things to take care of.

Clear pending items

One of these things is resolving open issues. These issues might have been identified even before the go-live cutover moment but remained unaddressed until after the go-live. We will always have issues at the moment of go-live and this cannot be a reason for postponing the go-live, unless these issues are really critical and considered to be showstoppers. Making customers aware about this before you reach that point is a smart thing and Sure Step will help you in doing so.

So now we have reached that moment, some things to do in the Operation phase. This activity can be found in Sure Step as *Clear pending Items*, indicating that we need to collaborate with the customer in finding a final resolution to our open issues. In most cases, not all issues are resolved as some have no impact on the business operations. This is an effort of communication and negotiation to ensure satisfaction on both sides. Don't park your common sense outside is the message.

Finalize knowledge transfer

We need to ensure that before we leave, the customer will have access to all important resources, enabling them to take over the control. They need to know the location where all documentation resides, security permission documentation needs to be available for the administrator, actual support information and logs need to be transferred to the customer support team, and they need to know how to log in on CustomerSource" (name of a Microsoft portal).

Conduct performance tuning and optimization

Once our solution is operational for a few days, it is time to measure the performance and to provide additional tuning and configuration. Real performance bottlenecks might reveal themselves only after go-live. It is smarter to do this proactively at this stage, than waiting for the performance to drop to an unacceptable level, where users start complaining about the performance of the solution.

Transition the solution to support

The time has come to say goodbye. The implementing consultants cannot remain onsite forever and the customer organization needs to take responsibility for their new solution. They can organize the support entirely by themselves or use the operational supporting services of the partner.

To close or not to close?

To close! Projects are, by definition, temporary, and so they need an ending date. A formal closing is an essential component of project management. Without closing, we end up in an operation for which we are not organized and do not have sufficient budget. Not closing our project will, in the end, evaporate all our profit for which we worked so hard.

Closing—a nice little job?

We wish it was, but unfortunately we all know better. Closing is where it all comes together and when we say all, it means all. How good were our project communications? How strong was our project culture? What quality did we deliver? What time and cost performance did we achieve? Was our Statement of Work any good? What is the status of our relationship with the customer at this point? Was our project management effective? Is the customer familiar with sign-off procedures by now?.

Building it up

The project closure is something that you build up in pieces by working on it throughout the entire project lifecycle. Closing phases by means of Tollgate Reviews reports, signing of important deliverables, project status reporting, steering committee meetings, and formal testing results will only make your case stronger. There is a large bridge to cross when trying to get a sign-off, now represents the first sign-off attempt since the approval of the statement of work. We, as project managers, need to understand that project closure is an essential task of our job and that it does not come as a free lunch. We need to work towards closure throughout the entire process.

The core challenge

The core challenge of closing is the review of the deliverables against the Statement of Work. We need to prove that we delivered what we promised to deliver in the SOW and that might be a hard job when the deliverables were not specified in the SOW. This stresses again the importance of the deliverable thinking against the activity thinking. SOWs stuffed with activities will be hard to compare with what was delivered and will open doors for long and exhausting discussions. Buying "something that can drive" refers to which kind of car? Hard to tell, right?

Sign please!

Yes, you need to have a formal sign-off representing the end of this project. To achieve this, we must communicate well in advance and organize a formal meeting with a fixed agenda, ideally attended by the project managers, executive stakeholders, and sponsorers. With the formal signature, our flight has come to an end. We can now disembark the plane and celebrate our successful journey.

The Agile Implementation project type

In the previous section, we discussed the options for the waterfall approach in Sure Step at length. We now turn to the Agile approach, which, as we noted earlier, represents an iterative solution development method that promotes a collaborative process between the resources that own and specify the requirements for the solution and the resources responsible for the development and rollout of the solution.

The Agile project type was introduced in the Sure Step 2010 release, primarily to facilitate the development and rollout of the solution to those customers who expect to use Microsoft Dynamics as a platform and customize the solution to their specific needs. In so doing, these customers tend to evolve their requirements during the course of the development process, necessitating a flexible and iterative approach to development, which is where the Agile project type is ideally suited.

The next screenshot shows the **Agile Project Type** in Sure Step. The left navigation tree view and the methodology pane on the right depict the Sprint cycles characterizing the Agile project type.

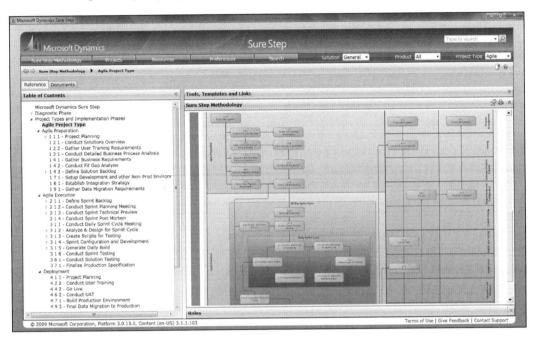

While the Sure Step waterfall approaches have activities flowing across five phases, the Sure Step Agile project type has Sprint cycles to encompass the Analysis, Design, and Development phases. The Agile project type does have two phases, Deployment and Operation, at the culmination of the Sprint cycles. So, in this context, the Agile project type deviates from a strict Agile approach, and is fashioned as a blended approach for ERP/CRM deployments.

The Agile project type begins with a set of activities that constitute the **Agile Preparation** phase. Beginning with a project kick-off activity, the Agile Preparation culminates with the achievement of its primary goal — the creation of the **Initial Solution Backlog**. This backlog represents the initial subset of the requirements for the solution, which will be used to begin the development process in the next phase.

The **Agile Execution** phase follows Agile Preparation. This phase is highlighted by the two Sprint cycles. The *Sprint cycle*, which is also referred to as *Scrum*, denotes a time period, up to four weeks in duration, in which the team executes the development of the solution on an identified set of backlog items. The Sure Step Agile project type has two Sprint cycles—a **Daily Sprint Cycle** that is encompassed within a **30-Day Sprint Cycle**, as seen in the preceding screenshot. The development activities are carried out on a daily basis, including planning, analyzing, designing, developing, and testing. These activities are performed against the **Sprint Backlog**, which is a compiled list of requirements from the Solution Backlog that is broken down into smaller increments of product features. The requirements in the Sprint Backlog are then further broken down into manageable tasks during a **Sprint Planning Meeting**.

At the end of a Sprint Cycle is a **Sprint Technical Preview** activity, during which the implementer and customer teams review the developed solution for the requirements. This is a critical activity wherein the requirements are approved, or rejected, and fed back into the Solution Backlog for possible inclusion in a future Sprint Cycle. A **Sprint Post Mortem** is also conducted to evaluate the team's performance and discuss any opportunities for improvement. After the final Sprint Cycle, an overall solution testing is performed, and the specification for the customer's production environment is finalized.

At the culmination of the Agile Execution phase, the solution then moves to the corresponding activities in the Deployment and Operation phases, including User Training and User Acceptance Testing. These activities were discussed in the *Sure Step Waterfall implementation phases* section. These two phases and activities also signify a shift from the classic Agile approach to a blended approach from business applications solution delivery.

The typical usage scenarios for the Agile project type include the following:

- The selected Microsoft Dynamics solution has a fair Degree of Fit—around 50-75%—with the customer's requirements. The customizations required to fashion the solution to meet the customer's solution vision are expected to be medium-to-complex in nature so that the development efforts can be encapsulated within the Sprint cycles. Also, the envisioned solution may or may not include an ISV solution in addition to the core Microsoft Dynamics solution.

- Custom code development may encompass integration or interfaces to third-party sources, as well as migration of data from legacy or third-party systems to the envisioned solution. Again, it is suggested that these coding efforts are not overly complex.

- Business process analysis activities and OCM activities may be included in the scope of the engagement. These activities will be executed in parallel with the development activities in the Agile project type.

- The Agile project type is typically applicable to single site implementations, but it may be extended to smaller multisite engagements with about three locations.

The usage of the Agile project type requires a very disciplined approach by the project teams to control the overall scope of the project and manage it to fruition. It is highly recommended that organizations that choose this approach have experienced Scrum Masters or Sprint Cycle Managers—individuals well versed with the Agile discipline.

Similar to the Standard project type, the customer organizations using the Agile project type should also have business and IT users with multiple years of experience in deploying and using business solutions. It is also important that the experienced users are selected to be part of the solution delivery team, and they actively support the service provider during the implementation.

The Agile project type can also be used for the development of the pilot solution for multisite deployments. Such solution rollout usage scenarios are described in an earlier section titled *Setting up a program for solution rollout*.

In the following section, we describe a few use cases of the Agile, Rapid, and Enterprise project types.

Agile project type for a multinational chemicals customer

After going through their due diligence, a chemicals manufacturer selected Microsoft Dynamics CRM as their solution. The customer selected the Microsoft Dynamics CRM solution for the ability to use it as a platform, and to use the Extended CRM or xRM capabilities as a starting point to build a solution catered to their specific needs.

As the customer and implementation partner worked through the requirements for the solution, they felt that while they had a good understanding of the overall needs, they were likely to unearth additional use cases for the solution during the development cycle. Both the customer and partner had past experience in a sprint cycle-based solution development approach, and had experienced project managers to manage the solution delivery with an iterative approach. Accordingly, they decided that the Agile project type afforded them the best approach to tailor their solution delivery.

The Statement of Work was structured to include nine monthly sprint cycles for the first release of the solution. The solution requirements constituted the initial Solution Backlog and became the starting point for the determination of the Sprint Backlog.

Rapid project type for a GP customer

A distributor in the Small-to-Medium Enterprise segment selected the Microsoft Dynamics GP solution to support their financial needs. The customer was using an old unsupported ERP solution that was unable to meet their growth and additional user requirements for the system. The company decided to work with a Gold-certified Microsoft Dynamics GP partner to quickly install a limited solution for financial reporting, customer and receivables aging, and vendor and payables tracking.

The partner used the Fixed Scope Proposal and Statements of Work provided in Sure Step (refer to the next screen) as a starting template, and catered the engagement accordingly.

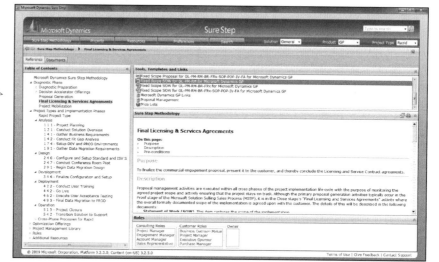

The implementation was structured using the Rapid project type, and included specific activities for solution design, installation, configuration, and data conversion. Also included was a **Conference Room Pilot (CRP)** activity, which afforded the users a preview of the upcoming solution and the chance to review the solution configuration to ensure that it met the proposed design.

Enterprise project type usage by a global advertising organization

A global advertising organization found itself unable to meet increasing customer demand for detailed information due to its antiquated financial management application. Seeking to improve its financial reporting capabilities, the company decided on Microsoft Dynamics AX as a "best-in-class financial management software" as it had scalability and localization capabilities (both language and statutory) required for their global organization.

Due to the scale of the solution delivery, the customer needed an implementation partner that had a global presence capable of understanding local requirements, languages, and laws. The customer selected Microsoft Services and its **Microsoft Global Solutions India (MGSI)** group to work with their own corporate project team, in order to develop and deploy the solution across multiple locations.

Using the Sure Step Enterprise project type and guidance, the teams worked together to gather the functional requirements for the solution and design the solution. The customer was impressed with the delivery approach, leading their VP and Corporate Controller to remark: *The Microsoft Services consultants who worked with us on our implementation knew the product inside and out. The project management methodology used by the consultants minimized scope creep, which is very common for major system implementations, enabling us to finish on time and within budget.*

Over 30 agencies were already using Microsoft Dynamics AX as of this writing, with more deployments in the offing. The company also runs an internally hosted solution of Microsoft Dynamics AX to support its smaller agencies. The implementation approach provided the basis for this successful delivery. The customer's global program manager added: *Sure Step is a well-thought-out and flexible methodology that allows us to present a consistent plan and approach tailored to our global strategy. It helps with resource planning for deployments, provides ongoing financial status of each deployment, and gives us the ability to set expectations of required staff time commitment.*

Summary

In this chapter, we focused on the project lifecycle planning in Sure Step and talked about Waterfall and Agile project types, cross-phase processes, and how to set up solution rollout programs. We learned that Sure Step truly helps in engaging smart projects as it enables us, through intelligent lifecycle planning, to be proactive, goal driven, efficient, and flexible at the same time. Sure Step taught us that we need to be flexible in our approach to the needs of the project, instead of deploying the same approach on all of our projects, while keeping an eye on continuous interactions with the customer stakeholders.

As a quick reference, the following project types afford you the required flexibility in solution delivery.

- The Rapid project type is designed for out of the box implementations of the Microsoft Dynamics solution, with zero or minimal customizations of the standard solution.

- The Sure Step Standard project type is suitable for a majority of Microsoft Dynamics projects, and is typically used for medium-scale, single-site implementations that require a moderate number of customizations and/or add-on solutions.

- The Enterprise project type is designed for large-scale engagements with complex requirements and solution scenarios that necessitate deep governance and oversight.

- The Agile project type represents an iterative solution development method that promotes a collaborative process for the development and rollout of the solution.

- Sure Step also includes a waterfall-based upgrade project type, which will be covered in a later chapter.

In the next chapter, we will learn about essential quality assurance and control principles supported by Sure Step. This chapter will also provide an introduction to the optimization offerings.

References

Microsoft Case Studies: http://www.microsoft.com/casestudies/

6
Quality Management and Optimization

In the last chapter, we learned about the Waterfall and Agile implementation approaches supported by Sure Step. We discussed the different project types based on these approaches, as well as the implementation phases and cross-phase processes that these project types span. We also learned about the activities, templates, and guidance provided by Sure Step to enable solution delivery.

In this chapter, we focus on the quality aspects of Sure Step, which encompasses both proactive actions that can be taken during the solution delivery, as well as post go-live steps to ensure the ongoing maintenance and success of the solution. The following topics will be covered:

- The manifestation of Quality Management in the different areas of Sure Step
- How Quality Control is embedded within the waterfall and agile-based project types
- The Sure Step Optimization Offerings Roadmap—what it means to service providers, especially those starting in the Microsoft Dynamics field, and how the customer can benefit from its usage

Quality management manifestation in Sure Step

Quality management practices including quality control and quality assurance are essential aspects of the solution delivery process to ensure that the solution being developed is in line with the expectations of the customer. Dr. W. Edwards Deming was one of the pioneers of the quality revolution, first in Japan, then in the United States, and then the rest of the world. Dr. Deming's teachings and philosophies originated in manufacturing, but have been extended to several disciplines over time, and his works have been produced and reproduced via a number of books and articles. Dr. Deming emphasized how quality and efficiency can improve simultaneously, by creating "a consistency of purpose designed to drive the organization toward product and service improvement" and "continually and permanently" improving the system.

In the Sure Step methodology, quality control and assurance are manifested in many areas, including in the activities of each cross phase of the implementation project types. Following are some of the areas where quality control and management are accentuated and specifically called out:

- The Program Management cross phase within the Sure Step project types includes specific activities and templates focused on quality control.

- The Quality and Testing cross phase within the Sure Step project types focuses on due diligence to ensure that the solution is configured and customized per agreed upon standards and requirements.

- Sure Step provides several offerings under the Optimization umbrella. The Optimization offerings include proactive oversight of an implementation from a technical and/or governance aspect, as well as actions that can be performed during production to ensure that the solution continues to operate effectively.

- Finally, Sure Step also includes reference content featuring quality management within the Project Management Library.

We will review the first three topics in more detail in this chapter. We will reserve the discussion of the Project Management Library and its quality management content to an upcoming chapter.

Quality control within the project types

Within the Sure Step implementation project types, the execution of quality management is often emphasized and entrusted to senior roles like the Project Manager, Solution Architect, and Tester. These roles assume leadership of the solution delivery process, and as such it is seen as natural extensions of their roles to oversee the quality aspects of the solution delivery. Accordingly, key activities in the Program Management and Quality and Testing cross phases are specifically called out to monitor the quality of the implementation, with the Project Manager, Solution Architect, and so on, as the "owners" for the execution of the deliverables. In the Program Management cross phase, key quality-focused activities include the documentation of the Conditions of Satisfaction and the execution of Tollgate Reviews. The Quality and Testing cross phase includes activities early in the delivery cycle to ensure that Quality Standards are established. Additionally, Monitoring and Testing activities are essential elements of this cross phase, with activities called out in each phase.

Quality activities embedded in program management

Conditions of Satisfaction (COS) are the measures of project success and the goals for the engagement that allow the teams to clearly determine success or failure of the project. The guidance in Sure Step calls for the elements of COS to be identified at the outset of the engagement, and noted within the Project Charter or similar project documentation. The Project Manager is responsible for working with the customer to ensure that this activity is executed, and also to ensure that the document is signed off by the customer, thereby denoting their acceptance.

Another key component of quality control during the implementation is the Tollgate Reviews. For the waterfall project types, the executions of the Tollgate Reviews are called out at the end of each phase. For the Agile project type, Tollgate Reviews take the form of the Sprint Post Mortem, which is executed at the end of each sprint cycle.

The Tollgate Reviews in the waterfall project types assess the current health of the project by reviewing the key milestones achieved and key deliverables completed during the corresponding phase. Any project issues and risks are also identified, documented, and a course for mitigating them is established. This may include scope and change requests to be initiated, and approval requested from the customer. Any adjustments to the overall timeline of the project are also performed during this activity. The Tollgate Reviews are also used to assess how the project is faring in terms of addressing the conditions of satisfaction identified by the customer.

Finally, the "lessons learned" are documented for the benefit of the customer and project teams, which is especially critical at the end of the Operation phase of the project because they may produce important guidelines for future related engagements.

In the Agile project type, the project team members use the Sprint Cycle Review to discuss the relative success and failures of the process at the end of each sprint cycle. The team focuses on the processes and working practices followed during the sprint cycle, including how the team worked together and if any improvements are needed before the next sprint cycle is initiated.

Key quality and testing cross-phase activities

Establishing the Quality and Testing Standards early in an implementation can reduce any ambiguity in the configuration, development, and testing of the solution. These standards, gathered and documented in a Test Plan, communicate the general procedures to be followed when conducting software testing and validation. The plan may include specific test cases or scenarios and their expected results. It may also encompass projected business processes and workflow changes in the customer organization.

The Test Plan also provides the general overview of the Monitoring and Testing activities that will be performed during the course of the implementation. The Testing activities are especially emphasized in the Sure Step methodology—the larger the scope of the engagement, the more the rigor and number of tests that are recommended. The following diagram shows the recommended tests for large-scale engagements:

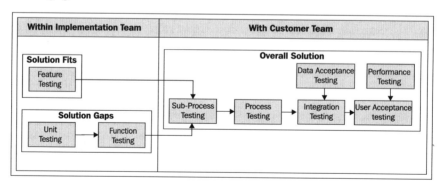

At the outset of the engagement, the implementation team ascertained the solution requirements and conducted a Fit-Gap Analysis to determine the requirements that fit with the standard solution and those that were gaps and required customization. The testing activities address these requirements beginning with the **Solution Fits** and **Solution Gaps** during the solution development phase, and then testing the overall solution in the deployment phase.

The first three tests performed during solution development are executed within the development team. These tests do not require the customer team to be involved. The customer team will be required in the next series of tests, though the development team may query the customer **Subject Matter Experts (SMEs)** as necessary during the development process if for example, a requirement needs clarification.

- **Feature Testing**: This test is performed by the application consultants in the delivery team focused on the configuration and setup of the system. The objective of this test is to ensure that the system is configured to meet the requirement described in the **Functional Requirement Document (FRD)** and **Functional Design Document (FDD)**.

  Let's take an example of a customer requirement for a specific workflow for approval of orders over a certain quantity or amount. The design for the requirement is defined in the FDD, and the system is configured to follow this approval workflow. A Feature Test is first conducted by the application consultant to verify that the requirement is met. At a later stage, the customer SME will also verify this configuration.

- **Unit Testing**: A Unit Test is a stand-alone test of the custom code written for a system modification. It is performed by the developers and is based on the solution design described in the **Technical Design Document (TDD)**.

  For example, say the customer's marketing department needs some custom fields in the customer master table to allow them to classify and segment their customers. The TDD may be used to describe the specific tables in the system that will need to be modified. After the system is customized accordingly, the Unit Test is conducted by the developer to verify that the fields have been created as required.

- **Function Testing**: The Function Test is the subsequent test to the Unit Test. Like the Unit test, it is also focused on custom code, but unlike the Unit Test, the Function Test is performed by the application consultants, and is based on the Functional Design Document. The objective is that the system modification is in-line with the functional or business need of the customer.

  In our previous example of the custom field, in the customer master table, after the Unit Test the Function Test is conducted by the application consultant to verify that the marketing department's functional need is being met by the customization. This may involve for example, verifying that the field is placed on the corresponding form at the right location and the appropriate values are available to the marketing personnel.

The need for such rigor in testing is evident from the examples noted here. However, if the reader concludes that the number of tests seems to be too much overhead for smaller engagements, they may consider combining tests where feasible. However, for large-scale engagements, which may have several hundred simple and complex requirements, this rigor is necessary, so the reader is strongly advised against taking any shortcuts that may pose unnecessary risks. Skipping the individual tests may lead to issues being detected downstream in the process. As any experienced consultant would tell you, it is better to test a smaller subset of the solution so as to isolate any potential issues. The alternative, which is more time consuming and laborious, is to test all the setups together to try to determine if the problem lies in a single subset of code or is due to the intersection with another element of code. In that sense, you could draw a parallel to a manufacturing process—in multi-part manufacture, it is critical to detect quality issues during the manufacture of the components. Waiting until assembly to discover parts that don't fit will likely shut down the assembly line and lead to expensive delays. Just as in the manufacturing process, testing the individual code components is important during solution development, before the solution is tested as a whole.

The tests described above are conducted within the implementation team. The remaining tests are conducted with direct involvement of the customer's personnel involved in the solution implementation. The success of these tests is predicated on this involvement, to ensure that the solution is developed as envisioned.

- **Sub-Process Testing:** A Sub-Process Test involves the testing of a subset of the company's overall business process, to ensure that the users of the new solution will be getting a system that performs as originally envisioned. This test is performed by the application consultants with the customer SMEs participating, verifying, and signing-off on the subset of the solution.

  A test of the customer's Order Taking process is an example of a Sub-Process Test. The new solution is set up in a Test environment and the customer SMEs work with the application consultant to run the system, checking that the Order Taking workflow is intuitive and as per the agreed-upon design.

- **Process Testing:** While a Sub-Process Test focuses on a subset of the company's workflow, the Process Test is a complete test of the related features and functions that make up a defined business process. This test is also performed by the application consultants with the customer SMEs.

Testing of the Order-to-Cash workflow or Procure-to-Pay workflow are examples of Process testing from an ERP solution perspective. In the Order-to-Cash Process Test, the customer SMEs verify that the system performs as desired for entering a customer order, fulfilling the order, and accepting payment for the order, including alerting the appropriate Customer Service personnel when the payments are overdue. In the Procure-to-Pay Process Test, the SMEs verify that they can place a Purchase Order with their suppliers as per their design, they can receive and account for the delivery of the supplies, and they are able to pay the suppliers for their goods within the appropriate payment conventions of the organization.

From a CRM solution perspective, the Process Test examples include Quote-to-Order workflow, where a quote captured in the CRM system can be tracked through to conversion into an order, or Self Service Portal workflows such as users obtaining documentation or answers to specific queries or statuses of their requests.

- **Data Acceptance Testing (DAT)**: DAT is a very important test for business solutions delivery. The first objective of DAT is to verify that the data migrated from existing systems to the new system is the correct data subset, and the data has been cleansed as necessary. The second objective of the DAT is validating that all the data needed for transactions, inquiry, and reporting is available. DAT should be performed by the customer's data owners and key users who are closest to the data elements and can identify any shortcomings. DAT may also involve the customer's IT staff, if the data sources need to be validated during the testing process.

The importance of the DAT cannot be understated as the behavior of the new system is dependent on the data that is populated in its database. If the data is incorrect, it doesn't matter how good the new system is—the users will only get wrong information faster or easier.

Let's say that one of the suppliers for the customer is ABC Corporation. Due to the lack of data entry checks and rules in legacy systems, it is not uncommon to find multiple records with the same supplier entered as ABC or ABC Corp or ABC Corporation. Why is this a problem? The Purchasing Manager does not have a true overview of all the orders placed with ABC Corporation, without which he or she may not have all the ammunition to negotiate additional discounts.

- **Integration Testing**: The Integration Test is an end-to-end test of specific business processes, and includes system setup, development, reports, and testing of integrations or interfaces to any external sub-systems. Integration testing is performed with the company's SMEs and key users and the application consultants. The company's IT staff may also be involved in this testing, especially as it relates to the touch points with the external systems.

  In the Process Test Order-to-Cash and Procure-to-Pay workflow testing examples, if the process required connecting to external systems or databases for reporting or other reasons, the Integration Test would address and validate these scenarios.

- **Performance Testing**: The Performance Test is a technical test that focuses on how well the system performs in high transaction volumes anticipated during peak times. This test is performed with the company's IT staff and SMEs, and the application and technical consultants.

  Performance Testing can avail of canned scripts to populate the system and simulate heavy load. However, depending on the number of customizations made to the standard system, the development of the scripts may require several person-hours. But depending on the criticality of the system response rate for a corresponding business process, this test may be a very important one to validate that the configured system under load meets the business requirements and agreed-upon performance metrics.

  An example of Performance Testing is a scenario to monitor the system response for multiple order entries, which includes validation of the customer's credit and outstanding payments.

- **User Acceptance Testing (UAT)**: The UAT is the final test performed by the customer SMEs and key users and the application consultants for system sign-off. The UAT is the most important indicator of the customer's acceptance of the new solution for go-live.

  The UAT is conducted with data migrated from the customer's existing systems, and uses actual transactions from a specific period (such as one or two days) identified by the customer as being a representative sample of their business. The test focuses on complete end-to-end testing to ensure that the system meets the business requirements and the test criteria established early in the implementation. The UAT is typically performed in a Testing or Staging environment. The UAT leverages scripts that are pre-populated with the test steps and expected results from the testing, and the actual results of the testing are documented for future reference and customer approval. The following figure shows a screenshot of one of the many UAT scripts provided in Sure Step.

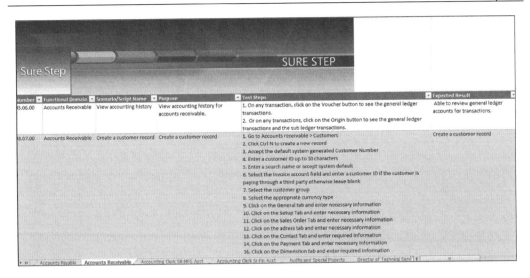

If the tests were determined to be successful, the customer signs off on the system to be moved into production. However, the customer may still request changes to a certain feature, data migration, or integration process. These changes will go through the change management process established at the outset of the engagement.

In the above sections, we saw how Sure Step has guidance and templates embedded within the activities of the project types to assure a quality solution delivery. We now discuss other avenues for ensuring customer satisfaction with the overall solution and delivery process.

The Sure Step Optimization Offerings Roadmap

The Encarta dictionary definition of optimize is "enhance effectiveness of something: to make something function at its best or most effective, or use something to its best advantage." Optimization can mean different things depending on your point of view. In terms of a system, optimization could mean the process of improving the ease of use or response rate of the system. For a program, it could mean an attempt to reduce runtime, bandwidth, or memory requirements, while for computer code, optimization could entail improving the performance or efficiency of the compiled code. For a business process, optimization could mean improving the efficiency of that process, including reducing costs or the throughput time. For the optimization offerings in Sure Step, all these definitions apply to a certain extent.

The **Sure Step Optimization Offerings** Roadmap includes a set of offerings designed to proactively help reduce the risk in an implementation or upgrade, as well as to assist the customer in ensuring that their system is performing optimally when it is in production. The following figure depicts the top-level optimization offerings in Sure Step.

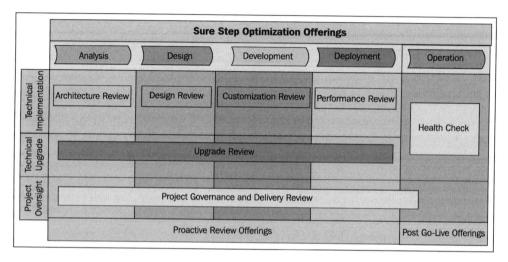

Technical review offerings

Sure Step provides five technical proactive review offerings and one technical post go-live offering. Four of the technical proactive review offerings—**Architecture Review, Design Review, Customization Review, and Performance Review**—focus on the implementation of a new Microsoft Dynamics solution, and the other, **Upgrade Review**, focuses on the upgrade of the existing solution. The one technical post go-live offering, **Health Check**, is designed for solutions that have already been in operation for a certain period of time. Each of these offerings provides a range of services to the customer or service provider assisting the customer. These offerings also include sub-offerings, which are more limited in scope and focused on a specific area.

The proactive technical review offerings promote quality management by enabling the customer or service provider with access to Microsoft Dynamics specialists at appropriate checkpoints during their implementation. These experts can review the proposed architecture and design for business and industry solution fit, as well as in technical areas such as performance, scalability, and integration with other systems and third-party software.

Architecture Review

Architecture Review provides an assessment of the overall technical design of the customer's Microsoft Dynamics solution, and covers design of the solution for areas including the performance, scalability, security, and release management. The objective of this offering is to ensure that the envisioned infrastructure for the customer's solution is in-line with best practices, and is it executed towards the end of the Analysis phase.

A sample schedule for an Architecture Review is shown below.

	Mon	Tue	Wed	Thu	Fri
Week 1	Kick-off meeting	Technology analysis and review of FRD	Technology analysis and review	Review of Fit Gap Analysis and Solution Blueprint	Review of Integration and Interface requirements
Week 2	Server architecture review	Server architecture review	Transaction volume review	Transaction volume review	Transaction volume review
Week 3	Analysis and document preparartion	Analysis document preparation	Analysis and document preparation	Analysis and document preparation	Report Submission and Architecture Review project closure

The key tasks carried out in this example include: technology analysis and review of the Functional Requirements Document (FRD), server architecture review, review of the Fit Gap and Solution Blueprint, high-level review of the integration and interface requirements, and high-level review of transaction volumes. As output of the review, the customer's and service provider's implementation teams receive an objective, third-party view of the proposed architecture and how it aligns with the customer's requirements.

Architecture Review also includes specific sub-offerings such as Reporting Strategy, to address reporting needs for the customer, and Advisory Services, to identify operational risks and address potential issues before they occur. These sub-offerings can be executed as part of the overall Architecture Review, or if a full-fledged Architecture Review is not desired, these sub-offerings may be used instead to focus on those specific areas of the implementation.

Design Review

The Design Review offering is used to examine the design of the Microsoft Dynamics solution in two primary areas—the customizations of the Microsoft Dynamics system and the integration scenarios between the Microsoft Dynamics system and other third-party systems. This offering is executed towards the end of the Design phase of the implementation. The stated objectives for the Design Review engagement may include the following:

- Assess the customization needs for the customer's Microsoft Dynamics solution

- Assess the integration needs for the Microsoft Dynamics application with other systems

- Review the Functional Design Documents for Gaps (FDD-Gap) and the corresponding Technical Design Documents (TDD) for the proposed customization and integration design

- Provide an assessment of whether the customization design is in-line with the previously completed and signed-off Fit Gap Analysis and Solution Blueprint

- Provide recommendations to optimize the Microsoft Dynamics solution architecture and integration design for performance, availability, and reliability

An example of the flow and steps carried out in a Design Review engagement is shown in the following diagram. The deliverable from the engagement is a Design Review and Assessment Report, which includes integration design and customization design recommendations for optimization based on best practices for developing custom components.

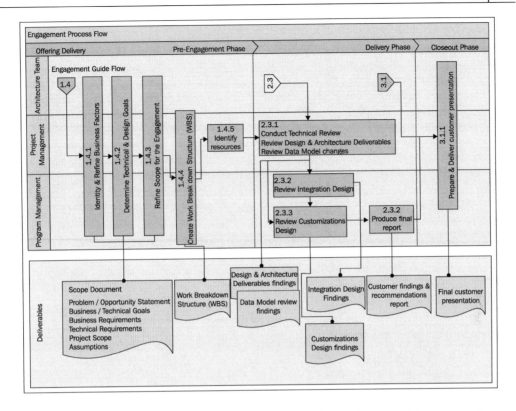

Design Review also includes sub-offerings that provide guidance and/or instruction via workshops to technical and development consultants on topics including reporting and migration design. Focus areas include building reports with Microsoft SQL Reporting Services, developing the design and preparation for migrating users, accounts, and data, as well as management of co-existing systems during the migration. Just as with the Architecture Review, these sub-offerings can be executed as part of the overall Design Review, or if a full-fledged Design Review is not desired, these sub-offerings may be used instead to focus on those specific areas of the implementation.

Customization Review

The Customization Review offering focuses on analyzing the custom code to improve performance, increase stability, improve security, and reduce operating and upgrade costs. This offering is executed towards the end of the Development phase, and the stated objectives may include the following:

- Identify any best-practice deviations in custom coding, including both server-side and client-side code
- Review conformity with standards, detect code development errors early, and document the deviations

- Ensure compliance with necessary quality guidelines
- Review the interfaces to system components

An example of the activities carried out in a Customization Review engagement is shown in the diagram below. The final report from the engagement provides recommendations and an action plan to implement the best practices and fix any issues found, to ensure optimal long-term operation of the Microsoft Dynamics system.

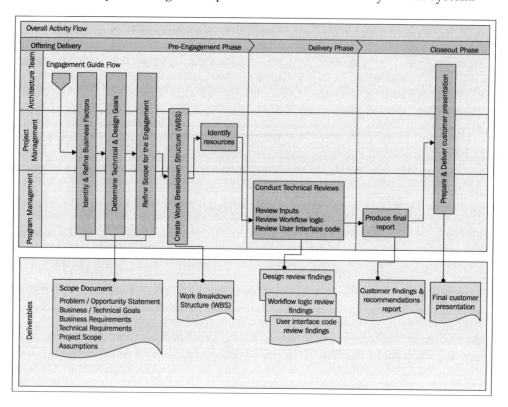

Customization Review also includes sub-offerings that provide release management and test guidance for managing the different environments and the transition to the production environment; workshops for training the Microsoft Dynamics solution administrators in the customer organization; and services based on established migration design for migrating legacy data to the Microsoft Dynamics solution. Similar to the other review offerings, these sub-offerings can be executed as part of the overall Customization Review, or if a full-fledged Customization Review is not desired, these sub-offerings may be used instead to focus on those specific areas of the implementation.

Performance Review

The Performance Review offering analyzes the performance impact of the solution design and customizations. The offering begins with a review of the existing Microsoft Dynamics solution and the current and proposed customer usage metrics, such as user counts, dataset sizes, transaction volumes, and so on. The output is the performance recommendations for the Microsoft Dynamics server(s) and for the Microsoft SQL Server database that will support the Microsoft Dynamics solution.

The Performance Review offering is executed in the Deployment phase, after the solution development is frozen for any additions. The review should be conducted before the solution is moved to production so as to catch crash, leak, performance, and other non-architectural issues that do not meet best practices. Performance Reviews should also be considered when prior solution testing has indicated potential performance implications in certain areas of the solution. Performance reviews can address the following concerns:

- **Cost**: The infrastructure works properly, but at too high a cost, causing an insufficient return on investment.
- **Agility**: The infrastructure works properly, but it does not have the flexibility to change quickly enough to meet the business needs.
- **Performance**: The infrastructure fails to meet users' expectations, either because the expectations were set incorrectly, or because the infrastructure performs incorrectly.
- **Security**: The infrastructure fails the business by not providing enough protection for data and resources, or by enforcing so much security that legitimate users cannot efficiently access data and resources.

An example of the activities carried out in a Performance Review engagement is shown in the following diagram. The final report from the engagement provides system environment recommendations addressing the network topology, latency numbers, and bandwidth.

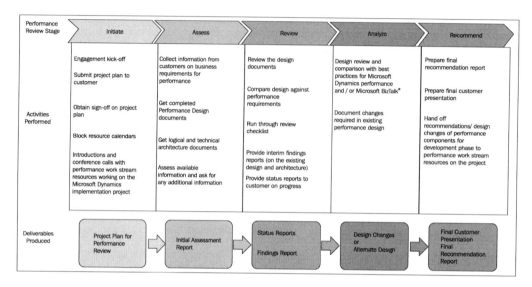

Performance Review also includes sub-offerings that address the customer's performance and scalability needs via a benchmark test in a lab environment; a workshop for training technical resources on the methodology and processes for collecting and analyzing performance data and teaching them the necessary skills to resolve performance issues; or deployment services that can assist the customer with planning for future growth and system needs. Similar to the other review offerings, these sub-offerings can be executed as part of the overall Performance Review, or if a full-fledged Performance Review is not desired, these sub-offerings may be used instead to focus on those specific areas of the implementation.

Upgrade Review

While the prior optimization offerings address new solution implementations, the Upgrade Review offering is provided as guidance for customers upgrading their existing Microsoft Dynamics solutions to the current product release. The Upgrade Review offering provides oversight of the customer's upgrade solution, including design, customization, integrations, physical infrastructure, and architecture throughout the upgrade project lifecycle.

The Upgrade Review offers a group of advisory activities or sub-offerings that are carried out throughout the Upgrade project lifecycle. The three activities or sub-offerings within the Upgrade Review are as follows:

- **Upgrade Review**: This sub-offering aligns with the activities of the Analysis and Design phases in the Upgrade project type, including upgrade preparation, requirements gathering, test planning, and environment setup. The review team evaluates the customizations in the existing Microsoft Dynamics solution, analyzes the upgrade of the code components, and documents issues along with resolutions and recommendations. The output of this exercise is an upgrade estimation report to the customer.

- **Test Upgrade**: This sub-offering follows Upgrade Review and aligns with the Development Phase in the Upgrade project type. The goal of the Test Upgrade is to provide a test or sandbox environment with the customer's existing data promoted to the new Microsoft Dynamics product version. This environment can then be used to verify and benchmark the data before promoting to production.

- **Production Upgrade**: This offering, executed in the Deployment phase of the Upgrade project type, provides on-site assistance with the promotion of the upgraded solution to the production environment.

A sample of activities performed in these sub-offerings is shown in the following diagram:

Pre-Upgrade	
Pre-Upgrade	**Topics:**
	• Assist in the preparation of the upgrade • Validate pre-requisites have been completed • Kick off the upgrade
During Upgrade	
During Upgrade	**Topics:**
	• Troubleshoot any Dynamics issues with the server upgrade • Assist with issues related to applying service packs or updates • Assist with kicking off multiple organization database upgrades, if applicable • Assist with upgrading up to 5 clients to the upgraded relates • Help test the functionality with project team • Identify any "show-stopper" issues • Help revert to previous version of Dynamics if too many show-stopper issues exist
Post-Upgrade Troubleshooting	
Post-Upgrade Troubleshooting	**Topics:**
	• Review the new functionality with power users • Assist in the testing and validation process for the new version • Document any outstanding issues • Create support incidents for any issues that cannot be resolved on site

The Upgrade Review sub-offerings align with the flow of the Upgrade project type in Microsoft Dynamics Sure Step. The Upgrade project type will be covered in detail in a forthcoming chapter.

Health Check

When the solution is in production, and after the initial stabilization period, it is a good idea to revisit the solution to ensure that it is running efficiently. Periodic checks during the solution operation phase are also a recommended best practice. Both of these objectives can be achieved with the Health Check post-go-live optimization offering in Sure Step.

The Health Check offering analyzes the customer's Microsoft Dynamics solution and measures the effectives of the solution in operation. The solution monitoring allows the proactive identification of any potential problems, and provides suggested resolutions for the selected components.

A sample Health Check report is shown in the following diagram:

⬤⬤⬤ Good (Green) – Customer's deployment criterion match "Best Practices" in 100% of criterion		
⬤⬤⬤ Fair (Yellow) – Customer's deployment criterion match "Best Practices" in <100% but >/= 70% of criterion		
⬤⬤⬤ Poor (Red) – Customer's deployment criterion match "Best Practices" in < 70% of criterion		

Category	Status	Explanation
Operational Excellence Scorecard		
General Operational Excellence	⬤⬤◯	
Business Continuity	⬤◯◯	
Monitoring and Alerts	⬤◯◯	
People	⬤◯◯	
Application Configuration Scorecard		
Application User Information	⬤⬤◯	
Performance Optimization	◯⬤◯	
Application Server Scorecard		
Administration	⬤⬤◯	
Hardware Utilization	⬤⬤◯	
Settings	⬤⬤◯	
Configuration	⬤⬤◯	
Event Logs	⬤◯◯	
SQL Server Scorecard		
Administration	⬤⬤◯	
Server Settings	⬤⬤◯	
Database Settings	⬤⬤◯	
CRM Database Settings	⬤⬤◯	
Hardware Utilization	◯⬤◯	
Security Settings	◯⬤◯	
Performance	◯⬤◯	
SQL Query Performance	◯⬤◯	
SQL Server Blocking	⬤⬤◯	
SQL Server Deadlocks	⬤⬤◯	
Event Logs	◯⬤◯	
Memory Guidelines	◯⬤◯	
Microsoft Dynamics Client Scorecard		
Configuration	⬤⬤◯	
Hardware Settings	⬤⬤◯	
Exchange Router Scorecard		
Settings	⬤⬤◯	

The Health Check offering also includes a Performance Tuning sub-offering that monitors the performance capabilities of the Microsoft Dynamics solution to enhance the solution performance and stability. This sub-offering can be executed as part of the Health Check offering, or on its own depending on the needs of the customer.

Project oversight with the Project Governance and Delivery Review offering

The offerings described in the previous section section are technical offerings that are typically delivered by solution architects and senior application or technology consultants. Sure Step also provides another option to drive quality through project oversight and overall project governance delivered by experienced project and engagement managers. This can be achieved with the Project Governance and Delivery Review offering.

Project Governance and Delivery Review

The **Project Governance and Delivery Review (PGDR)** offering provides customers with proactive project governance and delivery execution guidance through the full lifecycle of their Microsoft Dynamics engagement. PGDR is executed by senior resources experienced in project management for business solutions delivery. At a high level, these resources perform three tasks:

- Analyze and assess the proposed engagement structure and established deliverables.

- Monitor the project governance and communications with the customer and within the implementation teams

- Analyze and assess the quality of the deliverables for completeness and relevance

PGDR features two components—Lifecycle Phase-by-Phase Reviews and Project Closure Review. During the Analysis through Deployment solution implementation phases, the PGDR offering acts as guidance and oversight for the activities performed by the delivery team, helping them to stay aligned with the agreed upon vision for the solution by proactively identifying risks and actively managing the overall scope of the engagement. Once the solution is in operation and the engagement is at closure, the PGDR offering evaluates how the project was delivered against the initial vision, and determines the performance against schedule and quality.

At the start of the project, the PGDR initiates two key activities. The customer, reviewers and the implementation team work together to establish the customer's **Conditions of Satisfaction (COS)** for the engagement. These COS are key components of the Project Charter, and other key areas including governance, risk, communication, status reporting, and issue management are discussed and clearly documented in the charter.

During the engagement, the PGDR produces phase-by-phase recommendations and project health dashboards to help customers identify risks and address issues before they become problematic. The reviewers are armed with tools such as the Cobb's Paradox Tool, which is an effective risk assessment tool that provides questionnaires to detect and monitor the overall project risk factors. The screenshot below shows a sample of a graphical output of the Cobb's Paradox tool.

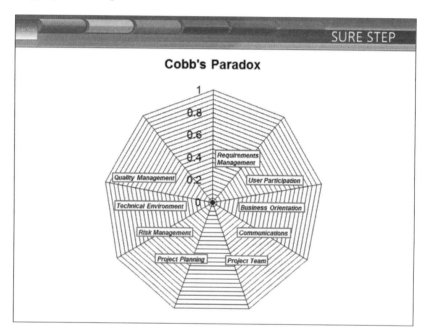

At project closure, PGDR is used to collaboratively discuss accomplishments and challenges and capture lessons learned. Some of the key tasks performed at project closure are listed as follows.

- Document the lessons learned, including the accomplishments, challenges, what the team could have done differently, and so on. This is sometimes viewed as trivial, but it can be a very important source of reference for future projects.

- Review the Conditions of Satisfaction to determine whether or not they have been met.

- Collate outstanding issues and open items, and determine how they will be addressed after project closure.

- Provide recommendations for future projects and follow-on work pertaining to the customer's deployed Microsoft Dynamics solution.

The PGDR and the technical review offerings can be of great benefit to the customer and the implementation team, augmenting the resources in key areas to provide valuable independent perspectives. In the next section, we will discuss some of these benefits.

It is also important to keep in mind that to be most effective, the Optimization offerings should be delivered by an independent third party — meaning, a provider who is not the primary implementer of the solution.

How customers and service providers can benefit from the optimization offerings

Delivering business solutions, especially ERP solutions, requires an industry-savvy implementation team, or in other words, situational fluency. The team must have the ability to translate the system functionality into a solution that meets the specific needs of the customer. When a customer selects a service provider for their solution implementation, they often add extra weight to industry knowledge, because of this reason. So what if it comes down to a service provider that is very knowledgeable in the specific industry or industry vertical, but is not quite as familiar with the Microsoft Dynamics solution? This is one area where the Technical Review Offerings can greatly benefit both the service provider and customer. The marriage of seasoned industry veterans with technical Microsoft Dynamics experts can provide a powerful team to solve deep, topical requirements for the customer.

Microsoft Dynamics is a relatively newer solution in the ERP/CRM marketplace. As such, the available resource pool is also limited, especially in specific regions in Europe, Asia, Africa, and Latin America. This is another area where leveraging the Technical Optimization Offerings, especially the Proactive Review Offerings, can benefit new ERP/CRM Service Providers getting starting with Microsoft Dynamics. Inexperienced service providers can include experienced resources on their team by using these offerings, and as the team members "shadow" the experienced resources, they can ramp up on their understanding of the Microsoft Dynamics solutions.

Where the service providers already possess deep technical expertise but are short on project management expertise, especially on large-scale engagements, the Project Governance and Delivery Review offering can be of great benefit. The Microsoft Dynamics resource pool includes several individuals with knowledge of the solutions prior to their acquisition by Microsoft. While these technical resources are very knowledgeable about the product itself, they sometimes lack the experience to manage the scope, communications, and risks inherent in complex, multi-site solution deployments. Leveraging the PGDR offering, these resources can work with experienced project managers to develop that skill set for future engagements. They can, in turn, lead their organizations to scale up their offerings to address larger clientele.

The Health Check post-go-live offerings, including the Performance Tuning sub-offering, are highly recommended offerings for the customer. Given the substantial investment made in acquiring and deploying the Microsoft Dynamics solution, it behooves the customer to periodically get expert resources to monitor the health of the application. Depending on usage behavior, the application can feel like it bogs down over time, and the system response may appear slower to the users. The post-go-live offerings can then be used to review it and the subsequent recommendations can help clean up the system to perform more efficiently.

From a service provider's perspective, the post-go-live offerings can be exercised to continue maintaining their relationship with their customer. A common paradigm noted in the industry is that it is harder to get a new customer than to keep an existing one. It is also next to impossible to gain a customer back once they are lost to the competition. As such, the service provider should leverage the Health Check offerings to further their relationship with their customers. In doing so, they may also unearth new related or unrelated opportunities on which they may assist the customer.

Technical Review offerings Usage by Global Advertising Organization

In the previous chapter, we talked about a Global Advertising Organization that used Sure Step, specifically the Enterprise project type, for their Microsoft Dynamics AX solution delivery. The customer successfully deployed the initial solution across specific locations with the help of Microsoft Consulting Services (MCS) and Microsoft Global Solutions India (MGSI) resources.

To roll out the solution across additional sites, the customer decided to use a combination of internal and partner resources. The customer also decided to leverage the Technical Review Offerings, specifically the Architecture, Design, Customization and Performance Review offerings, and had the Microsoft resources execute these offerings as independent third-party reviewers. This approach provided continuity and consistency, resulting in reduced costs for the solution rollouts at the corresponding locations.

Project Governance and Delivery Review (PGDR) offering Usage by Partner

A large Retailer selected Microsoft Dynamics AX as their solution, as well as a Partner familiar with their specific industry vertical to assist them in the delivery of the solution. The Partner was adept in Microsoft Dynamics AX, and they were also comfortable with the technical ability of their consulting resources for solution delivery. They were however, concerned with the ability of their resources to manage the overall scope of the engagement, especially given the tight timelines necessitated by the customer.

Having worked successfully alongside MCS resources on other engagements, the Partner felt that a Microsoft resource could assist in reducing the overall project risk inherent with the aggressive timelines. Accordingly, they set up a PGDR engagement wherein an experienced MCS Project Manager performed periodic independent assessments of the overall engagement. The result was an on-time and on-spec rollout of the solution, and a win-win for the customer and the partner.

Summary

In this chapter, we covered the quality aspects of Sure Step, from the perspectives of proactive actions that can be taken during the solution delivery, as well as post go-live steps to ensure the ongoing maintenance and success of the solution. We discussed how quality is embedded in the Sure Step implementation project types, as well as the review and optimization offerings available through the Sure Step Optimization Offerings Roadmap.

In the next chapter, we will learn about Upgrading with Sure Step, including assessing the existing solution and determining the right approach to the upgrade, and guidance for executing the upgrade itself.

References

W. Edwards Deming (2000). *Out of the Crisis*, MIT Press

Microsoft Case Studies, `www.microsoft.com/casestudies/`

7

Upgrading with Sure Step

In the last chapter, we discussed how quality is embedded in Sure Step, during the solution delivery, as well as when the solution is operation. We covered the quality focus in the project activities, as the Optimization Offerings.

In this chapter, we will cover Sure Step's approach to upgrading Microsoft Dynamics solutions. The following topics will be covered:

- Beginning with the Upgrade Assessment to determine the scope and components of the existing solution that need to be upgraded to the current product release
- Determining if the upgrade approach is a Technical Upgrade, or if additional functionality is to be delivered as part of a Functional Upgrade
- Delivering the upgrade using the Sure Step Upgrade Project Type
- Implementing additional functionality to an existing solution

Upgrade assessment and the diagnostic phase

In Chapter 4, we introduced you to the Sure Step Diagnostic phase process and models for a current Microsoft Dynamics customer, both from the customer's due diligence perspective and from a seller's solution selling perspective. In this section, we will discuss the process, particularly the Upgrade Assessment Decision Accelerator offering, in more detail.

We begin by reintroducing the diagram showing the flow of activities and Decision Accelerator offerings for an existing customer. You may recall that the flow is very similar to the one for a prospect, with the only difference being the **Upgrade Assessment** DA offering replacing the Requirements and Process Review DA.

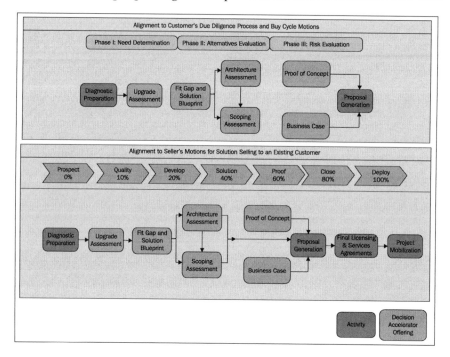

As noted before, the flow for the existing customer also begins with Diagnostic Preparation, similar to that for a prospect. The guidance in the activity page can be leveraged to explain/understand the capabilities and features of the new version of the corresponding Microsoft Dynamics solution that is being considered. When interest is established in moving the existing solution to the current version of the solution, the next step is the Upgrade Assessment DA offering, which is the key step in this process.

The Upgrade Assessment Decision Accelerator offering

The Upgrade Assessment DA is the most important step in the process for an existing Microsoft Dynamics customer. The Upgrade Assessment DA is executed by the services delivery team to get an understanding of the existing solution being used by the customer, determine the components that need to be upgraded to the current release of the product, and determine if any other features need to be enabled as part of the upgrade engagement.

In combination with the Scoping Assessment DA offering, the delivery team will also determine the optimal approach, resource plan and estimate, and overall timeline to upgrade the solution to the current product version.

Before initiating the Upgrade Assessment DA, the services delivery team should meet with the customer to ascertain and confirm that there is interest in performing the upgrade. Especially where delivery resources are in high demand, this is an important step that the sales teams need to carry out before involving the delivery resources such as solution architects and senior application consultants. Sales personnel can use the resources in the Sure Step Diagnostic Preparation activity to understand and position the current capabilities of the corresponding Microsoft Dynamics solution.

Once customer interest in upgrading has been determined, the services delivery team can employ the Upgrade Assessment DA offering. The aim of the Upgrade Assessment is to identify the complexity of upgrading the existing solution and to highlight areas of feature enhancements, complexities, and risks. The steps performed in the execution of the Upgrade Assessment are shown in the following diagram.

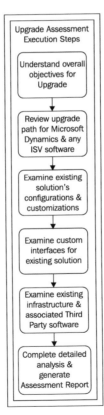

The delivery team begins the Upgrade Assessment by understanding the **overall objectives for the Upgrade**. Teams can leverage the product-specific questionnaires provided in Sure Step for Microsoft Dynamics AX, CRM, GP, NAV, and SL. These questionnaires also include specific sections and questions for interfaces, infrastructure, and so on, so they can also be leveraged in the following steps.

One of the important tasks at the outset is to **review the upgrade path for Microsoft Dynamics and any associated ISV software**, to determine whether the upgrade from the customer's existing product version to the targeted version of Microsoft Dynamics is supported. This will have a bearing on how the upgrade can be executed—can you follow a supported upgrade path, or is it pretty much a full reimplementation of the solution?

The next step in executing the Upgrade Assessment is to assess the **existing solution's configurations and customizations**. In this step, the delivery team reviews which features of Microsoft Dynamics have been enabled for the customer, including which ones have been configured to meet the customer's needs and which ones have been customized. This will allow the delivery team to take the overall objectives for the upgrade and determine which of these configurations and customizations will need to be ported over to the new solution, and which ones should be retired. For example, the older version may have necessitated customizations in areas where the solution did not have corresponding functionality. Or perhaps the solution needed a specific ISV solution to meet a need. If the current product version provides these features as standard functionality, these customizations or ISV solutions no longer need to be part of the new solution.

The next Upgrade Assessment step is to **examine the custom interfaces for the existing solution**. This includes assessing any custom code written to interface the solution to third-party solutions, such as an external database for reporting purposes. This step is followed by **reviewing the existing infrastructure** and architecture configuration so that the delivery team can understand the hardware components that can be leveraged for the new solution. The delivery team can provide confirmation on whether the existing infrastructure can support the upgrade application or if additional infrastructure components may be necessary.

The final step of the Upgrade Assessment DA offering is for the delivery team to complete the detailed analysis of the customer's existing solution and generate a report of their findings. The report, to be presented to the customer for approval, will include the following topics:

- The scope of the upgrade, including a list of functional and technical areas that will be enhanced in the new solution.

- A list of the functional areas of the application categorized to show the expected complexity involved in upgrading them. If there are areas of the existing implementation that will require further examination or additional effort to upgrade successfully due to the inherent complexity, they must be highlighted.

- Areas of the current solution that could be remapped to new functionality in the current version of the base Microsoft Dynamics product.

- An overall recommended approach to the upgrade, including alternatives to address any new functionality desired.

The Upgrade Assessment provides the customer early identification of issues and risks that could occur during an upgrade so that appropriate mitigating actions can be initiated accordingly. The customer can also get a level of confidence that an appropriate level of project governance for the upgrade is available, as well as that the correct upgrade approach will be undertaken by the delivery team.

In the next sections, we will discuss how the Upgrade Assessment DA becomes the basis for completing the customer's due diligence, and sets the stage for a quality upgrade of the customer's solution.

When to use the other Decision Accelerator offerings

After the Upgrade Assessment DA has been executed, the remaining DA offerings may also be needed in the due diligence process for the existing Microsoft Dynamics customer. In this section, we will discuss the scenarios that may call for the usage of the DA offerings, and which ones would apply to that particular scenario.

From the Upgrade Assessment DA, the delivery team determines the existing business functions and requirements that need to be upgraded to the new release. Using the Fit Gap and Solution Blueprint DA offering, they can then determine and document how these requirements will be ported over. If meeting the requirement is more than implementing standard features, the approach maybe a re-configuration, custom code rewrite, or workflow setup. Additionally, if new features are required as part of the upgrade, these requirements should also be classified in the Fit Gap worksheet either as Fit or as Gap. They should also be further classified as Standard, Configuration, or Workflow as the case may be for the Fits, and Customization for the Gaps.

The Architecture Assessment DA can be used determine the new hardware configuration for the upgraded solution. It can also be used to address any performance issues up-front through the execution of the Proof of Concept Benchmark sub-offering.

The Scoping Assessment DA can be used to determine the effort, timeline, and resources needed to execute the upgrade. If it was determined with the Upgrade Assessment DA that new functionality will be introduced, the delivery team and the customer must also determine the Release plan. We will discuss upgrade approaches and Release planning in more detail in the next section.

It is important to note that all three of the above Decision Accelerator Offerings — the Fit Gap and Solution Blueprint, the Architecture Assessment, and the Scoping Assessment can be executed together with the Upgrade Assessment DA as one engagement for the customer. The point of this section is not that each of these offerings needs to be positioned individually for the customer. On the contrary, depending on the scope, the delivery team could easily perform the exercise in tandem. The point of emphasis in this section for the reader is that if you are assessing an upgrade for the customer, you should be able to leverage the templates in each of the DA offerings, and combine them as you deem fit for your engagement.

Lastly, the Proof of Concept DA offering and Business Case DA offering may also apply to an upgrade engagement, but typically only for a small subset of customers. Examples include customers who maybe on a very old version of the Microsoft Dynamics solution so that they pretty much need a re-implementation of the solution with the new version of the product, or customers that need complex functionality to be enabled as part of the upgrade. In both these cases, the customer may request the delivery team to prove out certain components of the solution prior to embarking on a full upgrade, in which case the Proof of Concept DA may be executed. They may also request assistance from the delivery team to assess the return on investment for the upgraded solution, in which case the Business Case DA may be employed.

Determining the upgrade approach and release schedule

As noted in the previous section, the customer and the delivery team should work together to select the right approach for the upgrade during the course of the upgrade diagnostics. Sure Step recommends two approaches to Upgrades:

- **Technical upgrade**: Use this approach if the upgrade mostly applies to application components, such as executable files, code components, and DLLs. This approach can be used to bring a customized solution to the latest release, provided the application functionality and business workflow stay relatively the same.

- **Functional upgrade**: Use this approach if new application functionality or major changes in the existing business workflows are desired during the course of the upgrade. Additional planning, testing, and rework of the existing solution are inherent in this complex upgrade process, and as such more aligned to a Functional upgrade. Functional upgrades are typically performed in multiple Releases.

The following diagram depicts the two **Upgrade** approaches and the **Release** schedules.

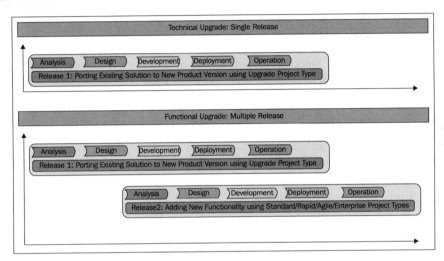

Depending on the scope of the upgrade, the customer engagement may have one or more delivery Releases. If for example, the customer's solution is on a supported upgrade path, the **Technical Upgrade** maybe delivered in a single Release using the Sure Step Upgrade project type. If the new solution requires several new processes to be enabled, the **Functional Upgrade** may be delivered in two or more Releases. For example, if the customer needs advanced supply chain functionality such as production scheduling and/or advanced warehousing to be enabled as part of the upgrade, the recommended approach is to first complete the **Technical Upgrade** using the Sure Step Upgrade project type to port the existing functionality over to the new product version in Release 1, then add the advanced supply chain functionality using the Rapid, Standard, Agile, or Enterprise project types in Release 2.

As noted earlier, the DA offerings can be executed individually or in combination, depending on the customer engagement. Regardless of how they are executed, it is imperative that the customer and delivery team select the right approach and develop the necessary plans such as Project Plan, Resource Plan, Project Charter, and/or Communication Plan. These documents should form the basis for the upgrade delivery Proposal. When the Proposal and Statement of Work are approved, it is time to begin the execution of the solution upgrade.

Delivering the upgrade

In the previous section, we discussed how we set up for the upgrade delivery. We now focus on the delivery of the upgrade itself, using the Sure Step Upgrade project type.

We discussed the two approaches to upgrading with Sure Step in the previous section, the Technical Upgrade and the Functional Upgrade. The common denominator for both these approaches is the Sure Step Upgrade project type, which provides the underlying workflow for the only Release for the former approach and the first Release for the latter approach. A screenshot of the Sure Step Upgrade Project Type is shown next:

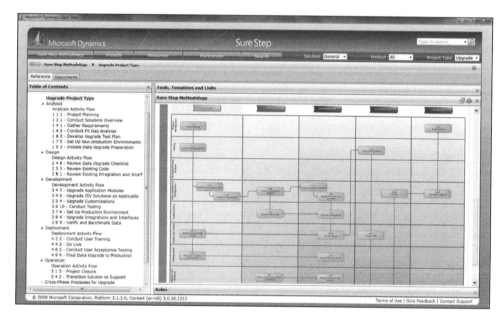

As shown in the diagram, the Sure Step Upgrade project type follows the waterfall method, and with the five phases, **Analysis**, **Design**, **Development**, **Deployment** and **Operation**. Just as in the Standard, Rapid, and Enterprise project types, the activities in these phases are grouped under the nine cross phase processes (refer to Chapter 5 for a review of the cross phase processes). We will discuss some of the important activities in each of the phases of the Upgrade project type in the ensuing sections.

The Analysis and Design phases

The Analysis phase builds on the discovery efforts undertaken in the Diagnostic phase with the goal to finalize the requirements (the what) and the fit gap analysis (the how), and initiate the data upgrade, while the Design phase is used to finalize and gain approval on the solution design before beginning development.

The following diagram depicts some of the key activities in the Analysis and Design phases of the Sure Step Upgrade project type.

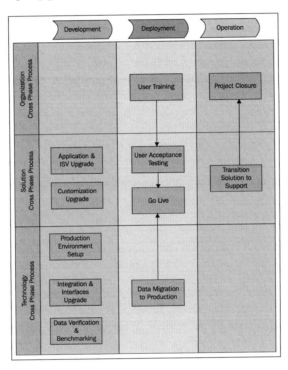

As you would expect on typical projects, the Upgrade engagement starts with a **Project Kickoff**. The objective of this activity is to ensure that the team members understand the overall objectives for the upgrade engagement, and each other's roles and responsibilities in the journey. Items such as what is the Communication Plan, who is responsible for keeping the team and the stakeholders in the know, and what will be the vehicle to achieve that, are just some of the important points to get clarified at this juncture.

This is followed by the **Solution Overview** activity, to provide an introduction of the Microsoft Dynamics solution to those on the team who were not involved in the assessment phase. This sets the stage for the key steps of finalizing the requirements and scope to move to the Design activities.

The next two activities, **Requirements Finalization** and **Fit Gap Finalization**, are very important, but they also come into question at times. The question is usually regarding why these activities are called out both in the Diagnostic phase and in the Analysis phase. Quite simply, the answer is that depending on how in-depth the discovery effort was, the work in this phase may mostly entail an affirmation of the scope. But that is a big IF! IF all the key users were involved in the Diagnostic activities, IF all the requirements were considered in the Diagnostic phase, and IF all the questions were answered and issues were resolved during the execution of the Decision Accelerator offerings. IF the answer to any of the above is no, it is important that these activities are executed and the deliverables finalized in the Analysis phase.

For the **Requirements Finalization** activity, typically a Requirements Workshop is conducted, to finalize the Functional Requirements Document (FRD). The FRD should clearly note the existing business functions and requirements that will be upgraded to the new release, and also any additional requirements (in other words, new functionality) to be delivered as part of the upgrade. The Fit Gap Finalization builds on the requirements, using the Fit Gap Worksheet to determine how these requirements will be delivered—by implementing standard features, configuration or re-configuration, workflow setup, or new/rewritten custom code. Again, depending on the effort that was carried out with the Upgrade Assessment DA, the FRD, and Final Fit Gap may be easily accomplished. But both are key documents that must be approved by the customer's business sponsor by the end of the Analysis phase.

Data Upgrade Preparation is another key activity in the Analysis phase. This activity constitutes the start of the Data Migration activities, beginning with the identification of existing data sources, including the existing Microsoft Dynamics solution, any ISV solutions, and any interface programs. Also in scope is the identification of additional data sources and how they will be accessed. Additional items for consideration include the state of the source data (amount of data cleansing required, who, how, where, and when will cleanse the data, and so on), any legal requirements for data retention, and strategies for warehousing of data external to the Microsoft Dynamics solution. Depending on the state of the source date, the team may also need to identify whether Extract Transform and Load (ETL) tools may be needed for the data cleansing and migration efforts. It should also be determined which parts of the data migration will be automated, and which, if any, require manual execution.

While the goal of the Analysis phase is to understand the requirements to establish the overall scope for the upgrade engagement, the Design phase is used to define how the technical upgrade will be implemented. Objectives include planning the steps for executing the upgrade and identifying conflicts for upgrading custom code. It also includes proactively planning for potential post-upgrade issues and reviewing the existing integration and interfaces between Microsoft Dynamics and third-party solutions to determine whether they need to be upgraded to work with the newer version of the Microsoft Dynamics solution. Accordingly, the key Design phase activities include **Data Upgrade Checklist** for planning and executing the upgrade, **Existing Code Review** to analyse and identify any conflicts created by the customizations to the existing solution, and **Existing Integrations & Interfaces Review** to determine which existing integrations and interfaces need to be upgraded. If product tools are available to support these activities, links to the corresponding tools are referenced in Sure Step. For example, Microsoft Dynamics AX provides an upgrade checklist utility with required and optional steps denoted in a sequential manner to provide guidance and assistance during the upgrade process, as well as a Compare Tool for Microsoft Dynamics AX to help determine and resolve code conflicts for the solution customizations. Since Microsoft Dynamics AX has a unique architecture where the code can be saved in different layers, (such as a USR layer for the customer users, VAR layer for the partners, and so on), the Compare tool also provides the ability to compare and detect code conflict during the upgrade one layer at a time or simultaneously in all layers.

The completion of the Design phase indicates that all the customer requirements for the solution have been analyzed and the functional and/or technical designs completed to initiate development efforts for the upgrade. A phase review at the end of each phase is recommended for any size project, but certainly for larger engagements. Besides getting agreement from the customer on the completion of the phase, it also allows the delivery team to document lessons learned, outstanding issues and risks, and mitigating actions for them.

The Development, Deployment, and Operation phases

The goal of the Development phase is to set up the application for the upgrade, which may include ISV solutions to complement the standard Microsoft Dynamics product. This phase also encompasses upgrading any customizations, integrations and interfaces, and corresponding data elements. The Deployment phase is the culmination of the upgrade delivery efforts, resulting in the transition of the customer to the new solution. The Operation phase encompasses the post go-live stabilization of the solution and transition to support.

The following diagram depicts some of the key activities in the **Development**, **Deployment**, and **Operations** phases of the Sure Step Upgrade project type.

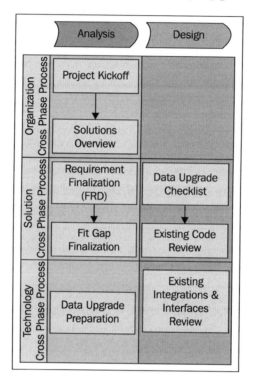

The key Development phase activities in the Upgrade project type include **Application & ISV Upgrade**, **Customization Upgrade**, **Production Environment Setup**, **Integration & Interfaces Upgrade**, and **Data Verification & Benchmarking**. Just as with the prior phases, the activities may include links to product tools or white papers where applicable, such as the Custom Coding Best Practice for Microsoft Dynamics CRM. Activities also provide templates such as Test Scripts and Environment Specification documents that can be leveraged by the delivery teams as a starting point to document their efforts.

While the Development phase represents a large percentage of the efforts of the upgrade engagement, the Deployment phase is where the efforts come to fruition. **User Training** is a key activity in this phase wherein the end users get hands-on training on the new system prior to go-live. Depending on the size of the organization, training could be executed in groups—typically, the delivery team will train the key users or a core set of users who will then act as trainers for the remaining end users.

Following the completion of user training, the organization can begin **User Acceptance Testing (UAT)**. UAT is a key validation point by the customer organization of the new solution—user acceptance of the solution indicates the customer is ready to go live with the new solution. Sure Step provides several product and industry focused UAT script templates that the delivery teams should leverage. These detailed scripts walk the user through the steps for executing a given process or functionality. In many instances, delivery teams have also leveraged the details in these scripts to develop Training guides for the previous activity. An example of one of the Test Scripts for Microsoft Dynamics NAV is shown in the following screenshot:

Once this acceptance is obtained, the last activity prior to **Go Live** is **Data Migration to Production**, wherein the cleansed data from the existing system are migrated to the new system.

After the solution going live, the project moves to the Operation phase. The key activities in this phase include **Transition Solution to Support** to transfer the solution from the delivery team to the Support team, and **Project Closure** to finalize and wrap-up the project.

Use Case of Microsoft Dynamics Upgrade by Nondurable Products Manufacturer

In this use case, we discuss how a Nondurable Consumer Products Manufacturer and Distributor approached a multisite upgrade of their Microsoft Dynamics solution.

The Manufacturer was headquartered in the US, and had multiple manufacturing and distribution agencies around the world. The organization's HQ was running an older version of Microsoft Dynamics AX, Axapta 3.0, while other manufacturing entities from acquisition were running different legacy ERP systems. The company decided to consolidate its systems to benefit from economies of scale from its IT operations, but also to enable consistent processes throughout the subsidiaries of the organization.

The company worked with a Gold-Certified Microsoft Partner and went through a thorough Upgrade Assessment and Solution Envisioning process. From the discovery process, the company realized that it was running a heavily customized version of Axapta in its HQ, which would not only make for a complex upgrade process, but was also not a sustainable solution to standardize across the multiple entities. At that point, the company decided to alter its overall solution and IT strategy. They began by reviewing the standard functionality in the newest Microsoft Dynamics AX release, Microsoft Dynamics AX 2009, and then considered replacing modifications with standard functionality wherever feasible, even if it meant changing some of their business processes. The diagnostic exercise by the joint partner consultants and customer process and technical experts led to the determination that they could replace about 40 percent of the customized functionality with standard functionality in Microsoft Dynamics AX 2009.

The organization moved forward on the solution upgrade delivery with a core objective of minimizing the customizations for business processes that were unique to each operation. Because some of the company's business processes were inherently unique, such as when dealing with government regulations for a specific product, the organization realized that while they could share best practices for a common solution, they also needed to account for the unique site requirements. Accordingly, the joint customer and partner team decided to leverage both the Upgrade and Implementation project types of the Sure Step methodology, for the development and rollout of the solution across the sites. The following diagram shows the Sure Step approach taken by the joint team.

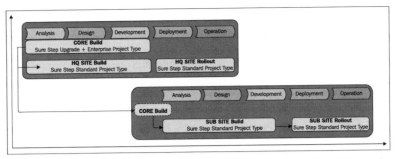

The team combined guidance and artifacts from the **Sure Step Upgrade** project type with the **Enterprise** project type to develop an approach for the rollout of a consistent solution between the headquarters and its subsidiaries. The team began with a planning session that included a group of cross-functional and cross-organization analysts from business and IT functions. They designed a core solution that accounted for the common requirements across the organization, which formed the basis for the **Core Build**. The Core Build leveraged standard functionality to the maximum extent, and included minor custom code modifications where necessary. The team also developed **Site Builds** for the HQ and the Subs, which accounted for specific requirements at that site. The corresponding Builds were then merged for the HQ and Sub **Site Rollouts**.

The joint team was able to complete the engagement within one year. The company's Vice President of Operations credited the Sure Step methodology for helping to keep the project on track. "By using the Sure Step methodology, we were confident in moving from one task to the next. Once everyone left the kickoff meeting, they needed to know exactly what to take care of. The methodology helped us to articulate exactly how we would accomplish each task." The company's IT Director also agreed saying, "This was not the first time that we've gone through an ERP implementation. But, it was certainly the best implementation that we've ever done, in terms of how smoothly the go-live went."

The combined solution provided a streamlined and consistent interface for the business users, affording them important timesaving capabilities. Greater employee productivity and gains were seen in shortened quote-to-sales order cycle, and from improved inventory turns stemming from better visibility that allowed proper reorder points to be established. The company's process experts were also enthusiastic about the reduced complexity and less burdensome processes in areas such as managing the company's pricing structure.

The solution also led to significant cost savings from an IT standpoint, in the licensing, infrastructure, and ongoing maintenance aspects. By migrating all of its business groups onto Microsoft Dynamics AX 2009, the organization eliminated its software-licensing costs for other legacy ERP systems, resulting in significant annual savings. In addition, the company substantially reduced its server infrastructure from 110 physical servers to 60 virtual servers running on just 5 physical servers. The combined solution also allowed the organization to reduce the number of developers needed to a third of their original number.

Finally, the consolidated solution and Sure Step methodology also enabled the IT department to minimize upgrade costs, which was evident when the organization decided to upgrade to Microsoft Dynamics AX 2009 Service Pack 1. The company's IT Director had this to say about the upgrade process. "Previously, it would take a large team months to roll out an upgrade. But when upgrading to Microsoft Dynamics AX 2009 Service Pack 1, we only needed to spare a few of our staff and they completed it in three weeks."

Summary

In this chapter, we learned the approaches to upgrade existing Microsoft Dynamics to the latest product release, including assessing the existing solution and executing the upgrade.

In the next chapter, we will learn about the Project and Change Management libraries in Sure Step. We will also learn about setting up projects, such as Upgrade projects, online using the SharePoint feature in Sure Step, for collaborating effectively with others in the solution delivery team.

References

Microsoft Case Studies, `http://www.microsoft.com/casestudies/`.

8
Project and Organizational Change Management

In the last four chapters, we covered due diligence and solution selling, solution delivery, optimization of the solution, and upgrade of the solution. Underpinning each of these areas are Project and Change Management disciplines, which provide the foundation for successful engagements and happy customers. These disciplines will be the focus of this chapter, as will be another important aspect — how Sure Step enables project teams to effectively collaborate with each other when they are not centrally co-located.

In this chapter, we will cover the following:

- The Project Management discipline in the Sure Step Library that provides fundamentals and guidance to project managers
- The Organizational Change Management discipline in Sure Step that stresses the importance of addressing employee viewpoints and concerns that can arise from replacing existing systems with new systems
- The Projects feature in Sure Step that facilitates automatic setup of projects on a local drive, shared drive, or on a SharePoint server

The Sure Step Project Management Library

Sure Step includes a content section that is referred to as the "Project Management Library". This section must be considered as the Project Manager's guidebook in terms of project management fundamentals. It offers an inside view of the project management discipline, the project management processes, and organizational change management. It provides knowledge and best practices and is designed to act as a constant source of inspiration for project managers seeking to improve their project management skills continuously. Compare it with the Project Management Body of Knowledge (PMBOK) by the Project Management Institute (PMI), which is the guide to many project managers providing the fundamentals of project management.

Do we, project managers, need to know about project management fundamentals? It may seem like a trivial question but it is not. Project Management is a true profession; it is not just something that you can do as a side activity. Over the years, the community of professional project managers has increased significantly indicating that a continuously growing number of professionals do understand the true essence and importance of successful project management. But despite this positive evolution, some people still seem to ignore this and continue to manage their projects while neglecting best practices. For those who do recognize project management as a true profession and seek to improve their skills, and are eager to learn new things and find inspiration to take their project management knowledge to higher levels, the project management library is an excellent knowledge hub.

The Enterprise Project Type in Sure Step is fully aligned with the processes, activities, tools, and templates that are discussed in the different disciplines of this project management library. Other project types in Sure Step only include a subset of what is described in the disciplines and how you leverage your project management approach with each of these disciplines is subject to your envisioning of Quality Assurance for the specific project.

The Project Management disciplines

Ever wondered what a project manager needs to do? It just takes one click in the Sure Step Project Management Library to get a bird's-eye view on what a project manager really needs to manage. The Project Management discipline unveils nine management domains associated with a project manager's responsibilities:

- Risk Management
- Scope Management
- Issue Management
- Time and Cost Management
- Resource Management
- Communication Management
- Quality Management
- Procurement Management
- Sales Management

So, a project manager needs to manage all these domains in a context that is always unique and temporary. Projects are never the same and we always run short on time, but still we must manage all these disciplines. Quite an arduous task! In an operation-driven company, each of these management domains is controlled by dedicated managers whereas our project manager needs to combine the skills and knowledge of them all, so all best practices and guidance will be more than welcome. That's exactly why Sure Step provides all the fundamentals of the project management disciplines in the project management library.

Risk Management

The Risk Management discipline teaches us fundamentals about initial and ongoing risk management. Here we can seek guidance on how to deal with risk identification, risk analysis, and how we can set up an effective risk response planning. Apart from valuable guidance, we can also find valuable tools that will help us become much more efficient in risk management exercises, like:

- A Project Risk Register
- A Risk Identification Checklist
- A Risk Management Planning spreadsheet

In the Project Risk Register, we can list, describe, and categorize our identified risks and generate a risk rating based on our probability and impact estimation. It also allows us to plan for contingency and responses. What is really interesting is that this risk register template also includes a checklist tab that is already populated with known risks for Dynamics implementations. The following screenshot illustrates prefilled content in the checklist tab of the risk register:

Risk Checklist

ID	Risk Category	Risk Description and Consequence (if/then)	Phase when risk typically occurs	Trigger Event Indicator	Risk Response Plan	Risk Contingency Plan
	Functional	Users don't understand (or can't describe) their own business processes or requirements	Analysis		Use diagramming tools to create visual representations of business processes.	
	Functional	Users have difficulty "bridging the gap" between Business Processes & Business system. As a result we cannot accurately define requirements	Analysis		• Select "Super User" who: • Understands the business processes • Has enough technical competence to assist in bridging the gap • Send Super User(s) to training immediately after the requirements are complete. • Develop effective trainers and training materials.	
	Functional	Consultants do not know the customer's business	Analysis		• Build in extra time in the Concept engagement for the Consultant to learn the industry (review web, study customer documentation, read other industry material). • Work with an extended consultant team.	
	Functional	Incomplete or inaccurate Analysis (for whatever reason)	Design		• Use structured tool to get requirements. • Hold a requirements review session • Conduct independent quality review activities	
	Functional	Customer does not have skills to adequately test.	Development		• Train key users right just the concept is agreed upon. • Make testing an easy process • Provide on-site consulting support	
	Functional	Consultant Team experience with this type of business				
	Functional	Availability of appropriate experienced people from Consultant				

This checklist with populated risks can act as an efficient starting point for a project manager's risk assessment. The Risk Identification Checklist is a questionnaire that is built up around environmental, people, process, and technology risk factors and acts as an efficient tool for risk identification. The following diagram shows some of the questions around the process risk factors:

3. Process Factors (Part C)

ID	Factor	Risk Cue	Evaluation (✓/✗)	Does it lead to a RISK Yes/No
C1	**MISSION AND GOALS**			
a	Fit to customer	The project is poorly aligned with the customer's strategy and goals?		
b	Fit to provider	The project is mismatched to Partner's capabilities and objectives		
c	Customer perception	The solution is poorly matched to prior services provided to the customer by Partner		
d	Work Flow	The solution introduces significant changes to the customer's workflow		
e	Program goals	The goals of the overall program are ill-defined or carry conflicting objectives		
f	Program conflicts	This project's goals conflict with those of other projects in the program		
C2	**DECISION DRIVERS**			
a	Political influences	Decisions are subject to political influences or made behind closed doors		
b	Convenient date	The project schedule is driven by an externally-dictated date not based on project team estimates		
c	Attractive technology	The solution is designed to showcase new technology or an excuse to bring new technology into the organization		
d	Short-term focus	The team been directed to ignore the longer-term outlook and focus on short-term deliverables		

Scope Management

Are you familiar with scope creep? Bet you are! Can we prevent scope creep in our projects? No, we can't, but we can manage it better. Well thought-out scope management elevates our success probability of customer satisfaction and acceptance of the implemented solution. The Scope Management discipline provides insights on how the project team needs to plan, define, document, verify, manage, and control project scope. This guidance is highlighted in the project management processes, as illustrated in the following diagram.

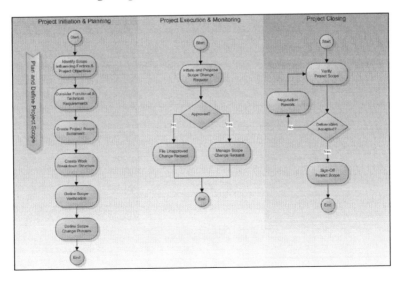

In this section, we can find specific information on how to make work breakdown structures for our product scope, what elements we need to include in a good scope statement, and much more.

Besides offering a helpful insight into scope management fundamentals, Sure Step also provides tools and templates to help us be more efficient. One of these tools is the **Change Request Form**, available in two versions as demonstrated in the following screenshot.

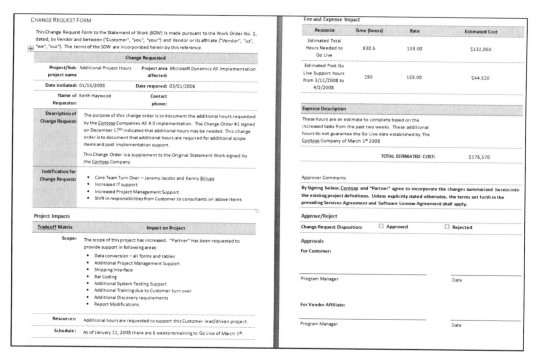

This first Change Request Form brings our attention to the trade-off matrix. Change requests mostly seem to only address the cost impact to the customer. However, change impacts more than budget; it can have an impact on the complexity of the scope, the deployment of skills and resources, and on the schedule. We need to investigate these other impact elements as well and monitor how a set of changes might impact us. The image below shows the table of contents of a second Change Request template that can be found in Sure Step:

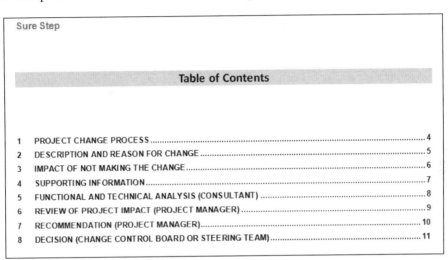

This template allows a more detailed description of the change and the trade-off analysis than in the previous template. So we might consider this one when facing larger changes with significant impact that needs extensive and in-depth documentation. This template also teaches us that it is a good idea not only to investigate all impact of making the change but that analyzing the impact of not making the change is equally valuable. A customer organization needs to be aware that in the course of an implementation visions and ideas might alter leading to changed and additional requirements but that it is not always to their benefit to implement them all. Some request might not have a significant impact on the efficiency of the company or the goals and objectives of the decision maker while representing a vast impact on the project and its risks. Analyzing the impact of not implementing those changes reduces potential risks and the scope creep in general.

Issue Management

While a risk has the potential to impact a project but is not yet substantiated, an issue is actual and impacting our project. Issues can arise any time after starting the project. Examples of issues are:

- Customer resources are not available
- Infrastructure is not in place
- Software license is not available
- Stakeholders change their opinion about the project
- Quality problems with the custom developed code

The project management needs to be proactive in managing issues rather than reactive. A solid issue management is a must-have in any project. Unaddressed issues are like snowballs; when they come rolling down the mountain, they can only become bigger. That is why we need to have a formal issue management in place that can make issues visible to the appropriate team members and stakeholders and to get the required support and resolutions. The Sure Step Issue Management discipline suggests a process of managing issues that includes the following steps:

- Identify the issue
- Document the issue
- List the issue
- Analyze the issue
- Determine the priority of the issue
- Plan and communicate activities
- Update project planning
- Assign Resources
- Follow up on the issue
- Proof and communicate the resolution of the issue
- Close the issue

The following screenshot shows the Issue Entry Form supporting this process:

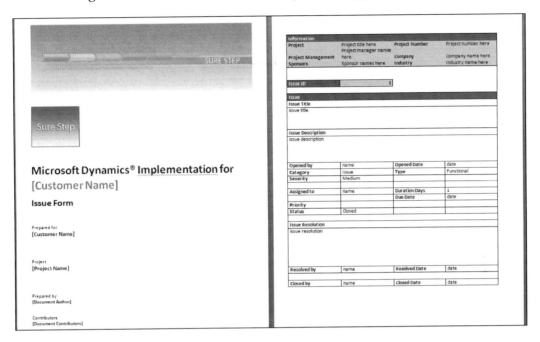

The overview of all the identified issues can be managed from the Issue List as shown in the following screenshot:

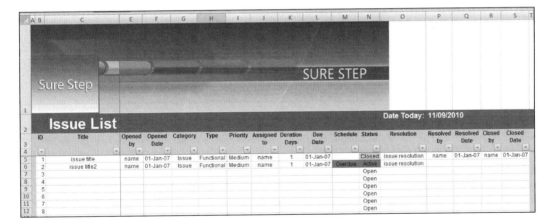

Time and Cost Management

In this discipline, Sure Step provides guidance and techniques to set up and manage initial and ongoing time and cost management. Any manager engaged in a project will and must be concerned about the time and budget constraints of the assignment. In a way they will all manage it, even without having a clue about the fundamentals and best practices described for this discipline. This activity is omnipresent and some even (unjustly) narrow down project management to time and cost management. So yes, it is important and the more we improve our skills to manage time and cost the more possibilities we will have to control our time and cost performance.

The first lesson to learn is that the initial time and cost management must be in line with the ongoing time and cost management. A common basis is needed for both the initial and ongoing time and cost management; this is where the Work Breakdown Structure (WBS) comes in. The WBS defines all deliverables and activities necessary to deliver the requested value to the customer. It is the basis for estimation and follow-up in our project and allows the setup of a common language amongst project stakeholders. If the breakdown of our deliverables in the beginning differs significantly from the follow-up breakdown in the ongoing project we might expect problems as we will have a difficult job aligning time and cost performance with the performance we had planned for. A simple search instruction in the Sure Step content reveals how important the WBS is. Searching on WBS generates over 30 Sure Step activities as a result as shown in the following screenshot:

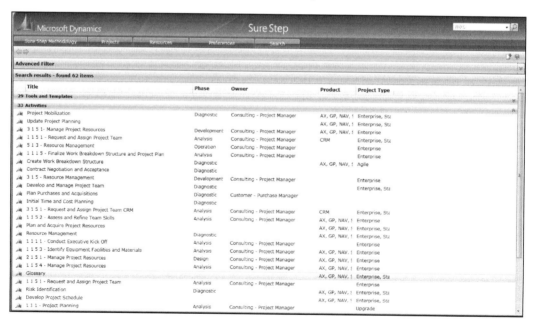

This discipline will also provide information on the estimation process. Estimation is generally accepted as a true challenge. At moments characterized by great uncertainty, we need to estimate cost and time durations. It would be great if we could produce estimates at times where all scope and risks were certain but unfortunately we are not granted that privilege and so we need to rely on our estimation efficiency. A good estimate is really important for both the consulting and the customer organization, making a good estimation process in place a sine qua non. This Sure Step discipline introduces the reader to generally accepted estimation techniques like the use of consulting experts, estimates from similar projects, parametric estimating, bottom-up and top-down estimating. It also gives attention to the challenges of estimating in an Agile context and provides solid tips like the use of three-point analysis and the involvement of the customer in the estimation process.

We can also find guidance in this discipline on how to develop a project schedule and how to prepare project tracking and reporting. Sure Step highlights the importance of structured and well-documented estimation and tracking techniques. Not only do we benefit from these techniques in a single project but as historic reference they will also have great value for future estimates. We might also get inspired by the content that is provided on the "Earned Value Concept", a method that integrates project scope, cost, and schedule in order to generate early warning signals by project tracking. This method identifies what we have delivered for what we have spent and calculates how much more time and cost we will need when progressing with the same performance.

Resource Management

The Resource Management discipline addresses how to organize and manage human resources, equipment, and material resources in the project context. For human resource planning, it is important to distinguish between roles and resources. Project Roles are the functional job categories or titles required to complete the project work. Examples are Technology Consultant, Development Consultant, or Business Analyst. Resources are specific groups or individuals who complete the project work. One resource might execute more than one role. Roles and responsibilities are often described using a Resource Assignment Matrix (RAM). A specific form of a RAM is the RACI Matrix. The RACI matrix assigns responsibilities to each role in terms of the following:

- **Responsible**: Those who do the work to achieve the task. This role is delivering effort and skill to complete the job.
- **Accountable**: Those who are ultimately accountable for the correct and thorough completion of the deliverable or task. The Responsible role will be reporting to the Accountable role.

- **Consultative**: The roles that provide both active and advisory assistance.
- **Informed**: Those who are kept up-to-date on progress by reporting on the task.

Sure Step uses an extended version of the RACI matrix, providing two additional roles:

- **Verifying**: Those roles that are executing a check against the defined scope and conditions of quality standards.
- **Signing off**: Those entrusted with the actions of review, validation, and acceptance.

The following screenshot is an example of how we can map responsibilities against roles by using an RACI matrix:

Task	Project Manager	Customer Project Manager	Solution Architect	Application Consultant	Technology Consultant	Sprint Cycle Manager	Build Manager	Development Consultant	IT Manager	BDM	Key User
Define Project Roles	A	R	C	I	I	I	I	I	C	I	I
Assign Resources to Project	A	R	I	I	I	I	I	I	I	I	I
Assign Work Package to Resource	A	A	I	I	I	R	I	I	-	-	I
Estimate Task	A	V	R	C	C	A	C	C	V	S	-
Schedule Task	A	V	I	I	I	R	C	I	V	S	I

This discipline also covers how to develop, manage, and release the project team and is supported by useful tools and templates like the "Roles and Responsibilities" template as shown in the following screenshot:

Roles and Responsibilities

	Consulting Organization												Customer Organization																													
R = Responsible / A = Accountable / C = Consultative / I = Informed / V = Verifies / S = Sign-Off	Executive Sponsor	Engagement Manager	Project Manager	Solution Architect	Business Analyst	Application Consultant	Technical Consultant	Development Consultant	Sales Representative	Account Manager	Technical Sales Specialist	Support Engineer	Executive Sponsor	Business Decision Maker	Project Manager	Purchase Manager	IT Team Member	Key User	End User	Customer Service	Accounting Manager	AP Coordinator	AR Coordinator	Customer Service Manager	Human Resource Manager	IT Manager	Materials Manager	Product Designer	Production Planner	Production Scheduler	Buyer	Sales and Marketing	Warehouse Manager	Quality Manager	Shipping and Receiving	Administration	Compliance Manager	Treasurer	Production Manager	Publications Manager	Payroll Manager	FDA Validation Manager	Purchase Manager
Diagnostic																																											
Diagnostic plan	A	R	C				I	I		A			I	V			I																										
High level business process analysis																																											
Gap/Fit analysis																																											
High level infrastructure analysis																																											
Analysis																																											
Training plan																																											
Data migration plan																																											
Data migration analysis																																											
Detailed business process analysis																																											
Detailed Gap/Fit analysis																																											
Detailed infrastructure analysis																																											
Functional Requirements Document																																											
Design																																											
Business process design																																											
Data migration specification																																											

Communication Management

An important theme in Sure Step is the importance of communication. As we unveiled in previous sections and chapters, the Sure Step lifecycle is planned with a lot of attention for interactions enabling communication between customer and implementer's resources. On top of that, the project management library dedicates a full discipline to the art of project communication. This discipline discusses how to conduct team meetings like the steering team meeting, project management meetings, and project team meetings. This discipline also informs us on how to execute project performance reporting and how to manage our stakeholders. We can also learn from this discipline how a good "Project Charter" should be made and how we can conduct effective kick-off meetings. This discipline is supported by templates like:

- Project Status Report
- Communication Plan
- Kick Off meeting presentation and meeting agenda
- Project Charter

It also points out that the success or failure of a project is determined by stakeholders and not by the Project Managers and therefore demands our attention for project stakeholders' analysis.

Quality Management

The Quality Management discipline tackles the question of how to assure, control, and improve the quality up to the required and balanced level. Quality Assurance (QA) can be considered as the plan we have to meet the project's requirements and quality standards. It is often defined as the planned and systematic activities implemented in a quality system so that quality requirements for a product or service will be fulfilled. In a way, implementing guided by Sure Step processes can be considered as an element of QA. However, this is not enough as we have to tune our planned approach with the specific quality expectations and demands of our customer. That means that first we need to understand what quality means to our customer and only then can we further refine our proactive quality approach. Quality Assurance is about the processes we have in place to deliver what we are asked for. Quality Assurance is not focusing on the deliverables themselves but on how we plan to deliver them. **Quality Control (QC)** activities are focused on the deliverables and are concerned with the acceptance of those project deliverables. Now let's assume that you are a customer project manager entrusted with the sign-off of the Functional Requirements Document for your implementation. Before signing off, you could inspect each page of this document for the correctness, accuracy, and consistency with your future business processes and demands. This would be an example of Quality Control. You could also verify the process on how this document was created. By doing so you would retrieve information about the workshops that were organized, the people that attended, how your key users validated this information, that it was double checked by a Fit Gap assessment and so on. This is an example of Quality Assurance with focus on the process of document creation. The following image illustrates how Sure Step integrates QA and QC in the project management processes.

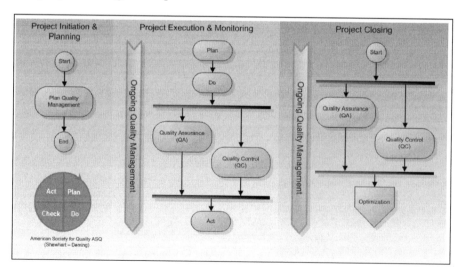

Procurement Management

This discipline discusses how to manage purchases and acquisitions of services and deliverables from outside the project team to fulfill the defined project requirements. Subcontracting can involve certain project risks, but it provides also the possibility to avoid, mitigate, or transfer risks. Important inputs and outputs for Procurement Management are to consider and define constraints, assumptions, and boundaries. This discipline explains how to do this by covering the planning, monitoring, and closing of subcontracting.

Sales Management

The Sales Management discipline provides more descriptive context on how to plan the diagnostic phase and who to engage in this process. It also informs about proposal management with sections explaining the selection of the project and contract type. Contract types like Time and Material (T&M), Time and Material Capped, and Fixed Price are discussed and set out against crucial project elements like uncertainty and the assessment of the gap between what the customer wants and what the standard Dynamics solution supports. This discipline also brings us good tips for the creation of our contract like:

- A good starting point for creating the contract is the work breakdown structure (WBS)
- Be specific by quantifying and limiting
- Clearly state assumptions in regards to the estimates
- It is not necessary to know everything; take a position and state an assumption
- Use all information gathered during scoping, quality planning, and risk analysis
- Process for sign-off and acceptance of deliverables can be part of contracting

This discipline also examines contract negotiation and lists the important steps and challenges for contract closing.

In the above sections, we focused on the Project Management sub-disciplines in the Sure Step Project Management Library. We now turn our focus to the Organizational Change Management discipline in the library.

Organizational Change Management

Organization Change Management (OCM) is a discipline that provides a structured approach to transitioning individuals, teams, and organizations from a current state to a desired future state while minimizing resistance and maximizing adoption.

OCM is a critical, and sometimes overlooked, aspect for the success of business solutions delivery engagements. As discussed on several occasions in this book, business solutions encompass multiple processes and workflows of an organization, and any changes to these systems can affect the daily operations of many individuals and their behavior. In smaller organizations, where the CEO or President is often the driving force behind a project of this magnitude, companies get away with pretty much brute force or pressure from the top to "adopt or else". But the larger the organization, and the larger the scope and impact of the project, the more critical it is for project teams to consider OCM as an integral part of the delivery activities. This will ensure obstacles to adoption are removed in a timely manner, and employee buy-in is an integral part of the solution deployment approach.

In their article titled *The Business Impact of Change Management*, the authors have brought together multiple research studies to understand the impact and importance of OCM on projects. They explain that the purpose of OCM "is to mitigate the risks of a project, including costs, scheduling, and performance," which OCM achieves by "facilitating greater economic value faster by effectively developing, deploying, and aligning the company's assets for a given project."

The article references a McKinsey study that examined many project variables and in particular, the effect of an OCM program on a project's ROI. The results were striking! Projects that included good OCM programs resulted in a 143% Return on Investment (ROI), meaning that companies gained 43 cents for every dollar they spent on the project. On the other hand, projects with no or poor OCM programs included produced a 35% ROI, meaning that companies *lost* 65 cents for every dollar they spent.

Another study entitled *Six Barriers to CRM Project Success* was highlighted by the authors, citing the reasons for failure of CRM projects:

- Lack of guidance
- Integration woes
- No long-term strategy
- Dirty data
- Lack of employee buy-in
- No accountability

The authors also describe a study by ProSci, a recognized leader in change management research. To efficiently and effectively manage the changes that a project produces in an organization, the organization needs the following:

- Effective and strong executive sponsorship
- Buy-in from front-line managers and employees
- Exceptional teams
- Continuous and targeted communication
- Planned and organized approach

As a process, the goal of OCM is to empower the employees to accept and embrace changes in their current business environment. Jeff Hiatt is the author of the *Employee's Survival Guide to Change*, and he talks about how it is easy and fascinating to talk about change happening to someone else, but how worrisome and uncomfortable an individual becomes when a change happens in their environment. Hiatt describes the field of change management as "the convergence of two fields of thought…an engineer's approach to improving business performance and a psychologist's approach to managing the human side of change."

In the book titled *Integrating People with Process and Technology*, Jon Anton and others look into how the organization's acquisition of technology does not necessarily translate into usage by its people. The following is a telling observation from the authors. "The truth about technology implementations is that although technology does what the vendor promised, ROI issues arise when change management is not figured in as part of the overall technology project budget. In cases where technology implementations include change management, the implementation becomes an exhilarating experience that improves the efficiency and effectiveness of the company." For a successful solution deployment, the authors' recommendation is that the company should "integrate their people, process and technology… in such a way that changes are embraced and viewed as good." They define a "good" change as one where the technology "makes it easier for employees to do their job and to be more efficient, makes it more operationally effective for employees serving their customers, and allows the company's products and services to be easily accessible."

These discussions underscore the importance of managing the people side of the change management equation for the success of the project. At the end of the day, it is the system users who ultimately define the success or failure of the solution. Without user buy-in, it doesn't matter how good the solution is if the users don't see the need to use it. As such, it is very important that users are closely involved during the implementation, and any concerns are heard and considered. It is also not uncommon for companies to conduct change workshops to convey the importance of being open-minded about the upcoming change.

One of the more popular books on the subject of people and change is *Who Moved My Cheese?* by Spencer Johnson. Written as a parable featuring two mice and two little people, the story provides an amusing view of how one of the characters is able to navigate the maze and find the cheese, while the other struggles due to his reluctance to change. The story can be related to a corporate setting in which the "maze" is the organization that the employee works in, while the "cheese" is the end goal that the organization is trying to achieve. The enlightening story has helped many employees deal with the inevitable change, and has also been used as a guide for change workshops.

So far, we have discussed the general concepts of OCM. In the next section, we look at how Sure Step enables and supports the notion of organizational change during the course of the implementations.

Organizational Change Management in Sure Step

Organizational Change Management (OCM) is described in Sure Step as an integrated communications, training, sponsorship, and organization alignment approach to assist employees in transitioning effectively into a new way of accomplishing work. The Sure Step approach depicts the strategies for success in four critical Organization Change Management areas—a review of the previous section shows that these strategies are very well aligned to the approaches of the change management research analysts.

- **Executive and Stakeholder Engagement**: This strategy requires business sponsor ownership and accountability for the envisioned solution by calling on the organization's business unit leaders to create an environment where process changes resulting from ERP/CRM solutions are accepted and owned. The strategy includes open communication, setting appropriate expectations, assisting in resolving critical project issues in a timely manner, and providing appropriate levels of reinforcement to ensure project success.

- **Organization Alignment and Mobilization**: For this strategy to succeed, the delivery team needs to analyze the workforce impact and transition to the future processes with the current business practices as the baseline. The appropriate business stakeholders will need to be actively engaged to understand the solution capabilities and to assess the solution effectiveness for their respective areas.

- **Communications**: This key success area focuses on communicating solution design, implementation timing and progress, involvement required by the stakeholders, and acceptance of new methods of work. Communications include getting the right information delivered at the right time in a suitable format and through an appropriate means, as well as feedback and response strategies via periodic surveys and iterative lessons-learned discussions.

- **Training**: This strategy focuses on ensuring that end users are comfortable with the new business processes, have the required skill set to work within the designed processes, and have been well trained on the use of the application. The strategy encompasses initial and ongoing user training for successful adoption of the new processes and tools.

Sure Step guidance for OCM is aligned along five pillars, as shown in the following diagram:

Each of these pillars is described in the following sections. The guidance provided within the OCM discipline is broken down into activities, as shown in the following screenshot:

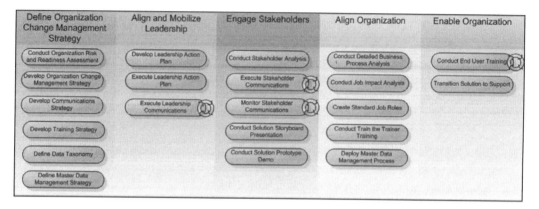

It also bears mention that these activities are in turn integrated with the Sure Step project types, meaning that they are called out as prescribed steps within the corresponding project workflow.

Define OCM Strategy

The OCM Strategy defines the overall vision, objectives, and activities for the various change management components of the project or program, to ensure successful adoption of the solution. The sub-components of OCM strategy include:

- **Organization Risk and Readiness Assessment**: Assesses the readiness of the organization to undertake a project of this magnitude, understand the risks that may exist, and define the mitigating strategies to overcome the barriers to project success.

- **Organization Change Management strategy**: Defines the nature and sequence of specific change management activities, resources, and interdependencies required to facilitate the change process.

- **Communications strategy**: Defines the content, method, and timing of the messaging and communications to align management, stakeholders, and business units.

- **Training strategy**: Defines the training audience and the approach that will be used to assimilate the new processes and solution to the user groups.

- **Data taxonomy**: Defines the data entities that will be required, as well as any optional data elements.

- **Master Data management strategy**: Defines the overall strategy and processes to manage and maintain Master Data once the solution is in production.

As mentioned earlier, the activities in the OCM Discipline section of Sure Step are also called out in the Sure Step project types, especially the Enterprise project type. For example, "Conduct Organization Risk and Readiness Assessment" is an activity under the Program Management cross phase of the Enterprise project type. The project activities also include excellent tools and templates, such as the Organization Risk Readiness Analysis Tool, a screenshot of which is shown next:

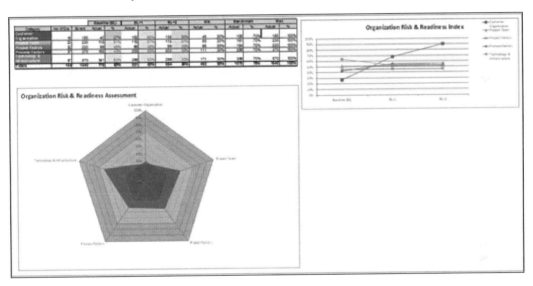

Align and mobilize leadership

With the strategy components defined, the overall change management action plan is created for the business executives and sponsors in this sub-discipline.

- **Leadership action plan**: Drives the change strategy by defining the communications from all levels, including executives and middle managers, to the stakeholders, those most impacted by the new solution. The plan should include regular checkpoints to audit the performance, and necessary course corrections should be made as needed.

- **Leadership communications**: Ensures that the project business executives and sponsors communicate periodically with the stakeholders over the course of the project.

For the Leadership Communication activity, Sure Step includes a ready-to-use Outlook e-mail template that can be shaped to suit the organization's messaging style. A screenshot of the template is shown next:

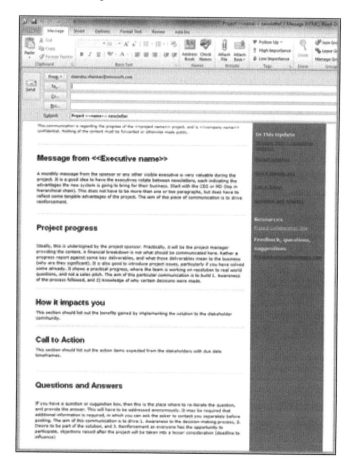

Engage stakeholders

The purpose of this OCM sub-discipline is to ensure that the project stakeholders are identified and are proactively engaged throughout the project lifecycle.

- **Stakeholder communications**: Encompasses crafting appropriate communications to stakeholders from leadership and the project teams, obtaining feedback, and creating action plans where necessary to address any issues that are raised.

- **Solution storyboard presentation**: Involves presenting the solution storyboard to the stakeholders prior to design completion in order to obtain proactive feedback and buy-in on the solution.

- **Solution prototype demo**: Involves demonstrating the configured solution to the stakeholders during solution development in order to obtain proactive feedback on the usability of the solution.

Similar to the previous sub-disciplines, these activities are aligned to the Sure Step project type activities, with templates included for communications, to create storyboards, and so on.

Align organization

The key goal of this OCM sub-discipline is to ensure that the stakeholders are adequately prepared to adopt the new solution. This is achieved by implementing the solution as envisioned for the future processes, defining roles and responsibilities, and preparing and executing training for the organization.

- **Future state business process models**: Future-state business processes based on the new solution are developed, which in turn provide the baseline to train and align the stakeholders to adopt the new solution.
- **Job impact analysis**: A key step to ensure that stakeholders have the information necessary to understand the impact of the project initiative on their job performance, job description, and career path.
- **Roles and responsibilities**: Builds on the job impact analysis to define the new or modified roles and responsibilities resulting from the new solution.
- **Train-the-trainer training**: Ensures that the organization's trainers are adept with the new solution and prepared to train the end users.
- **Master Data management process**: Ensures that the Master Data management processes are implemented by the data owners and that appropriate ownership and accountability for the data is established.

As referenced in previous chapters, Sure Step affords a vast library of Process Models that can be leveraged to develop the future state business process flows. Other templates such as a Job Impact Analysis spreadsheet are also included within the associated project type activities.

Enable organization

This sub-discipline ensures that the new solution is deployed, users are trained, and appropriate support processes are made operational.

- **End user training**: Ensures that adequate and ongoing training to the end users on the new solution is provided to facilitate user adoption.

- **Transition solution to support**: The appropriate support organization is engaged, and the solution handed over to the team that will provide ongoing support.

- **Master Data management process handover**: Ensures that the data management processes are handed over to the data owners so that the data integrity and accuracy can be maintained in the new solution.

The management of data is sometimes confusing to the user as to why that belongs under organizational change management. In ERP/CRM solution deployments, there is an old adage often used by consultants, "Garbage in, garbage out." As harsh as that sounds, as good as the new solution may be, if the data provided is still bad, it will only result in the solution users getting bad information faster. Managing the data elements is therefore an important change component that can impact the stakeholders.

In the above sections, we introduced the concepts of OCM, and also covered OCM from a Sure Step perspective. As we learned, OCM is a critical discipline that should not be overlooked during solution delivery. Given the investment that companies make in the solution, including OCM experts to guide the organization to successfully adopt the new solution should be a given.

The Sure Step "Projects" feature

In Chapters 4 through 7, we covered the five waterfall and agile Sure Step project types, including the templates that are provided for the project activities. Those templates include some of the project and change management templates we discussed in the above sections. In this section, we now turn our attention to initiating a project with the appropriate cross-section of these templates pre-populated depending on the user's selection.

Sure Step provides a feature called "Projects" for easy setup of project templates and efficient collaboration with project team members. This feature can be found under the second tab of the Sure Step application, and is appropriately titled, **Projects**, as shown in the following screenshot:

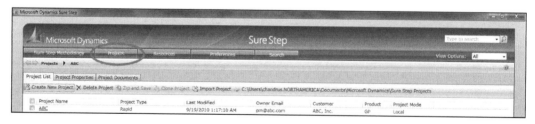

As a point of reference, the guidance, templates, and tools that we have referred up to this point reside under the first tab, labeled **Sure Step Methodology**, in the previous screenshot of the Sure Step application.

Creating projects using the Project Creation Wizard

The Sure Step Projects feature can be executed to initiate projects on a local drive (or a shared drive), or on a SharePoint server. The process for initiating these projects is described next.

For creating projects, Sure Step provides an intuitive "Project Creation Wizard" that walks the user through the setup. The following screenshot shows one of the screens on the Wizard.

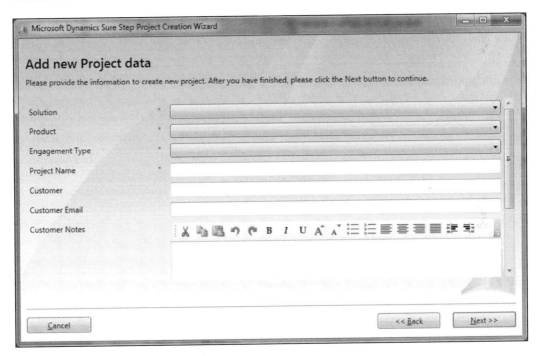

If the project is for a customer in a specific industry such as Process or Public Sector, or if the solution is a cross-industry solution such as XRM, the **Solution** dropdown provides those choices. Selecting one of those choices will then associate the corresponding templates in the project that is created. On the other hand, if the customer project is not for one of these industry or cross-industry solutions, a "General" solution value is provided, which attaches templates associated with the standard products.

The **Product** dropdown is where you select the appropriate Microsoft Dynamics product that the project is based on. The Wizard narrows down the choices depending on the solution selected — meaning if, for example, you select Public Sector, only CRM is provided as the product value because Sure Step only provides CRM solution guidance for Public Sector at this point. At a future point, when additional product coverage for a given industry is provided, the solution filter will provide the corresponding product values.

The **Engagement Type** dropdown provides multiple selections for the three different types of engagements supported by Sure Step.

- If the engagement is related to pre-sales/due diligence, the user selects Diagnostic Phase Offerings, which are the Decision Accelerator Offerings we described in the previous chapters. For this selection, the Wizard will then allow the user to select multiple Decision Accelerator Offerings, to support customer scenarios that call for the service provider to combine more than one offering in the due diligence process.

- If the engagement is for solution delivery, the user selects Implementation. In the next selection, the user is then asked to select one of the four waterfall project types, or the agile project type, as the basis for the implementation.

- If the engagement is for optimization or review, the user selects Optimization Offerings. Just like the Diagnostic Phase Offerings, the Optimization Offerings selection then allows the user to select multiple optimization or review offerings.

The wizard also provides a selection of whether the project should be created on a local drive or on a SharePoint server.

Creating projects on a local drive

The use case for creating projects on a local drive is typically limited to smaller projects with a limited number of resources on the implementation team. In these cases, projects are typically set up and reside on the consultant's personal computer, and the deliverables are shared with the customer at appropriate times. Sure Step does, however, allow the user to change the default drive from "C:\" to a shared drive, allowing for more resources to work on the same project. Other collaboration options such as exporting and importing these projects are also available in Sure Step.

Two screenshots of a project initiated for a general implementation of Microsoft Dynamics AX using the Standard project type are shown next:

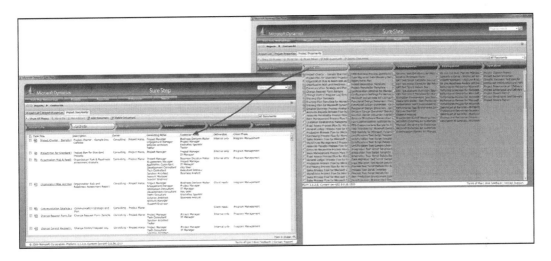

Also shown in the screenshots is an alternate view of the documents—when the user clicks on a particular phase, such as the Analysis phase in this example, the view changes to a more detailed one that displays the document **Description**, the **Owner** role for this deliverable, and the participant **Consulting Roles** and **Customer Roles**.

Creating projects on a SharePoint server

The more popular use case for the Projects feature is to initiate a project on a SharePoint server. At the end of the project setup process, the Project Creation Wizard provides the user with an option of selecting *SharePoint-based project*. Upon specification of the corresponding URL for the SharePoint site, Sure Step will run through a check to ensure that the user has the appropriate privileges to create the site, and following a positive return, automatically populate the corresponding Sure Step templates to the site. The following screenshots show the steps in this process.

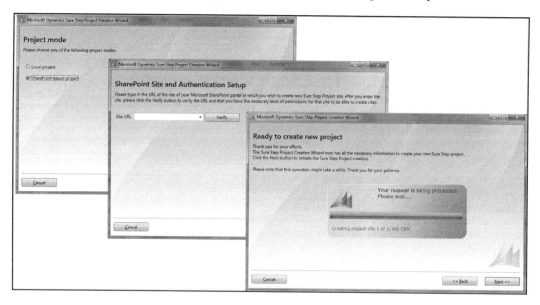

An example of the resultant SharePoint site is shown next. This example is of a SharePoint site created for a CRM project using the Enterprise project type.

Customizing Sure Step templates using the Projects Feature

The Sure Step Projects feature also provides a number of other useful options for the users. The "Change Logo" feature is a prime example of that.

The Sure Step templates come pre-populated with a Sure Step logo, which is also metadata-controlled. The metadata allows the users to make a universal change of the logo across all the documents in one quick step, using the "Change Logo" feature under Project Properties. The "Change Logo" feature supports a number of use cases, such as replacing the Sure Step logo with the customer's logo for a given project, or changing the logo to the service provider's logo to create a custom set of templates for their own organization.

The last point is an especially key one for service providers. The Projects feature allows for the saving, importing, and cloning of an existing project, thus facilitating the creation of project folders by industry, engagement size, engagement approach, and so on. Accordingly, the service provider may decide to create a set of project documents that, for example, their consulting teams would leverage as the starting point for all Automotive Manufacturing customers using Microsoft Dynamics AX Standard project type templates. Or they may create another folder for small, out-of-box deployments of Microsoft Dynamics SL using the Rapid project type. Or they may have another project folder for their CRM customers who prefer the Agile approach. Each of these templates could be pre-populated with the organization's logo, and key learning gleaned from past engagements.

Sure Step refers to this as the "60-20-20" rule, meaning that Sure Step provides the starting 60% of the templates, which the service provider then customizes and adds their 20% based on their expertise in a given area, and in the last 20% the consulting team transforms the templates into deliverables specific to the customer's environment.

Summary

In this chapter, we covered the Sure Step Project Management Library, which includes the Project Management and Organizational Change Management disciplines. We also discussed the Projects feature in Sure Step that allows for easy setup of project templates and enables efficient collaboration with other team members.

In the next chapter, we discuss the adoption of Sure Step methodology from both a service provider's and an Independent Software Vendor's perspectives. We talk about the Sure Step Adoption Roadmap, and how that can help the organizations adopt the methodology as their own.

References

Anton, Jon, Petouhoff, Natalie L., Schwartz, Lisa M. (2003). *Integrating People with Process and Technology*. Santa Maria, CA: Anton Press.

Hiatt, Jeffrey M. (2004). *Employee's Survival Guide to Change*. Learning Center Publications (ISBN 1-930885-20-2).

Johnson, Spencer, Blanchard, Kenneth (2002). *Who Moved My Cheese?* New York, NY: G.P. Putnam's Sons.

Petouhoff, Natalie L., Chandler, Tamra, Montag-Schultz, Beth (2006). The Business Impact of Change Management. *Graziado Business Report*, Volume 09, Issue 3: Graziado School of Business and Management at Pepperdine University.

9

A Practical Guide to Sure Step Adoption

In the previous chapters, we discussed the various features of Sure Step, including due diligence and solution selling enablement, approaches for high quality solution implementation and upgrade, options for review and optimization, and the project and change management disciplines. We now shift our focus to another important area—how an organization can adopt the Sure Step methodology and use it to consistently deliver solutions to its customers.

In this chapter, we will cover:

- Strategy development and execution for adopting Sure Step, including managing change within the organization
- The Sure Step Adoption Program, and the resources available to the partner organizations
- How Independent Software Vendors (ISVs) can benefit from adopting Sure Step

Don't park your brain outside

Both Microsoft Dynamics partners and customers have easy access to the Sure Step application via PartnerSource and CustomerSource respectively. From these Microsoft portals, Sure Step can easily be downloaded and installed, unleashing all the Sure Step content and tools in minutes. Project managers and consultants can also make themselves familiar with and knowledgeable about Sure Step through Microsoft Official Courseware (MOC), Microsoft Online learning, and Learning Snacks and Instructor Led Training (ILT) courses provided by Microsoft Certified Partners for Learning Solutions (CPLS). This means with a modest time investment, organizations can obtain the Sure Step Methodology tools, content, and knowledge. So then, is putting your organization on the Sure Step tracks is easy as pie? As many of us know, that couldn't be further from the truth. Any organization, looking to adapt their processes to adopt a new implementation methodology, is bound to face a certain set of challenges. To succeed, they will need an effective strategy, which they must execute properly while managing the organization change, and these are not exactly small matters!

Strategy execution

Plans are only good intentions unless they immediately degenerate into hard work.
    – Peter Drucker

Strategy execution is not the same as strategy building, but they need to go hand in hand. Strategy execution can be defined as *all the actions necessary to turn your strategy into success*. A great strategy cannot compensate for a poor execution, and vice versa. In his book, *Strategy Execution Heroes*, Jeroen De Flander lists four important differentiators when comparing strategy execution with strategy building. Strategy execution involves everyone in the organization, while strategy building is mostly reserved for a selected executive team. Strategy execution takes much longer than strategy building—it's a marathon versus a sprint. Execution requires short-and long-term thinking, as short term wins are a necessity to make execution a success. Strategy execution also requires a different skill set from strategy building. Successful strategy builders are champions in analytical thinking and opportunity identification, whereas executioners are masters in communication and coaching skills.

One of the key focus areas for partner organizations is increasing quality, satisfaction, and profitability levels in their Microsoft Dynamics implementations. During strategy building, we may look to define our quality goals, as well as generate plans on how we could achieve those quality excellence goals using Microsoft Dynamics Sure Step as our vehicle. But having a strategic plan, in and of itself, does not guarantee success. A strategy, even a great one, doesn't implement itself! To turn the Sure Step strategy into execution, the organization will need to put a plan in place for a company-wide effort, using management coaching support to detail out the incremental steps needed to achieve quick wins on the way to a larger transformation. The execution of this process is a completely different ballgame as compared to acquiring resources with knowledge on how to drive implementations successfully.

Change management

In *Chapter 3*, *Managing Projects*, we already introduced change as a challenge in adapting to Sure Step. This cannot be a surprise as most of us must be familiar with the great difficulty in changing good old habits in our personal and professional lives. Now think for some time on some of your change initiatives in your professional life. Did they fully succeed to the extent that you planned for? If not, try to list three reasons of their failure. Do these look familiar?

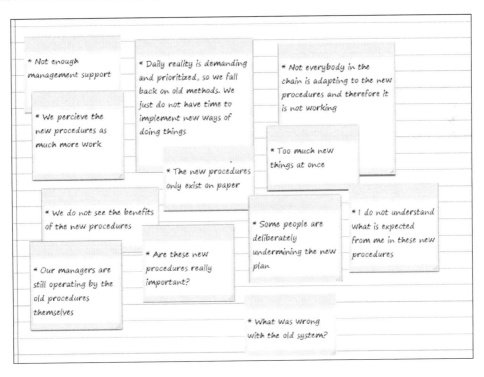

This illustration highlights only a few common pain points when reflecting on reasons for failing change projects. A majority of companies do have a track of failed change initiatives. Most of these failures were caused by typical change management challenges. If we want to successfully adapt to Sure Step, we need to have a strong execution plan to overcome these change management challenges. And awareness is the first step in this direction. People are creatures of habit and feel most secure when doing what is known.

Why change initiatives fail

In Chapter 3, we have already referred to John Kotter's book named *Our Iceberg Is Melting*. He describes 10 reasons for failing change initiatives. Let's have a closer look at these.

Underestimating the need for a clear vision of the desired change

Why do we need the change? What will be the outcome and how does it relate to our objectives and company strategy? Will we sell more and become more profitable? What is our compelling reason to implement this change? What are the business reasons for it? We need to make sure that our change initiative is connected to goal commitment and our company objectives, and that we have a strong vision behind the desired change. Just like in soccer, we won't go far unless we know where the goalposts are. So the first thing to do is to understand what we want to accomplish!

Failing to clearly communicate the vision

Do you feel comfortable in changing your ways of doing things without knowing why? Of course you don't, and this applies to most people. When we introduce change to our staff, they need to know why the organization really wants and needs the change. What are the business need and the compelling reason to go for this change? What are the issues we want to resolve? Will it increase our performance and quality levels? Explain how this initiative fits in to the strategic plan. Will it help reach our targets and how? Leadership that introduces change into an organization must sell the vision to those that will be executing the change. They need to make this vision believable and achievable for the entire company by good communication and information. A lack of this essential communication is a disconnection between strategy and execution.

Failing to build a substantial coalition

Our change initiative needs to be supported by a sizeable group of people within our organization to overcome tradition and inertia. They need to be confident, inspired, and excited by the change introduced. As such they will evangelize the new procedures within the teams and help others bridge the pit to the new ways of working. They will also argue and overcome the criticism of those who do not believe and resist to the change. This coalition of supporters will act as your running mates in your campaign for a more effective and quality-driven company. The coalition needs be powerful, including an authoritative mix of executives and non-executive roles within the different departments and disciplines in the company. We must invest time in the creation of such a group of believers, before forcing any new tools or procedures in our organization. We need to identify the promoters and potential promoters within our organization. Both have a positive generic attitude towards change; they do not fear change and feel less insecure than others. The real promoters will welcome the particular change right away and will seek for the advantage of the new ways of working with the speed of light. Potential promoters are not negative to change but they will not find the advantages that quickly. They just need that extra bit of encouragement to find the real value of the change. We need to get and keep both types of promoters on board during our change journey.

Permitting roadblocks against the vision

People don't like to change their ways of doing things, and new procedures make them feel insecure. This is true for a majority of people, even for the ones promoting the change. However, some people fear change much more than others and we are speaking about change in general. This may lead to resistance to any change. We need to know our opponents here and manage their resistance from day one. The real opponents are usually not so difficult to identify. They have a strong negative attitude against any change and, on top of that, they have strong personal reasons against this particular change.

These opponents will try to deny the change and bring up anger and resistance. We need to be prepared for that and manage them through exploration into acceptance.

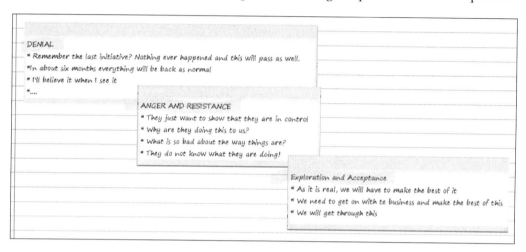

We also need to anticipate the hidden opponents or opportunists. Identifying them will be more of a challenge. They have a negative generic attitude towards change although they seem to be supporting the change on a superficial level. They are balancing between promoter and opponent and this means that our challenge is to give them enough information and encouragement to make them understand the benefits.

We need to shut the door for any rebellion against the improvement plan lead by the opponents, and we need to make sure that the opponents don't outnumber our coalition supporting the change.

Not generating a sense of urgency tied to improved performance

Even with the best intentions of a whole team, change projects are endangered by a lack of sense of urgency. Even if we support the new processes and tools, the real practice of it is frequently put off. There are certain widespread excuses such as "Yes, we support it because it is good, but right now we don't have time for it as there are other things with a higher priority." We've heard them before, but before you know it, "one of these days" becomes "none of these days", bringing our change project to an end. That's why we need to connect our change goals to an accepted urgency. People need to understand why we need quick change and how the whole organization will benefit from it. There is no time to waste as this is crucially important; we need to act now. John Kotter stated that 75% of a company's management must be convinced that the current business practice is totally unacceptable. If there is no such sense of urgency for the transformation, the change process is endangered.

Not building a plan for short-term wins

Exploring the first results and benefits from change is major. It will motivate people to adapt to any newly introduced procedure or tool, and experiencing the benefits will encourage them to continue our quest for more improvement and change. We don't eat our dish in one big bite, but in small bites as it enables us to explore, smell, taste, and appreciate it much more, which leads to better digestion. The same goes for our change project. The longer we keep the organization waiting for the first results and wins, the more support and enthusiasm we will lose, and the more ammunition our opponents will gain. A watched kettle never boils.

Failing to lead and coach changes in business behavior

As explained earlier, change doesn't come easy and the execution of a strategy doesn't implement itself. At the heart of every successful change project, we will find the individuals. Our people need to realize the change and therefore they need to be coached and lead into this change. There is no other choice; in fact, it is a management and leadership responsibility. Our challenge is to create awareness and build responsibility for this change in our people organization. It is quite unlikely that the "do as I say" approach will bring us instant success in our transformation effort. We need people who really want to take responsibility for this change and performance, making coaching the better option. In essence this is what leadership through change is all about—aligning the people force with a new vision and inspiring them to make it happen despite the obstacles. By coaching, we can involve our people in the change instead of imposing the change on them. People do what they think and feel, not what is imposed on them.

Failure of managers to operate in and above day-to-day execution

Changing the day-to-day execution practice is a management responsibility. Managers need to connect with the values and beliefs of the new vision and introduce new behaviors in the daily practice of their departments. Easily said, but a large group of managers find it hard to go beyond that day-to-day execution themselves, in spite of their being in charge of it. This leads us to the next topic—not practicing what you preach.

Not practicing what you preach

"Do as I say, not as I do" is clearly ineffective and yet very frequent. Managers might have connected with the new vision and seize every opportunity to communicate their support for it, but in practice, they still deploy good old habits and business practices. If managers do not support the practice and execution of the new behaviors, it is unlikely that their people will. The new procedures are clearly not in their hearts and any people organization will feel that immediately.

Fail to anchor changes in business culture

Most of us, who have worked in more than one company, must have experienced that there is something called a company or business culture—something in the air of that company that makes the organization unique. We must have also experienced that this unique culture has an impact on how we behaved, performed, and interacted in that company, and how we felt. There are many definitions of what a business culture is and they all point to the set of values and norms that are shared by people and groups in an organization. As this culture influences what we do and how we interact with colleagues, vendors, and customers, it represents the outer limit of what is achievable within that company. That's why our change project, our quest for more quality, needs to stick into the company's culture. We must reinforce the new norms and values and show the organization that they are an essential part of the culture. New recruits should be hooked up immediately to these new values, and for that to happen, incentives and promotions might become valuable instruments.

The Sure Step adoption program

The previous sections on strategy execution and change management made clear that adopting any implementation methodology is an important but complex, time-consuming endeavor that impacts the entire partner organization. To facilitate partners to be successful in this adoption, Microsoft provides a guiding and facilitating adoption program. This program is built and envisioned in such manner that it will help partners to overcome typical change and strategy execution pitfalls. The program includes essential elements such as:

- Confirming the business need and vision
- Executive communication
- Assessing your current business practice
- Identifying and communicating risks and rewards
- Goal setting and coaching model

We can identify two major components in the Sure Step adoption program:

- The adoption roadmap
- The adoption workshop

In strategy execution as well as in the change management theory, it is emphasized that teams need to be informed and aware about the transformation process that they will go through. Our people will all play a key role in this transformation and so they will need to know the scenario.

The adoption roadmap

The adoption roadmap is a structured way to lead your organization toward change. It includes recommended roles and responsibilities for each step of the way, emphasizing the importance and timing of executive communications, implementation team activities, sales and IT involvement, and the ultimate deployment of the transformation across your company. With the roadmap as your guide, you will be able to maintain momentum toward realizing the full benefits of adopting Sure Step.

As shown in the next diagram, the activities in the roadmap are broken down into six groups, following the six phases of Sure Step:

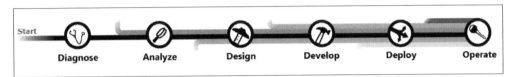

Let's have a closer look at each group.

Diagnose

This is a call to action for business leaders to identify a compelling reason to implement Sure Step. Why do we need Sure Step? Do we have strategic reasons to do so? What is the business need for it? What is our vision behind it? Identify the beliefs and values that urge the usage of Sure Step in our daily practice and behavior. Where are the goalposts, what do we want to achieve, and how will it be measured?

At this stage, we also want to start building up our substantial coalition. We need a team that has a general positive attitude towards change, who can lead and facilitate the change within the organization by generating quick results and motivate others to explore the new procedures. They will encourage and help their colleagues to find their own personal benefits and reasons for adapting to this change. This is a team that wants to take responsibility for the new performance—our backbone for the desired output. The roadmap plans for the assignment of a Sure Step Champion and a V-team.

The Sure Step champion

The champion is the day-to-day leader for the transformation. The champion is responsible for developing and executing the adoption plan for the company. The ideal champion is a senior-level person with the expertise, gravitas, and credibility to facilitate, lead, and coach the company-wide change initiative. It must be somebody who understands the business deeply, has the support of the most senior members of the company and at the same time is well respected up and down the hierarchy of the company. The champion needs to understand people's fears and be able to coach them into exploration and acceptance. A champion who has worked in a diverse set of roles across the company or for competitive companies might be better placed to put himself in another position. The champion needs to be well aware that he/she sets an example to others. Therefore, the champion needs to practice what is preached.

The V-team

Our champion's first task is to identify and recruit V-team candidates, who will each take responsibility for assessing, configuring, and deploying Sure Step. This must be a well-thought-out move, involving the identification of a good mixture of proponents.

The V-team needs to be a powerful representation of our entire company, including all roles and departments. The roadmap recommends including at least:

- A Sales Manager
- A Senior Application Consultant
- A Senior Development Consultant
- A Senior Project Manager

An ideal V-team will also have part-time participation from IT, Marketing, and HR, as we want to stick our change initiative to the company's culture, and our initiative might have an impact on job roles as well.

By assigning the champion and the V-team, we have founded our substantial coalition. At this point in the process, we need to inform and train our champion and team about this new world of Sure Step. What is Sure Step and what are the true essentials and benefits of this methodology? This training needs to be inspiring and informing, rather than detailed and overloaded. We want our coalition to feel the benefits, and not overload them with detailed technical aspects.

The diagnose moment also schedules for *executive communication*—a truly essential activity for change success. The executives need to communicate why this change is so important and explain the compelling reasons for it. They need to make clear that this is not just something that is imposed but involves everybody's initiative. They need to provide a shared picture of what success looks like. Your people need to understand the strategy, and be motivated and committed to take action.

The next diagram summarizes the steps of the diagnose phase:

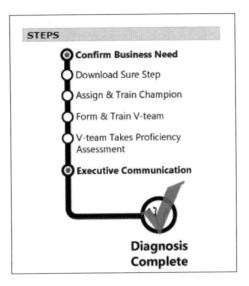

The average time to complete this phase is estimated to be 30 days.

Analyze

This is where we will go over our habitual implementation process, with a fine-tooth comb, to discover in detail why this transformation is so urgently needed. Where do we need to focus, where can we find the quick wins, and what will require more redesign time? We need to prepare to make *a deep and honest assessment* of ourselves, including our processes, skills, and organizational structure. All will be affected. In the end, we need the right input to develop our adoption plan.

The adoption program facilitates this investigation in two ways:

- By providing an online *Adoption Self–Assessment* for all V-team members
- By organizing a *Facilitated Assessment Workshop*, managed by an expert Sure Step Partner Adoption Facilitator

We will cover both in upcoming sections of this book. The output received from the workshop is an action plan to be carried out in this execution of the adoption program. Just executing this program once would be a missed opportunity for continuous improvement. Quality improvement philosophies such as Kaizen show us that quality improvement should be a continuous effort, and not a one-time stop of small improvements and standardization. Therefore, we will hopefully go through the roadmap many times, each time improving our level of quality in general and Sure Step adoption in particular.

From the results of our assessment, we can identify any specialized skills training required for individual V-team members to fulfill their responsibilities. For example, this could include sales methodology or project management training. The action plan will also advise us how we need to further develop the skills of our V-team in terms of Sure Step. At this stage, we can *complete our training plan*.

This phase asks for strong collaboration of the V-team and important stakeholders of our company. We need their input, their honest opinions, and we really need to listen to them. Practice has shown that this opportunity of giving input and co-driving this change opportunity truly motivates them. Experience with previous projects showed us that the feedback of most V-teams was extremely positive and resulted in great commitment to get the Sure Step practice really executed.

Together with the V-team, the champion must keep their eyes open for the attached risks and pitfalls of this adoption. Some of the important questions to be asked are:

- What might become an obstacle?
- What is too ambitious for the organization?
- What is achievable and what is not?

Do not become overambitious and do not throw everything overboard. Your improvement plan needs to be achievable and acceptable to your organization.

We also need to finalize our business case here and report our adoption plan and ROI case to the CEO. The CEO will then confirm the decision to proceed.

The next diagram summarizes the steps of the analyze phase:

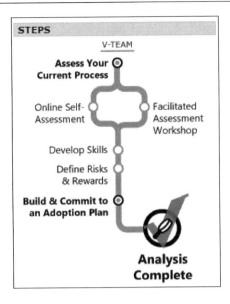

The average time to complete this phase is estimated to be 30 days.

Design

At this point, we have collected valuable information from the assessments and workshops conducted in the analyze phase. What we want to improve and change in our current sales and implementation processes is right on our radar. We also know where the goalposts are, as we have determined our short and longer term goals and returns. We are now ready to start redesigning our current processes to the ideal processes for our company, by mapping them against the Sure Step template with regard to what is achievable in our company.

Our champion must lead the V-team in the redesign of sales processes, project implementation processes, and performance management processes based on Sure Step principles and guidelines. We will focus on those that require our attention, as identified in the previous phase. A part of this process redesign is a Proof of Concept exploration, examining common sales and implementation scenarios, and mapping out how to address them using Sure Step. During design, we need to find consensus in the V-team about our new ways of doing things. We also might even need to check a broader basis within the company as these new processes need to be acceptable and achievable. We need to hunt for the added value for all stakeholders. This is exactly why the roadmap suggests running a pilot of these new processes with a few prospects. Based on the outcome of this pilot, we should revisit our design, making necessary adjustments. This is an interactive process, allowing the stakeholders to cooperate in our new execution plan.

Once agreement is found on the new process design, we can start to document this into new working instructions. These documented instructions will guide our organization through implementations and will ramp up new hires quickly. At the same time, we need to be aware that these new procedures may have an impact on job roles and therefore we should inform the HR department of our outcome. At the same time, we need to check what the impact of the new processes on the IT infrastructure might be.

Before Sales can engage with a pilot including the new processes, they need to fully understand how our organization will be working in the Sure Step way. So, we need to organize roll-based training on Sure Step and the new procedures for our sales teams involved with the pilot. After the pilot, the V-team compiles and absorbs the feedback from the pilot and adjusts the processes based on this feedback.

It is then the moment for the executives to inform the company about these new procedures and the results of the pilot. This crucially important communication will drive the company into acceptance.

The following diagram summarizes the steps of the design phase:

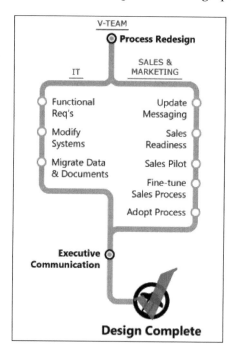

The average time to complete this phase is estimated to be 30 days.

Develop

With the new processes defined, the next step is to develop them. This not only involves using the resources found in Sure Step, but also completing any custom work that is required. As we explored in the previous chapters, Sure Step includes an impressive collection of tools and templates that might help you. Some are critical and required, some facultative and helpful, while some might not be of any immediate use to our specific needs. In the previous phase, we designed a set of these tools and templates to support our new processes. Some of the tools and templates might need some customization to tailor them to our specific needs. We also might need to configure and set up our SharePoint collaboration infrastructure. These are a few examples of what we need to do at this stage.

The pilot started by the sales team in the previous phase continues. Marketing captures the reaction of customers to our new engagement based on Sure Step, while HR will go thoroughly into changes to role definitions and organization. Based on the results of our pilot program and customer acceptance measurement, it is now time to make final modifications to our Sure Step processes.

The next diagram summarizes the steps of the design phase:

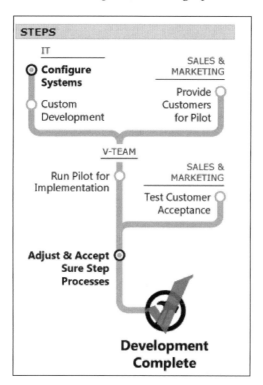

The time to complete this phase depends on the amount of work needing to be done.

Deploy

It is now time to ensure readiness to go live with Sure Step across our company. All our employees need to be knowledgeable so that they can perform, and all customer-facing roles need to comprehend the Sure Step essences in order to communicate the value of Sure Step amongst their customers and prospects.

This readiness needs to be accompanied by effective communications. Our CEO should send a company wide communication signaling our readiness to go live with Sure Step, fulfilling the promise and goals made at the beginning of the process. The CEO needs to recognize the company wide effort and the importance of each individual's contribution in reaching this great result. This communication needs to trigger excitement and a great belief in this new way of working.

Ensuring the readiness of our teams involves focusing on the necessary skills training such as project management for our people before deploying Sure Step Training. Both sales and implementation team people need to believe and evangelize the great benefits of Sure Step by now. They need to be able to take responsibility over these new procedures by practicing them in their daily work and helping customers collaborate to the full extent.

The following diagram summarizes the steps of the deploy phase:

The average time to complete this phase is estimated to be 30 days.

Operate

Your people are now practicing the new procedures, tools, and templates in their daily jobs. This means the new way of working is based on and inspired by Sure Step principles and tools. It is important to reinforce this use by discussing the results, showing the improvements, and learning from the daily routines. We need to continue the chain of communication within our company by detailing the progress made to date, the results of everyone's efforts, and the future goals for Sure Step partner adoption.

The Sure Step adoption roadmap advises us to perform a second health-check on our implementation adoption maturity. How has it improved since we began this journey? It is advised to compare our re-assessment against the deep and honest self-assessment that we established as our baseline. We are looking for any gaps still outstanding, so that we can plan to address them.

This is not the point where our change initiative stops, quite the contrary. We are in charge of ensuring the continued effectiveness and adoption of Sure Step, by coaching our managers to continually reinforce and manage to the process. Mature consultants and managers will require coaching on an ongoing basis. Their natural tendency will be to fall back on what they already know.

Communicating the results of customer satisfaction surveys, among the customers who have received a Sure Step partner adoption-based implementation, will drive our organization's learning curve.

Our newly gained, quality-driven values, along with the experience of our people of having participated in a quality improvement project, is a good basis for a second round of this adoption program. Remember the goal of the first round is unlikely to have been to adopt to Sure Step as a whole; instead, we redesigned our processes in those areas where we identified improvement opportunity and that urged us to do something. We will always find improvement opportunities and therefore planning a second round of this improvement cycle is the right way of moving forward.

The next diagram summarizes the steps of the operate phase:

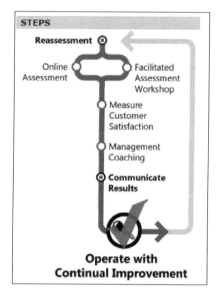

The adoption workshop

The adoption workshop is a facilitated organizational assessment. It is a deep dive into our existing implementation methodology, designed to discover critical gaps and areas for improvement. This workshop will help create a sense of urgency for our desired changes as it unveils real weaknesses in our current business practice. It will also help us to understand how Sure Step can offer real added value for our business.

Executing the adoption workshop

In the adoption roadmap, the adoption workshop is described and executed in the analyze phase and it can also be re-executed in the operate phase. In fact, we can go through this workshop each time we want to assess our current business practices.

This is a critical step in terms of change management and strategy execution. It not only unveils the need for change and builds up the sense of urgency, but it is also a great moment for the participation of our substantial coalition. This is the moment for the V-team and the Sure Step Champion to participate and impact on the transformation plan. The new way of working will not be imposed but is subject to consultation and participation.

The workshop itself is a one-day meeting of the V-team, facilitated by an external adoption expert. When the V-team comes together, it represents a mixed company audience of senior and junior levels, of sales and implementation roles, of different departments within the company. This means that the V-team is powerful in representing the entire company. During this one day, they will discuss their current business practice and work towards key points for their adoption action plan that will guide their next steps in designing and developing the transformation. They need to build up an important consensus for the new road ahead.

The online adoption assessment

We must prepare well for this workshop so that it can be really efficient. The online Sure Step adoption assessment is an important preparation tool. Each member of the V-team, including the champion, must take this online assessment individually. It is a business questionnaire, examining our current business practice, by asking questions:

- That pertain to our presales activities
- For scoping, designing, developing, and delivering the solution to the customer
- For effective project management in order to safeguard our profitability

Once the champion confirms that all V-team members have finalized their assessment, the individual results of the V-team members are aggregated into one company result sheet and this will be crucial input for the one-day adoption workshop itself. To understand this process a little better, we are going to have a closer look at the design of the assessment questions.

The cone of adoption

The cone of adoption is built around four elements that are crucially important in measuring the maturity of a company in terms of its business processes. These elements are:

- Design
- Acceptance
- Usage
- Manage

All questions in the online assessment are linked to these four elements. Questions related to *design* will test if we have specific formal procedures in place; do they exist in our company? Questions measuring the *acceptance* will ask the V-team members if they understand and support the benefits of specific procedures within the company. *Usage* questions will verify if specific procedures are really used in our practice. The last category of questions, *manage*, will discover if management is reinforcing and coaching the procedures into real execution. Is there a culture in our organization that reinforces the use of these processes?

As such, all V-team members will be asked design, acceptance, usage, and manage questions in each of the three domains—pre-sales, solution implementation, and project management.

Map your position

In the aggregated results, we can then identify crucial indicators such as:

- How strongly is the V-team aligned in certain areas?
- What are areas of collective risk in our current business practice?
- How strongly do we execute according to our processes?
- A maturity rating of our company

The maturity rating indicates where we stand today and what our focus points need to be. Are we acompany driven by a few processes only? In that case, we probably need to focus on our process design. We might have robust processes in place, but lack the real daily use of those? Or maybe management is not coaching the processes enough? The maturity rating will indicate what type of company we are today.

The diagram here explains the maturity ratings:

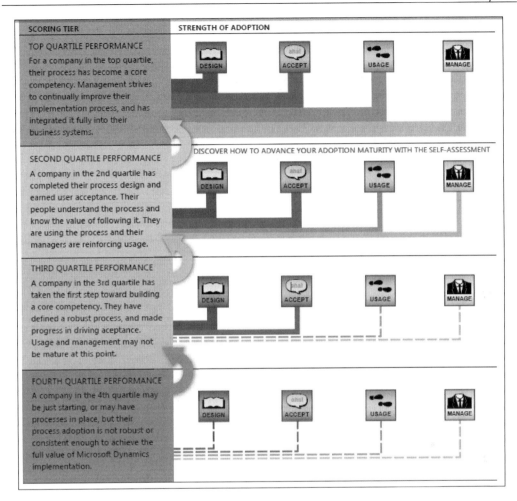

These insights will strongly facilitate, direct, and prioritize the discussions of the V-team during the workshop and will help us understand our current position much better. If we want to reach our goalpost, we certainly need to know our starting positions.

Headlights on

During the adoption workshop, we must, as explained, examine our current position. At the same time, we also need to close this workshop with a guiding plan for our change initiative. This plan can be finalized after the workshop by the champion, but the key outline needs to be approved by the V-team during this meeting. The aggregated results will set out the first beacons of what to focus on — the discussions during the workshop will then provide more input to this plan. It is important to keep in mind that we need actions leading to results and we need results in the short term to reinforce our success probability for this change initiative. The action plan needs to be specific: what are our goals, who are responsible, what actions we need to take to reach these goals, when we can start, and what is the expected due date.

The value of the adoption program

The previous sections only raised a small corner of the veil in terms of challenges that go along with any change program. The adoption program provides us with a predefined framework based on best practices to overcome the typical pitfalls. It also allows us to communicate and visualize to our people how the desired change will be implemented in our company. It is very important that all involved and affected know, in advance, how their journey is organized. At the same time, this program brings to us valuable tools to help us assess our current situation, our urgency for transformation, and the true value of Sure Step. To make it even better, this program teaches us how to execute transformation into real performance by means of a repeatable change process. For any strategy executioner or change manager within our business, this program is priceless!

GROW into new behaviors

Being a thoughtful reader, you have noticed that coaching was positioned as your most effective management instrument on the quest for transformation. At the heart of every transformation project are people, and people do what they feel and think not what is imposed on them. The GROW model is one of the most well-known coaching models, a framework to become a better coach. The name GROW stands for:

- G: Goal setting
- R: Reality
- O: Options
- W: Will

Goal setting involves defining of the goal. What is it that the end user wants to achieve? What are this person's short- and long-term goals for this transformation process? Together, the coach and end user need to agree upon the goals to be achieved. **Reality** refers to the real current situation of the end user. What problems does this person experience in the current way of working or with the proposed transformation? What is his or her perceived reality? **Options** stand for choice. As a coach, we need to help people find different possible solutions for the perceived problems. **Will** commits to action. What decisions does the end user take? What will he or she do and by when?

Now you might wonder why this coaching based on these GROW principles is emphasized in the Sure Step adoption program. The answer is simple: because this model is most effective in generating the awareness and responsibility of our people. We want people to take responsibility in our transformation project, as only they can realize the desired change. As long as people blame others when things go wrong, or they don't work as expected, they are not committed to the outcome.

Responsibility goes hand-in-hand with choice. When people make choices, they are committed to them because they feel responsible. This is exactly what we want when we want to execute our change strategy. Our people need to feel responsible for executing Sure Step principles in their daily professional reality. An important detail is that, *they* need to make the choices. By asking questions and exploring their daily perceived reality, a coach can help commit to action, in order to realize agreed objectives. A coach must not make the choices; we want true commitment. A good coach is an active listener, provides perspective, is someone who can make their peers think, and someone who can make them be perceptive to new input and see new options because of that.

Sure Step for Independent Software Vendors

In the previous section, we discussed how service providers can benefit from adopting the Sure Step methodology, as well as the process for adoption itself. We now shift our attention to the Independent Software Vendors (ISVs), who develop solutions to augment the Microsoft Dynamics core solution.

ISV classification

In the Microsoft Dynamics ecosystem, the ISVs provide solutions that can be broadly classified into three areas:

- Vertical solutions
- Horizontal solutions
- Complementary solutions

Industry-Vertical and Cross-Industry-Horizontal solutions were introduced in an earlier chapter, and the notion applies to ISVs as well. A **vertical** is a subcategory of an industry, characterized by enterprises with similar products or services. For example, automotive, chemicals, and electronics are subcategories or verticals of the manufacturing industry. A vertical solution generally covers end-to-end processes, and accordingly, it is designed to meet the specific needs of a vertical-oriented business.

In contrast to a vertical solution, a **horizontal** solution is designed to meet a broad business process or need, and may need little variation to cover multiple verticals or industries. For example, bookkeeping, payroll, and human resources applications are horizontal solutions.

The third category, **complementary** solutions, can also be viewed as horizontal solutions because these solutions can also be used in multiple verticals or industries. But while horizontal solutions can address multiple processes for multiple verticals or industries, a complementary solution is a "point solution" that addresses a specific function for a vertical or horizontal market, and as such complements a vertical or horizontal solution. Examples of complementary solutions include credit card validation, address look-up, or barcode solutions.

How ISVs can benefit from the Sure Step program

As an ISV, regardless of which of the three categories you develop solutions in, you can benefit from aligning your solutions documentation to the Sure Step methodology. Due to the inherent scope of the solution, if you are a vertical or horizontal solution provider, this alignment can especially help you. In this section, we will learn how you can benefit.

As you already know, Sure Step is designed to assist with the requirements gathering for the customer's solution, which leads up to a Fit Gap exercise to determine how much of the standard solution fits with the customer's requirements, and whether any gaps exist that must be solved by other means. During the Fit Gap exercise, the Value Added Reseller (VAR) and/or service provider may determine that a subset of requirements can be best met by an ISV solution. If this determination occurs in the diagnostic pre-sales phase, having appropriate documentation such as Requirements Questionnaires and Fit Gap worksheets would assist the VAR or service provider in selecting the right ISV solution. As an ISV provider, this is your primary benefit, as it enables the selection of your ISV solution. Even if the determination occurs only during the implementation, foreseeably during the Functional Requirements and Fit Gap Workshops in the analysis phase, these documents will once again help the service provider ascertain that they are making the right ISV selection.

Obviously making sure that your ISV solution is the one that gets picked is your primary goal. We will talk about other artifacts you can provide to increase the confidence level for the VARs or service providers. But let's continue with the additional benefits that you, as an ISV provider, can gain from aligning to the Sure Step methodology.

The more recognized your ISV solution becomes in the Microsoft Dynamics ecosystem, the more demand you are going to have for your product, which, without any doubt, is a good problem to have. But with that also comes organizational scale issues—do you have the resources to assist on multiple sales opportunities, or do you have the resources to support implementation questions as they arise? Having your process and documentation aligned with Sure Step can help you address these questions.

The other inherent benefits from the Sure Step alignment are alleviating project risks and improving solution delivery times. As we have learned in the prior chapters, having a consistent, repeatable, and end-to-end lifecycle method that Sure Step provides helps the service provider decrease the overall risks and issues that may arise during the engagement. This, in turn, can also lead to reduced deployment times, thereby reducing the overall solution delivery costs for the customer. If your ISV application is a component of the overall solution being deployed for the customer, ensuring that it also aligns to Sure Step will only help make life easier for the implementation team. They will not only be able to find artifacts for the appropriate activities, thereby reducing the overall delivery time for this component. They will also be using a single taxonomy in describing and implementing the overall solution, which is not something to overlook—the customer user base goes through enough churn as it is during the course of an ERP or CRM solution implementation that they do need to have to figure out multiple terms thrown at them to describe the same task.

Having good Sure Step-based documentation can also reduce the time taken for a service provider to become an expert on your ISV solution. As these consultants go into other engagements, they become evangelists for your product, resulting in more demand. Also, the documentation can help the consultants deliver quality training for this part of the overall solution to the customer's users.

These are just some of the potential benefits from Sure Step for ISVs. All in all, it is a win-win-win for the ISV, the VAR/service provider, and most importantly, the customer.

ISV artifacts for Sure Step

We have already discussed Requirements Questionnaires and Fit Gap worksheets as key artifacts that an ISV provider should make available. Other important documents that you may provide are noted below.

Consider the following for the diagnostic phase, to assist with solution selling and the customer's due diligence:

- **Product overview**: This is self-explanatory! A good product requires a strong overview document that describes the solution capabilities.

- **Requirements Questionnaires and Fit Gap Worksheets**: Discussed previously, but added here to complete the list, these documents can be used with the Requirements and Process Review Decision Accelerator offering and the Fit Gap and Solution Blueprint DA offering respectively.

- **Infrastructure and third-party software requirements**: These specifications will be used in the Architecture Assessment DA, by the technical consultants, to determine the infrastructure needs for the add-on solution. The technical consultants will need to ascertain if the existing hardware may be sufficient or additional hardware components are needed for the combined solution for example. If any third-party components are also needed for your ISV application, this should be known upfront, so that the teams can plan in advance for their procurement.

- **Cost Estimation Worksheets**: Use these worksheets to guide the service provider, during the Scoping Assessment exercise, in developing the budgetary estimates, timelines, and resource needs for the ISV component as part of the overall solution deployment.

- **Demonstration data**: This is an important need for pre-sales if the sales team, during the Proof of Concept DA, or at any other point in the sales cycle, has to demonstrate the solution add-on to the customer. This dataset should be easily installable, as time is often of the essence in a sales cycle. It may also be noted that demo data can also help during the implementation, for example, during solution overview or for setting up a Sandbox environment for user training purposes.

While the aim of the diagnostic documents is to assist the sales team with the positioning and envisioning the overall solution for the customer, the implementation subset noted below will help the consulting team deliver the promised solution to the customer. The recommended artifacts for ISVs noted next are aligned to each of the nine cross-phase processes in the Sure Step implementation project types.

- **Program Management cross phase**: If your ISV solution may need additional activities during deployment, consider providing a project plan addendum. You may also consider other documents to describe Conditions of Satisfaction (COS) or Key Performance Indicators (KPI) with your solution.

- **Training cross phase**: If applicable, include guidance on training for your ISV solution.

- **Business Process Analysis cross phase**: Use case scenarios provide examples of real-life usage of the product, which can be very helpful to the solution architects developing the overall solution vision. Business Process Maps, especially for the Vertical ISV solutions and, to an extent, for the Horizontal ISV solutions, can also help in this aspect. These may also be leveraged during the sales cycle.

- **Requirements and Configuration cross phase**: Providing templates for setup/configuration will be of great help to the implementation team in areas such as parameter setting, so that the consultants can correctly configure the solution specific to the customer's needs.

- **Custom Coding cross phase**: Templates such as Functional Design Document for Customizations and Technical Design Documents may help the development resources on the consulting team with designing and documenting any required customizations of the solution.

- **Quality and Testing cross phase**: Scripts for User Acceptance Testing and other related tests for testing your ISV solution are very important. These will help ensure quality delivery of the combined solution. As feasible, you may also consider other templates such as technical review and project governance compliance checklists.

- **Infrastructure cross phase**: Key documentation in this area are Installation Guides describing how the ISV application should be installed in tandem with the core Microsoft Dynamics solution. Remember to include uninstall procedures in these guides, which may help when switching environments, among other things.

- **Integration and Interfaces cross phase**: Use this area to explain how your product integrates with the core solution. If applicable, you can also include guidance on how your product integrates to other third-party solutions that are typically used in the customer's industry or vertical.

- **Data Migration cross phase**: If applicable, provide guidance on data migration scripting and specific mapping templates for migrating data from other third-party solutions into your product.

Sure Step provides you with starting templates, including Requirements Gathering Template, Costing Worksheet Template, User Acceptance Test Script Template, and so on that can help you get started in your journey to alignment with Sure Step! The following screenshot shows some of these templates:

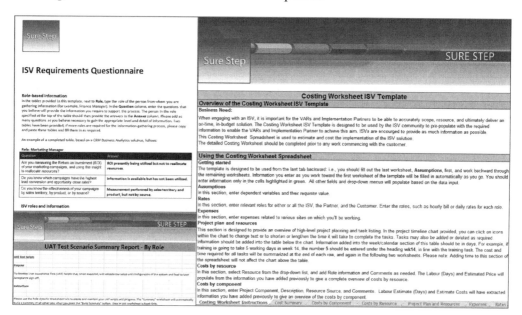

The list of ISV artifacts shown in the preceding screenshot may seem overwhelming at first, so it is very important to remember that you do not need to develop all of these documents in one fell swoop. This list should help you think about areas that will help the sales and implementation teams that represent and deploy your product. Use judgment to decide which areas need to be worked upon immediately, and which ones you can develop and provide as your business evolves. In the next section, you can also find a table with recommendations of templates for the Certified for Microsoft Dynamics program, which may also help you determine which ones to start with and which ones to build over time.

Sure Step and the Certified for Microsoft Dynamics program

The **Certified for Microsoft Dynamics (CfMD)** program introduced by Microsoft applies high quality and testing rigor to partner-developed business management solutions. CfMD solutions are tested by an independent company, and also go through verification by customers. By committing to the quality requirements of the CfMD program, the ISV solutions are provided higher visibility and afforded increased marketability to the resellers and customers. These solutions offer customers and resellers a lower risk profile in that they are used and recommended by other companies in the industry, are thoroughly tested and proven to meet Microsoft's highest standards for partner solutions, and very importantly, are tested as being compatible and integrated with Microsoft Dynamics and Microsoft technology solutions.

One of the main objectives of the certified solutions is to provide trusted, lower-risk solutions that can be implemented faster and maintained easier when the solution is in production. As such, in conjunction with the Sure Step 2010 release, the CfMD program introduced best practice guidance on Sure Step artifacts to be developed by Microsoft Dynamics ISV solution providers. The CfMD program also instituted a requirement for the ISV organization to have one or more resources with Sure Step methodology certification, to ensure alignment to Sure Step.

The following table illustrates the documentation requirements of the ISV provider from a CfMD perspective. The documents noted with a check mark under the **ISV Software Test** column are required for the CfMD test process, while the others are recommended.

Proposed Document	ISV Software Test	CfMD
Diagnostic Phase		
Product Overview	√	
Questionnaires for Requirements gathering		√
Fit Gap Analysis worksheet with specific considerations for the ISV solution		√
Augmentation of the Fit Gap and Solution Blueprint for ISV considerations		√
ISV Infrastructure and third-party software requirements	√	
Guidelines for the VAR on how to accurately scope, determine resources, and cost the respective ISV solution		√
Short Demonstration Video		√
Medium Demonstration Video		√
Product Positioning and USPs		√
Case Studies		√
Analysis through Operations Phases		
Installation, configuration, and uninstall procedures	√	
ISV Sample Project plans and guidance on how these can be incorporated into standard Sure Step Plans, such as providing examples		√
Integration Guide	√	
Operations Guide		√
Installable demonstration data	√	
Training Plans		√
ISV-specific Business use case scenarios	√	
Setup/Configuration requirements for ISV	√	
Functional Design Document and Technical Design considerations, including Security requirements		√
User Acceptance tests		√
Testing scripts for all relevant testing, unit, functional, performance, data, or integration testing as examples		√
Delivery Audit Checklists		√

Proposed Document	ISV Software Test	CfMD
Additions to Environment Definition and Deployment Plans for ISV infrastructure requirements	√	
Guidance on specific Dynamic solution and ISV integration	√	
ISV Data Migration guidance	√	

The CfMD program also created a "Certified for Microsoft Dynamics Partner-to-Partner Connections" site as an added benefit, allowing resellers to directly contact the certified solution provider. This provides the ISV an additional forum to showcase their solutions, and an opportunity to recruit the best reselling partners.

As an ISV solution provider, consider the Certified for Microsoft Dynamics program, and take advantage of the benefits to grow your business.

Use case of Sure Step adoption by a small Dynamics partner

In this case study, we look at the journey undertaken by a small Dynamics partner (let's call them Partner1) to adopt the Sure Step methodology. The clientele of Partner1 is predominantly in the Small-to-Medium Enterprise (SME) space. Partner1 is a VAR and solution implementer whose main focus is not only on the Microsoft Dynamics CRM solutions, but that also undertakes smaller ERP engagements. Partner1 has 24 employees, including six in sales, fifteen in consulting, and three in administrative/accounting/infrastructure roles.

Partner1 was struggling in two areas, a spotty win-loss ratio on the opportunities it was chasing, and inconsistency in its solution delivery resulting in less-than satisfied customers. In a way, the two issues were tied together—the lack of good customer references was causing it to lose out to the competition more often than not.

Partner1's CEO first learned of Sure Step at a Partner Conference, where he was also able to see a demo of the methodology. He came away impressed at the capabilities, and also felt that it could help his organization in both of its current struggles. But before embarking on the evaluation exercise, he wanted to get affirmation from others in his organization that this was worthwhile to pursue, and accordingly he asked his Consulting Director to evaluate whether Sure Step would be a good fit for them.

Partner1's Consulting Director and a Senior Project Manager reviewed the 100-level online training course on Sure Step, accessible through PartnerSource. They were also convinced that the time and effort to further evaluate Sure Step would be money well spent, with the Consulting Director going as far as feeling that it was essential to their survival as an organization.

As the first step, they downloaded Sure Step from Microsoft's PartnerSource website to get a better grasp on the guidance, artifacts, and tools available to them. The second step was to institute a **Train-the-Trainer** model, where the Senior Project Manager would undertake deep-dive instructor-led classroom training on Sure Step, then come back and educate the rest of the organization on Sure Step. After other key consulting resources received training on Sure Step, the company would evaluate if and how the methodology needed to be customized to fit their processes. They would also select a project and use Sure Step on a trial basis.

While the plan was fairly logical, the execution did not quite pan out as Partner1 had intended. First, while the training that Project Manager attended delivered the Sure Step knowledge, Partner1 still needed to go through an exercise of mapping their processes and deliverables to the Sure Step methodology. This required dedicated resources and time—a task that Project Manager, whose primary job was to keep her current customer project on the right track, did not have the luxury to carry out. Partner1 also felt a bit overwhelmed by the documentation that they thought was needed in Sure Step, and also struggled with aligning their internal taxonomies between sales and delivery. Finally, as the sales team was not involved in this exercise, the selling motions, and more importantly, the deliverables promised by the sales teams were not aligned with the new approach that the delivery team wanted to take. The project stayed mired on the shelf, and it was business as usual for Partner1. The problem was that their sales and delivery struggles continued as well.

At this juncture, the CEO was able to meet with a Microsoft executive and another partner at an event. The discussion and follow-up notes exchanged affirmed his belief that Sure Step could help alleviate his company's struggles, and also led him to go after a more sound adoption approach.

Partner1 decided to use the Sure Step Adoption Roadmap as guidance. Having already identified a compelling reason to adopt Sure Step, the first step for Partner1 was to assign a Sure Step Champion for the project. The Project Manager was designated as the Sure Step Champion, and she was also relieved of some of her day-to-day pressures so as to be able to focus on the adoption. Partner1 nominated a V-team that comprised of a Sales Manager, the Consulting Director, and other consultants. The team availed of the Sure Step Online Self Assessments, to analyze where they were as an organization and the steps they needed to take to improve their processes.

After the CEO signed off on the plan, the team went about redesigning their processes to align them to Sure Step. Partner1 decided to begin with a subset of the documents that were important to the sales and delivery processes — the "Key Documents" designated by Sure Step, as shown in the next screenshot:

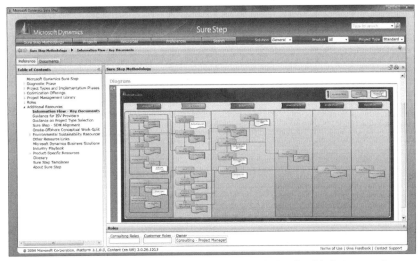

For their CRM implementations, Partner1 decided to build their templates around the Agile project type, while they selected the Standard project type for their ERP implementations. Using Sure Step's Projects functionality, the teams adapted the Sure Step templates and created Partner1-centric deliverable documents for their CRM and ERP solutions. The Statement of Work template provided to the customers at the end of the sales cycle was also recreated and aligned to the new Sure Step deliverables.

Partner1 piloted these documents for a CRM and ERP project, and fine tuned them as needed before requiring their usage on all projects. They also instituted periodic reviews of their projects and processes to ensure that their lessons learned were being transferred to future engagements.

Partner1 has been able to streamline their processes, and have also leveraged Sure Step to show their customers that they have a viable approach to deliver the promised solutions. Not only are they closing more opportunities, but customer satisfaction is high, as is employee morale and retention rates.

Summary

In this chapter, we covered the adoption of Sure Step methodology from both a service provider's and an Independent Software Vendor's perspectives. We learned of the resources that have been made available to help them with the adoption process, and how they can manage the resulting change in their organizations.

We will wrap up our discussions in the next chapter by summarizing our learning of Sure Step. We will also talk about some key areas for the reader to focus on in the immediate timeframe.

References

- De Flander, Jeroen (2010). *Strategy Execution Heroes*. The Performance Factory
- Kotter, J. (2006). *Our Iceberg is melting*. St. Martin's Press; 1 edition

10
Summary and Takeaways

Most (service providers) have well-trained and/or experienced project managers, use proven project management methodologies to guide the plan, and have the discipline and rigor to carry out the project plan. Those that are substantially late tend to be fraught with serious issues and with out-of-control changes in requirements and scope — all of which are issues that an ESP must have a plan for and be prepared to deal with. Savvy (service providers) will highlight the proven track record of their project management methodologies, as well as demonstrate their effectiveness.

Gartner, Inc.

Congratulations! If you have been following through the previous chapters, you now have a good understanding of the principles and architecture of the Microsoft Dynamics Sure Step Methodology. You understand the importance of a full lifecycle methodology for business solutions engagements, and how Sure Step 2010 provides you the depth of coverage to help you achieve success in this arena.

In this final chapter of the book, we will:

- Summarize the learning from the previous chapters
- Discuss the Sure Step near-term plans and what may be in store for its future
- Provide key takeaways that you can go execute in the immediate timeframe

What we now know about Sure Step

Since its initial release in 2007, Sure Step has evolved beyond a focus on deploying Microsoft Dynamics solutions. With each release of Sure Step, the design and development resulted in a number of additional use cases that the tooling and methodology was able to support, either willfully or as a circumstance. The basis for Sure Step of course continues to be successful delivery of Microsoft Dynamics solutions, but the value proposition for its usage extends beyond that.

The Sure Step value proposition

The first and foremost value proposition of Sure Step remains the consistent framework for solution delivery that it provides. The processes in Sure Step are repeatable and extendable, giving organizations the ability to build on past learning, and leading to high quality engagements that maximize the resources and speed up the time to value for the customers. Sure Step provides solid approaches for project scope control and management, early risk identification and mediation, and quality assurance and control throughout the lifecycle of the engagement. These approaches are of course valuable for the delivery organizations, but they are also very valuable to the customer teams involved in the solution delivery.

For a consulting organization, Sure Step provides that common thread across the groups. Consultants often have varied backgrounds when it comes to ERP/CRM solution deployments. The experienced consultants may have deployed other competitive systems, and they may each have their own preferred approach to the engagement. While having different perspectives is certainly a good thing, having a team work cohesively is of paramount importance to the customer when it comes to easing the organizational change that is intrinsic to business solution engagements. That is why having the consulting team use the same taxonomy and terminology of Sure Step helps them mature together as an organization and work closely with each other.

The second key value proposition for Sure Step is a thorough and viable process for customers and sellers to follow in product selection and sales. With the expansion of the Diagnostic phase in version 2 of Sure Step and beyond to focus on Decision Accelerator offerings, Sure Step provides a legitimate process for due diligence for the customer, and solution selling for the sales teams. Given the criticality of business solutions, which we have belabored many a time in the previous chapters, this value proposition cannot be over-stressed. The tie-in to **Microsoft Solution Selling Process (MSSP)** and its inherent focus on customer due diligence alleviates the risks for the customer and sellers if executed per the guidance provided.

The connection and flow of the Diagnostic phase to the implementation phases also facilitates the information flow between the sales and delivery teams. Knowledge gained during the pre-sales cycles by pre-sales resources can be captured and transitioned to the implementation teams, to avoid misalignment between expectations set in the sales cycle and the solution delivered during implementation. This helps the sales and consulting teams, and to an extent, the post-implementation support groups, to work together in the customer's best interests, rather than in silos.

Sure Step has also evolved into a full customer lifecycle methodology. From the post go-live Operation phase to the addition of post go-live optimization offerings and Upgrade guidance, a customer and partner can begin their relationship in the sales cycle, continue through the implementation of the solution, maintain the relationship with offerings such as Health Check, and resume the partnership by working together on the solution upgrade.

Another very important value proposition of Sure Step is knowledge management facilitation. You may remember from previous discussions that the activities in the Sure Step project type workflows are numbered, and these numbers also persist through to the project plans and deliverables produced. Thus any documentation, such as a Functional Requirement Document or a User Acceptance Test Script follows a number sequence that allows easy tracking, storage, retrieval, and potentially harvesting on future engagements. This can form the basis of any good Knowledge Management (KM) system. A good KM system helps the service provider be more effective in their execution of engagements, but it can also help them show to their customers that they are experienced in a given area, thereby building the customer confidence in their services rendered. It is also important to remember that KM systems do not have to be the domain of only the service provider—customers can also maintain KM systems, as they can stand them in good stead on future engagements.

Last but not the least is training as a value proposition for Sure Step, for both the service provider and the customer. We have heard many partner organizations talk about how Sure Step gives them a good structure for creating a training/ramp-up program for their new consulting resources. We have all started on new jobs at some point in our careers, and we can remember the butterflies in our stomachs as we began the employment, in spite of the level of confidence that we may have had that we were the right person for the role. Knowing that there is a structured process to follow can only ease that initial uneasiness, and helping develop confidence in the roles. This extends to the customer organization as well. The customer will have any number of **Subject Matter Experts (SMEs)** and Key Users participate in the engagement. Some of these resources may have had past experience with deploying ERP/CRM solutions, while others may be new to this. Sure Step provides these resources the visibility to the approach as well as their own roles and expectations in the process.

Another benefit from a customer training perspective is the organizational change aspect. The introduction of a new business solution can bring renewed tensions and apprehension of the employee's role in the to-be organizational workflows. Being able to train and provide visibility into the new processes can help allay the fears in these customer resources.

Of course, training is not just for new consulting or customer resources. We talked earlier about experienced consultants each having their own bag of tricks. Training them on the Sure Step approach ensures that they each follow a consistent process, and that the entire team works off the same page for the benefit of the customer and consulting organizations.

All in all, Sure Step creates a better overall ecosystem for the consulting and customer organizations.

A look back at the previous chapters

As we look back at the previous chapters of this book, you can find the building blocks for success in business solutions using Sure Step 2010 as the basis. These building blocks are portrayed in the following screenshot:

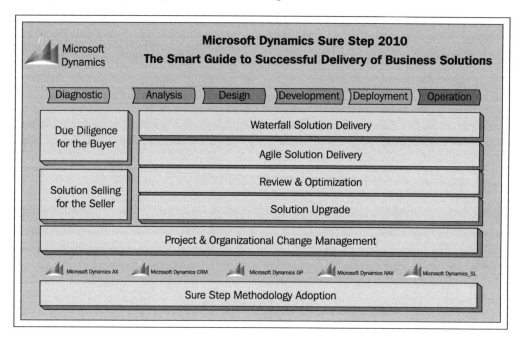

We began with an introduction to the concept of methodology and its importance in the selection and implementation of ERP/CRM solutions in Chapter 1. We discussed the importance of a thorough selection process as the foundation for solution deployment, as well as implementations going awry due to poor scope, risk, and change management.

Chapters 2 and 4 focused on **Solution Selling for the seller** and how it also drives **Due diligence for the buyer**. In Chapter 2, we covered the theory and concepts, and talked about how solution selling is different from transaction sales, where the seller needs to build a relationship with their customer and establish trust. We built on these concepts in Chapter 4 and covered specifics on how Sure Step helps with selling Microsoft Dynamics solutions. We covered the Decision Accelerator offerings in the **Diagnostic** phase of Sure Step in detail, focusing on how they help accelerate the sales cycles and bring them to close, while also helping the customer with their due diligence process. We also talked about how the Diagnostic phase sets the stage for a quality implementation by outlining the risks involved, as well as how it drives the selection of the right approach for the deployment, and the determination of the roles that will be involved both from the consulting and customer teams.

Chapters 3 and 5 discussed the essence of projects and successful delivery of the envisioned solution. In Chapter 3, we introduced the concepts of project management, talking about managing projects from a result-driven and real-life perspective. We discussed the resistance to project management, covered the four pillars of project success, and explained the project management essentials. In Chapter 5, we focused on the implementation lifecycle, covering the **Waterfall and Agile Solution Delivery** approaches in Sure Step. We covered the implementation phases and cross phases that make up the Sure Step project types. We also talked about the real-life challenges that implementers and customers face when implementing ERP and CRM software solutions and demonstrated the true value of the Sure Step methodology in terms of supporting tools and templates.

In Chapter 6, we discussed the **Review and Optimization** offerings as options for the service providers and customers to ensure a quality implementation. We introduced the Sure Step Optimization Roadmap, and discussed the technical proactive and post go-live offerings, as well as the project governance and upgrade review offerings.

In Chapter 7, we focused on using Sure Step to help existing Microsoft Dynamics customers with their **Solution Upgrade** to the latest product release. The approach begins with the Upgrade Assessment Decision Accelerator offering to ascertain the right approach, followed with the Sure Step Upgrade project type for technical upgrades. We also suggested approaches for adding new functionality during the upgrade process.

In Chapter 8, we covered **Project and Organization Change Management (OCM)** disciplines in Sure Step. We discussed the sub-disciplines of Project Management, such as Risk, Scope, Issue, and Communication management. We also explained why Organizational Change Management is a key area for customers and partners to consider when it comes to ERP/CRM engagements. In this chapter, we also covered the SharePoint feature built into Sure Step, to assist the solution delivery teams to effectively collaborate with each other.

In Chapter 9, we switched gears to provide a practical guide to **Sure Step Methodology Adoption** for Microsoft Dynamics partner organizations. We talked about how organizations can make their implementation methodology as one of their core competencies. We also covered the Independent Software Vendor (ISV) perspective, and discussed how the ISV solution provider can leverage Sure Step.

The future of Sure Step

Sure Step is continuing to evolve, developing and surfacing more artifacts to support pre-sales and customer due diligence, and solution delivery. As of this writing, the Sure Step team was getting ready to launch the first content pack, CP1, for the Sure Step 2010 version. Content development plans and efforts for the second content pack, CP2, were also underway.

In this section, we will review the planned enhancements in Sure Step in the near-term. We will also discuss some projections for the future.

Sure Step 2010 Content Pack 1

The Sure Step 2010 CP1 release includes content in some key areas, including the Service Industries and Microsoft Dynamics GP 2010. Other areas are also enhanced with updated or refined templates, tools, and guidance in this release. We will review the salient enhancements to CP1 in this section.

Service industries

The field of economics broadly classifies the types of goods produced or consumed in a society into three major economic sectors—primary, secondary, and tertiary. The primary sector of the economy focuses on extraction, harvesting, and refinement of materials from the earth. Agriculture and mining are primary sector examples. The secondary sector deals with manufacturing and processing these materials into finished goods. Metal working, auto industry, construction, and breweries are all examples of this sector. The tertiary sector of the economy is the service industry, which is about services provided to consumers and businesses. A somewhat related and interesting note is that information technology is typically classified under the quaternary sector of the economy, along with government and education.

The 2010 CP1 release of Sure Step provides coverage for this tertiary sector of the economy, focusing on the solution capabilities of Microsoft Dynamics AX for the Service industry and sub-industries, and its related verticals. New guidance and artifacts are provided in the CP1 release for positioning, customer due diligence, and solution selling to prospects in the Service industry and related verticals. This guidance is then carried through to the implementation phases as well, to help with a quality solution delivery.

The following sub-industries and verticals of the Service industry are covered in the 2010 CP1 release.

- Professional Services
    - Government Contracts
    - Legal Services
- Architecture, Engineering, and Construction
    - Architecture and Engineering
    - Construction
- Media and Entertainment
    - Advertising

Coverage may be expanded in the future into additional verticals such as IT and Data Services (under Professional Services sub-industry), Commercial Real Estate and Property Management (under Architecture, Engineering and Construction sub-industry), and Publishing and Broadcasting (under Media and Entertainment sub-industry).

The Service industries value chain has been leveraged to help on the solution positioning and capabilities discussions with the prospects. The value chain of the Service industries is depicted as spanning six main pillars or capability groups, **Sell**, **Develop**, **Resource**, **Deliver**, **Maintain**, and **Manage**, as shown in the following diagram:

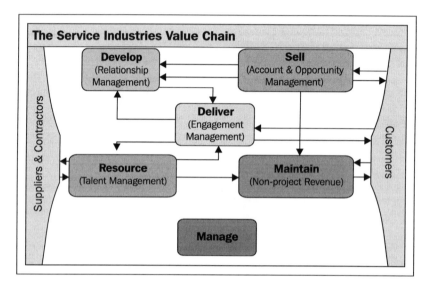

This value chain is then percolated down to each of the sub-industries and verticals, showing the subset of Microsoft Dynamics AX solution capabilities that correspond to the shared common business processes and practices that make up the value chain. As an example, the value chain for the Media and Entertainment sub-industries is shown in the following screenshot.

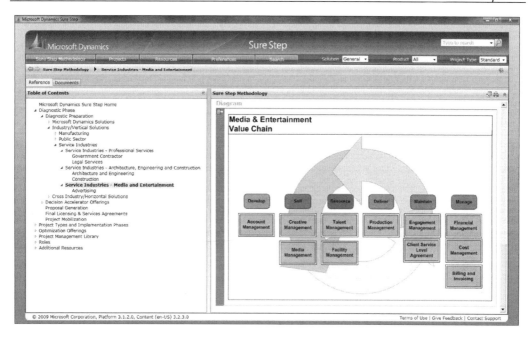

Beyond the positioning, templates are provided for key activities in the Diagnostic and implementation phases. Templates can be found under the Decision Accelerator offerings, such as the Role-Tailored Requirements Questionnaires. Templates are also provided for corresponding implementation activities, including Business Process Maps and User Acceptance Test Scripts at the vertical level, either as a fully contained document, or as an addendum in cases where the standard Microsoft Dynamics AX template should also be leveraged.

Microsoft Dynamics GP 2010

The Sure Step 2010 CP1 release also includes refreshed Microsoft Dynamics GP content, with the guidance and templates updated to the current GP 2010 release.

To assist with customer due diligence and solution selling, the CP1 release includes templates such as an updated Requirements Questionnaire for new customers and Upgrade Assessment Questionnaire for existing Microsoft Dynamics GP customers looking to upgrade their solution to the GP2010 release.

The following screenshot shows screenshots of these two templates from the corresponding Decision Accelerator offerings.

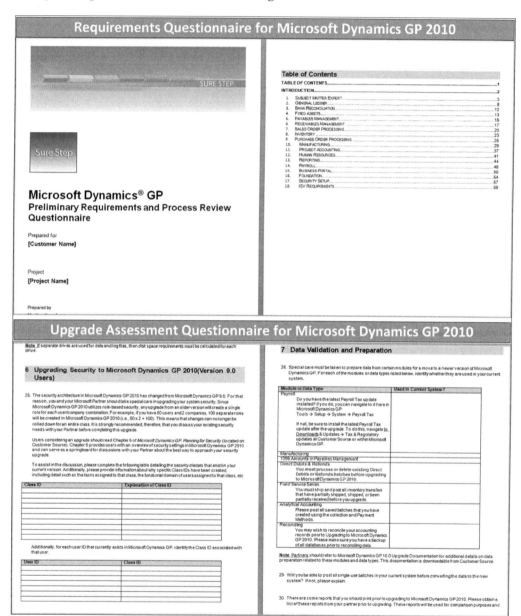

The Sure Step 2010 CP1 release also provides updated content for solution delivery, which can be found under the implementation phases. An example of this is the Setup Checklist that can be found under the very first activity in the Requirements and Configuration cross phase of the Design phase (activity # 2.4.1). A screenshot of this template is shown next:

Additional content and feature enhancements

The Sure Step 2010 CP1 release includes additional guidance, template, and tool enhancements. These include the Estimator tools for Microsoft Dynamics AX and Microsoft Dynamics CRM, which have been updated for ease-of-use, as well as with updated base data. These Estimators are an excellent starting point for service providers who have several years of experience in the AX or CRM field, or those just getting started in this arena. Service Providers should of course, use judgment when using these tools — make sure to consider all external and internal factors that may not necessarily be accounted for. The flexibility of the tools allows the user to adjust up or down the suggested values, or completely override them if they choose to.

Content updates for Microsoft Dynamics NAV are also provided in the CP1 release, including updated business process flows and new go-live checklists. For Microsoft Dynamics AX, additional business process flows for Human Resources (HR), Master Planning, and Quality modules have been included. For Microsoft Dynamics CRM, the CP1 release includes an initial subset of templates to assist with the positioning of the Customer Care Accelerator (CCA), which was recently added to the CRM solution. Plans to enhance these templates in the Sure Step 2010 CP2 release are also underway.

The Sure Step 2010 CP1 release also includes some user experience and client enhancements. A new labeling convention has been applied to the tools and templates, making it especially easier to navigate through on activities that have multiple templates. The Projects functionality has also been enhanced to support SharePoint 2010, allowing companies with the latest release of SharePoint to now be able to automatically generate projects with the Sure Step templates included under the corresponding phases.

Sure Step 2010 Content Pack 2

Plans are underway to release the second content pack (CP2) for Sure Step 2010 in the first half of 2011. The CP2 release is expected to have major emphasis on two areas, Microsoft Dynamics CRM 2011 and the Retail industry, as well as incremental content in other areas including Microsoft Dynamics NAV and the Integrated Customer Care (ICC) cross-industry segment.

Microsoft Dynamics CRM 2011 and Microsoft Dynamics CRM Online 2011

With the projected and much anticipated launch of Microsoft Dynamics CRM 2011 and Microsoft Dynamics CRM Online 2011 solutions early next year, Sure Step 2010 is gearing up for updates of all related content with the CP2 release.

For product positioning, customer due diligence, and solution selling, the corresponding guidance and Decision Accelerator templates will be updated from their relevance to the current CRM 4 version to the upcoming CRM2011 version. This is expected to include the Requirements Questionnaires, Fit Gap spreadsheets, and Estimator Tool for Microsoft Dynamics CRM. The corresponding Microsoft Dynamics CRM Online artifacts will also be refreshed to the CRM Online 2011 release.

Likewise, on the solution delivery side, the implementation templates including the business process maps, functional requirements and design documents, setup guidance, test scripts, and installation and infrastructure guidance, are being planned for refresh to the latest releases of the solutions.

Also being planned for updates are the Extended CRM (or xRM) guidance and artifacts. Upgrade guidance from CRM4 to CRM2011, including the Upgrade Assessment Questionnaire, is also planned for refresh.

Retail industry

The Sure Step 2010 CP2 release will expand the Industry solutions coverage with the addition of guidance for the Retail industry, sub-industries, and related verticals. The retail industry as an economy sector relates to sales to the end consumers. As such, the scope of this industry is very large. The CP2 release will focus on the Microsoft Dynamics AX for Retail solution capabilities for the retail industry. Guidance is expected to cover positioning, customer due diligence, and solution selling in the Diagnostic phase for Specialty Retail, General Merchandise, Health & Personal Care, and Food & Beverage sub-industries, as well as select verticals in these areas. The guidance will also extend to solution delivery encompassing the implementation phases with related templates and workflows.

Projected Diagnostic phase templates would include Role-Tailored Questionnaires and/or addendums to cover specific retail aspects such as pricing and promotions, store configuration, Point-of-Sale (POS) configuration, loyalty, and bank management.

For the implementation phases, business process maps for all the above areas may be incorporated. Project plans referencing specific retail activities may also be provided, as would be configuration checklists, test scripts, and data migration design guidance for key aspects such as migrating data from POS systems to the Microsoft Dynamics AX database.

Microsoft Dynamics NAV Role-Tailored Client guidance

Key content for other areas is also being planned for the Sure Step 2010 CP2 release, including the positioning and implementing the Role-Tailored Client (RTC) of Microsoft Dynamics NAV. This guidance will encompass the standard Role Centers that are provided with the Microsoft Dynamics NAV solution, both in the Diagnostic phase for positioning, and in the implementation phases for solution delivery.

The guidance and artifacts in this area are expected to cover important topics such as mapping of personas to role centers, selection of the appropriate components, layout and design aspects for the user experience, setup checklists, and so on. Also planned for inclusion is guidance on upgrading from the classic NAV client to the RTC.

Integrated customer care cross-industry guidance

The Sure Step 2010 CP2 release will also expand the cross-industry solutions coverage with the addition of Integrated Customer Care guidance. As noted in the previous section, the CP1 release introduced a subset of templates to address the Customer Care Accelerator (CCA) addition to the Microsoft Dynamics CRM solution. The CP2 release will build on that, with additional positioning and delivery guidance for the solution.

The ICC solution encompasses CRM and CCA capabilities to enable enterprise organizations to improve sales and customer service via enhanced customer interaction. ICC addresses the multiple channels available to an organization's customer, by providing a common and consistent platform to aggregate these interactions, thereby helping to reduce costs and increase customer loyalty. ICC coverage may also extend to integration of other Microsoft technologies including SharePoint, Office Communication Server, and SQL.

Sure Step 2011 and beyond

In 2011, the Microsoft Dynamics product teams are poised for two major product releases. The first is the Microsoft Dynamics CRM 2011 release that we discussed earlier, for which content coverage will be provided in the Sure Step 2010 CP2 release. The second major product release planned for 2011 is Microsoft Dynamics AX 2011.

Also referred to as AX 6, Microsoft Dynamics AX 2011 is expected to continue its functional depth with new features and functionality, including coverage for specific industries such as the Public Sector. The release is also projected to include additional improvements to the user interface, as well as in technical areas including the X++ code development environment, reporting through SQL Server Reporting Services (SSRS), and workflow creation.

Sure Step 2011 is expected to be released corresponding to the Microsoft Dynamics AX 2011 release, providing positioning and delivery content for the solution. Besides updating all the technical content, templates and tools, focus on solution upgrades to AX 2011 is also planned for inclusion.

Beyond Sure Step 2011

The Sure Step program is testament to the commitment that the Microsoft Dynamics business group makes to enable its partner ecosystem with appropriate guidance, and to ensure that the customers get the solution that they envision. Sure Step has come a long way since its 2007 beginnings, and it promises to continue evolving as the corresponding Microsoft Dynamics solutions evolve.

Future releases of Sure Step promise to increase the guidance delivered with industry and cross-industry solutions. Special emphasis is expected in the area of positioning of the solutions for a given industry or vertical, so as to help sales teams relate the solutions to customers in a manner that resonates with the way they run their businesses. As has been emphasized on many occasions in this book, successful solution delivery begins with proper selection and envisioning of the solution, which speaks to the added focus on the solution diagnostic area.

One feedback item that is surfaced often is the want for a viable Business Process Modeling tool. The Microsoft Dynamics and Sure Step teams are evaluating options to further the deep guidance provided in the Sure Step business process maps, perhaps moving from the current Microsoft Office Visio maps to a self-contained tool that could allow users to not only model a customer's business process, but potentially also view the corresponding settings needed in the Microsoft Dynamics solution. This evolution will require sustained effort on the part of all the product teams, but it is certainly a worthy goal to shoot for.

Another area that is being investigated is the progression of the current Sure Step client into an online client that may leverage the capabilities of SharePoint to render the content. This does not necessarily mean that the offline client will no longer be available; the online client could be an addition to provide added benefits including faster content refresh, and better tracking of content usage and feedback.

The Microsoft Dynamics solution suite is used by over 317,000 customers worldwide, and based on the strengths of the upcoming solution releases this number promises to increase dramatically in the coming years. The Sure Step users can in turn expect the program to continue serving them with appropriate guidance for the solution enhancements.

Key takeaways

In the last section, we talked about the projected immediate and long-term roadmap for Microsoft Dynamics Sure Step. In this section, we discuss some key takeaways that you can go execute with Sure Step in the immediate timeframe and achieve quick wins in your organization.

Takeaways for customer due diligence and solution selling

Selling and implementing a business solution should be about driving value in the customer's organization. Strive for win-win deals, making both parties better off and more profitable in the end, with these five takeaways on your radar:

- Use the Sure Step Diagnostic phase as an opportunity to propose an adaptable value proposition instead of selling a blurry pre-analysis phase. This represents a unique opportunity to start collaborating with the customer and ensuring appropriate due diligence efforts by the involved parties.

- Do not limit yourself during pre-analysis activities to a written reproduction of what has been said in terms of the as-is situation. Focus on envisioning the to-be processes and how they map to the solution. Architectural firms do not plan, design, and budget a client's new house based solely on the description of the old house, nor should you architect the customer's solution based on existing information. Use the Sure Step product and industry-specific process flows to ascertain the future state processes as early as possible.

- Manage perceptions from the beginning by making sure that the customer understands what they will get as a solution when they sign the contract. This involves explaining and visualizing how critical business processes will be executed with the new solution. The Diagnostic phase helps you manage this perception with the Fit Gap and Solution Blueprint Assessment offering, and continues this effort in the implementation phases.

- Make sure that the customer and partner's stakeholders agree upon real objectives and conditions of satisfaction for the new solution by leveraging the corresponding Sure Step guidance.

- Use the Sure Step implementation options and select the most appropriate approach to delivering the solution for the customer before contract completion. Envision, communicate, and validate your most effective approach with your customer as it impacts budget, timeline, and risks.

Implementation takeaways

The following takeaways focus on the impact and value of Sure Step on implementations, both in terms of initiating and delivering a project, and for building on lessons learned for previous engagements:

- Use the off-the-shelf advantage of the Sure Step project lifecycle planning with the project type options. The longer a project, more the uncertainty in the solution delivery process. Having predefined Sure Step project lifecycle workflows and plans will help you jumpstart the envisioning, planning, and budgeting required to successfully deliver the project objectives.

- Make sure to emphasize your project kickoff meetings as noted in Sure Step. Each project is unique, so treat this activity as an opportunity for initiating team communication and coordination.

- Use the Sure Step Project Charter to align all stakeholders with an all-encompassing document.

- Leverage the Sure Step templates to develop reference models for your organization. This will not only help improve the efficiency of your implementations, but will also prepare your consulting teams to be goal-driven, while helping with new hire ramp-up.

- Focus on driving value to your customers and keep away from scope documents containing several pages of blurry analysis. Documentation is important but only if it includes real value in the form of current situation, analysis, outcomes, and solution vision. Use the Sure Step workflows, activities, workshops, and reports to ensure that the delivery teams avoid these pitfalls. Begin by capturing the solution requirements (what needs to be delivered), then build on them with the Fit Gap exercise to drive early consensus on how the solution will be delivered. If these exercises are executed thoroughly in the early stages, the outputs can serve as a compass for the delivery teams throughout the course of the engagement.

- Leverage the visibility provided by the Sure Step cross phase processes to further cross-functional coordination and integration across the various roles and teams involved in the engagement.

- Use Sure Step templates and guidance to continually interact with the key users during the project lifecycle, keeping them informed of the solution progression and building their knowledge of the solution at appropriate points in each implementation phase.

- Sure Step is a methodology that assists with packaged solution deployments. Use the guidance provided for configuration, setup, and customization of the solution, as well as for the corresponding testing of the solution during development.

- Leverage the templates and guidance provided for Tollgate reviews at the end of each implementation phase. Getting sign-off on key customer-facing documents improves the visibility and confidence of your customer in your delivery performance.

Sure Step adoption takeaways

Adopting any implementation methodology is an important but challenging endeavor. The following takeaways will help contextualize this challenge:

- Do not confuse knowledge on Sure Step with company-wide use of the methodology. Adopting the methodology as a core competency involves the institutionalization of a formal change program. See this as an opportunity for continuous improvement in your organization.

- Sure Step does not have to compete with your own internal implementation methodology. Leverage Sure Step as a baseline to enhance your own implementation processes with appropriate guidance, templates, and tools.

- Do not underestimate the effort needed for adopting a methodology. Leverage the Sure Step Adoption Roadmap to execute a step-by-step approach tuned to your needs, your industry focus, your customers, and your projects.

- Focus on finding value within Sure Step that can drive your organization, and make sure that your teams understand the value.

General takeaways

We highlight a few general observations about Sure Step in this section:

- Remember that your offering should be all about delivering value. Review your implementation processes to ensure that they are designed to deliver value.

- There is no need to look at standard project methodologies (like PMBOK or Prince2) and Sure Step as alternative methodologies. Instead they can both be viewed as complementary. Sure Step is a product-specific customer engagement methodology while PMBOK and Prince2 provide a general project management framework for a wide range of project classifications.

- Improvement is an attitude, and if at first you don't succeed, try, try, try again. Use "lessons learned" as a foundation to bring together any insights that can be usefully applied on future projects.

Summary

When somebody new to the ERP/CRM space is exposed to Sure Step, they are often overwhelmed. For that matter, given the volumes of content, even experienced consultants don't fully understand all the resources available to them. As such, one of our objectives with this book was to provide more clarity to those starting in the industry, while augmenting the savvy consultants and arming them with additional ammunition for their bag of tricks.

Therefore, this book was much more than just another step-by-step guide into project management. Our goal was to address daily challenges of different stakeholders, not only those of the project manager. We fashioned the book as an easy-to-follow guide for high-performance team members using Sure Step as the basis for delivering Microsoft Dynamics solutions.

We hope you have gained insights into the design and architecture of Sure Step, as well as into the applicability of the methodology to your engagements. Sure Step is a methodology developed by the Field, for the Field, and its success will continue to be driven by you, the users of the methodology.

References

Tan, Susan (2010). Survey Analysis: The Seven Highly Effective Habits and Seven Deadly Sins of Consulting Project Teams, *Gartner Publication*, 26 July 2010, Gartner, Inc.

Index

on implementation 316, 317
TCO 101
TDD 174
TEC 24
Technical Design Document. *See* **TDD**
technical review offerings
about 206
activities 213
Architecture Review 207
Customization Review 209, 210
Design Review 208, 209
Health Check 214, 215
Performance Review 211, 212
Production Upgrade 213
Upgrade Review 212, 213
Technology Evaluation Centers. *See* **TEC**
technology priorities, Gartner study
list 11
Total Cost of Ownership. *See* **TCO**
Train-the-Trainer model 298

U

UAT 204
UAT, goals
commitment 184
early planning 184
focus 184
key user interaction, scheduling 184
results, analyzing 185
results, documenting 185
Upgrade Assessment
about 221, 222
Decision Accelerator offering 222, 223
Decision Accelerator offerings, using 225
execution steps 223-225
Release schedules 227
upgrade approach, functional upgrade 227
Upgrade Assessment execution, steps
custom interfaces, examining 224
delivery team report, completing 224, 225
solution configuration, assessing 224
upgrade delivery
Analysis phase 229, 230
Analysis phase, Data Upgrade Preparation 230
Deployment phase 232

Design phase 229-31
Development phase 231, 232
Operation phase 233
phases 228
Requirements Finalization activity 230
Sure Step Upgrade Project Type, screenshot 228
Upgrade Review
about 212
activities 213
Production Upgrade 213
Test Upgrade 213
User Acceptance Testing. *See* **UAT**

V

value measurement
about 32
examples 33

W

Waterfall-based implementation project types
about 140
Enterprise project type 145, 146
Enterprise project type, usage scenarios 146, 147
Rapid project type 140, 141
Rapid project type, screenshot 140
Rapid project type usage, conditions 141
Standard project type, usage scenarios 143, 144
waterfall implementation phases, Sure Step
about 151
Analysis phase 152
Deployment phase 181
Design phase 171
Development phase 176
Operation phase 187
WBS
about 82, 83
as central concept 85, 86
as estimation instrument 83, 84
Dynamics ERP project, structure 82
estimation, following up 85
levels 82
Work Breakdown Structures. *See* **WBS**

Thank you for buying
Microsoft Dynamics Sure Step 2010

About Packt Publishing

Packt, pronounced 'packed', published its first book "Mastering phpMyAdmin for Effective MySQL Management" in April 2004 and subsequently continued to specialize in publishing highly focused books on specific technologies and solutions.

Our books and publications share the experiences of your fellow IT professionals in adapting and customizing today's systems, applications, and frameworks. Our solution based books give you the knowledge and power to customize the software and technologies you're using to get the job done. Packt books are more specific and less general than the IT books you have seen in the past. Our unique business model allows us to bring you more focused information, giving you more of what you need to know, and less of what you don't.

Packt is a modern, yet unique publishing company, which focuses on producing quality, cutting-edge books for communities of developers, administrators, and newbies alike. For more information, please visit our website: www.packtpub.com.

About Packt Enterprise

In 2010, Packt launched two new brands, Packt Enterprise and Packt Open Source, in order to continue its focus on specialization. This book is part of the Packt Enterprise brand, home to books published on enterprise software – software created by major vendors, including (but not limited to) IBM, Microsoft and Oracle, often for use in other corporations. Its titles will offer information relevant to a range of users of this software, including administrators, developers, architects, and end users.

Writing for Packt

We welcome all inquiries from people who are interested in authoring. Book proposals should be sent to author@packtpub.com. If your book idea is still at an early stage and you would like to discuss it first before writing a formal book proposal, contact us; one of our commissioning editors will get in touch with you.

We're not just looking for published authors; if you have strong technical skills but no writing experience, our experienced editors can help you develop a writing career, or simply get some additional reward for your expertise.

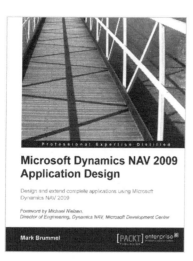

Microsoft Dynamics NAV 2009
Application Design

ISBN: 978-1-849680-96-7   Paperback: 496 pages

A focused tutorial for Microsoft Dynamics NAV
application development

1. Learn how Dynamics NAV ERP suite is set up
   and customized for various industries

2. Integrate numerous parts of a company's
   operations including financial reporting, sales,
   order management, inventory, and forecasting

3. Develop complete applications and not just
   skeleton systems

Implementing Microsoft
Dynamics NAV 2009

ISBN: 978-1-847195-82-1   Paperback: 552 pages

Explore the new features of Microsoft Dynamics
NAV 2009, and implement the solution your business
needs

1. First book to show you how to implement
   Microsoft Dynamics NAV 2009 in your
   business

2. Meet the new features in Dynamics NAV 2009
   that give your business the flexibility to adapt
   to new opportunities and growth

3. Real-world examples with step-by-step
   explanations

Please check **www.PacktPub.com** for information on our titles

Programming Microsoft Dynamics NAV 2009

ISBN: 978-1-847196-52-1   Paperback: 620 pages

Develop and maintain high performance NAV applications to meet changing business needs with improved agility and enhanced flexibility

1. Create, modify, and maintain smart NAV applications to meet your client's business needs

2. Thoroughly covers the new features of NAV 2009, including Service Pack 1

3. Focused on development for the three-tier environment and the Role Tailored Client

4. For experienced programmers with little or no previous knowledge of NAV development

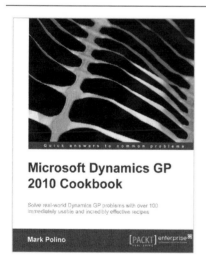

Microsoft Dynamics GP 2010 Cookbook

ISBN: 978-1-849680-42-4   Paperback: 324 pages

Solve real-world Dynamics GP problems with over 100 immediately usable and incredibly effective recipes

1. Discover how to solve real-world Dynamics GP problems with immediately useable recipes

2. Follow carefully organized sequences of instructions along with screenshots

3. Covers the new features in Dynamics GP 2010

Please check **www.PacktPub.com** for information on our titles

Printed in Great Britain by
Amazon.co.uk, Ltd.,
Marston Gate.